Hitler's Library

Hitler's Library

Ambrus Miskolczy

Central European University Press
Budapest – New York

© 2003 by Ambrus Miskolczy

English translation © 2003
by Rédey Szilvia and Michael Webb

First published in Hungarian as
„A Führer olvas": Tallózás Hitler könyvtárában
in 2000 by Napvilág Kiadó

English edition published in 2003 by
Central European University Press

An imprint of the
Central European University Share Company
Nádor utca 11, H-1051 Budapest, Hungary
Tel: +36-1-327-3138 or 327-3000
Fax: +36-1-327-3183
E-mail: ceupress@ceu.hu
Website: http://www.ceupress.com

400 West 59th Street, New York NY 10019, USA
Tel: +1-212-547-6932
Fax: +1-212-548-4607
E-mail: mgreenwald@sorosny.org

ISBN 963 9241 59 8   cloth

Library of Congress Cataloging-in-Publication Data

Miskolczy, Ambrus.
  [Führer olvas. English]
  Hitler's library / by Ambrus Miskolczy ; English translation by Rédey
Szilvia and Michael Webb.
    p. cm.
Includes bibliographical references and index.
  ISBN (Hardbound)
  1. Hitler, Adolf, 1889-1945--Books and reading. 2. Hitler, Adolf,
1889-1945--Knowledge and learning. 3. Germany--History--1933-1945. I.
Title.
  DD247.H5M52513 2003
  943.086'092--dc22
                              2003012659

Printed in Hungary by
Akadémiai Nyomda, Martonvásár

Contents

Foreword

This work is an investigation of Hitler's library. To be honest, I found myself in this "library" quite by accident. While reading in the Library of Congress in Washington, I discovered that Hitler's books, or rather a number of his books, are lodged there in the Rare Book Division. American soldiers gathered them up from a salt mine near Obersalzberg. From the stamps in the books it is discernible that a significant part of the Hitler Library came from the Berghof in Obersalzberg, in addition to the books that arrived there from the Reich Chancellery, and from the Party Headquarter [*Parteikanzlei*]. What was it that drove me to take books into my hands that one of the foremost mass murderers of history had touched or leafed through? Well, as it happens, I am not terribly partial to the so-called modern era that we were taught was—perhaps only too correctly—a period that began with the "Great October Socialist Revolution" and continued, in the name of historical inevitability (but actually in the cause of shabby power-mongering) through the destruction of the Austro-Hungarian Monarchy. These events, as we now know, created more space for the Führer who set out from this era, and who might just as easily have become a slightly confused, amateur Social-Realist painter. Instead he stepped forward as, in Ernst Nolte's apt words, the "last faithful vassal" of Wilson and the national self-regulation that he advocated.[1] In fact the American president was an idealist, and turned away in disgust from the decidedly foul power politics of Europe. One product of such politics was the Führer himself, about whom A. J. P. Taylor would say: "In principle and doctrine, Hitler was no more wicked and unscrupulous than many other contemporary statesmen."[2] It is no accident that he was an admirer of Clemenceau, who reputedly emphasized with the following far-reaching statement: "I don't know whether war is an interlude during peace, or peace an interlude during war."[3]

Hitler and I, You and He...

It is difficult to identify a motivation for interest in the Hitler library. First of all, I believe that a somewhat morbid curiosity is at work. A researcher who had been studying the Führer's books for a decade closed his analysis on a descriptive yet somewhat understated point: "For a Jew born in Germany it was a peculiar feeling to hold books in one's hand that had once been Hitler's own, and which bore his *ex libris*, signature, notes in the margins, and underlinings: this, too is part of the challenge, experience, and adventure that faces historians."[4] Without doubt something similar was at work within me as well.

Iván Horváth, the editor of the journal *2000*, described this feeling even more precisely. He very systematically edited the precursory studies to this work, giving it the title "Gondolatok a könyvtárról" (Thoughts on the Library) and attaching a brief introduction to it:

> The historian's heart, upon encountering Hitler's books, is filled with joy, since he can unveil a wealth of resources barely quarried by others. Then doubts slowly begin to creep in. Were all these books indeed Hitler's own? And if they were, then did all the notes in the margins originate from him—each and every mark and underlining? Could it have been he who put all the question marks along the margins of the decoratively bound volume of *Mein Kampf*? And how should one interpret the highlighted sections which were undoubtedly annotated by Hitler? Are they signs of approval, or perhaps the opposite? Even on the occasions when a note undoubtedly reflects Hitler's opinion, it has to be taken into account that the reader's view might have changed by the end of the book. Questions abound—some could not be resolved in the brief time given for research, and others will perhaps remain unanswered forever.
>
> The historian is able to do no more than to admit to his limitations, and to admit that he is incapable of offering a precise and completely objective description of the library. Thus he can only undertake to share his speculation with the reader of this book.
>
> Even that is no easy endeavor. In diving into the libraries of great minds, and in examining the origins of grand concepts and the circumstances of their rise, we follow a suggestive trail: a trail that leads to the unfolding of these great minds. However, the researcher of this particular library must, of course, renounce any attempt to provide guidance to those who should wish to follow along its path.[5]

This is quite correct, and I indeed disclaim any association with the provision of any such guidance. It has to be said that if I felt any joy, it was because I could work in a very pleasant atmosphere: I was never made to feel uncomfortable for requesting too much material.

Nonetheless, my curiosity, *horribile dictu*, is a committed curiosity with family roots. *Mein Kampf* was a key book for my father, the neurologist and psychiatrist Dezső Miskolczy. One of his students told me that while Hungary was being occupied on March 19, 1944, my father held a lecture at the University of Kolozsvár (Cluj, present day Romania) about certain relevant psychological disorders, during which he did nothing but read out long passages from the great work without comment (he became the rector of the University during 1944/45). He never discussed this coincidence at home, but he did tell us about a friend of his, Professor Oscar Vogt of Munich, who demonstrated that symptoms of hysteria are revealed by the passages where the Führer confesses to his three-day period of blindness following a gas attack. My father also told us in those days that *Mein Kampf* was the creation of a schizophrenic mind, and that (unfortunately) he had destroyed his copy of it. He must have used it to prepare for a lecture entitled "Psychology of a Dictator," which he announced several times but never held. There is a case which bears witness to the spirit of this lost lecture that was published and then withdrawn in the satirical magazine *Ludas Matyi*: during one lecture my father introduced a psychopath who responded to being questioned about his name by swinging his arm up and saying "Heil Hitler!" My father remarked that "He does not know his name, but he has an ideology." I presume that he would have used the typology of Ernst Kretschmer's great work *Geniale Menschen* (Translated into English as *The Psychology of Men of Genius* by R. B. Cattel) which he knew and respected, just as Edgar Alexander did in his *Der Mythus Hitler* (The Hitler myth), published in Zurich. To illustrate the kind of dangers inherent in the psychiatric approach of the time I would like to cite a couple of aphoristic observations: "Psychopaths are always present. In tranquil times we give a professional opinion on them, in inflamed times they rule over us." Another example is "To be a psychopath is always a misfortune, but occasionally it brings high esteem!"

Kretschmer's contemplations probably exposed him to danger, too. Here are just a few examples:

Great intellectual and political movements are mostly initiated by people who do not feel well; that is, in the language of psychiatry, those who are either psychologically abnormal, neurotic, psychopathic, or insane.

Let us observe those radical individuals who, at history's revolutionary turning points, ruled the political situation from the extremes of both wings. Placing their own neuroses into the soul of the masses they dragged peoples, who were often exhausted, and desired peace and tranquility, into another combative tempest. We ask whether these are not to some extent fanatics, raging and desperate compulsives, enthusiasts, and the prophetically inclined; or are they just decadent scribblers, products of lives that have gone off track, burnt out and blasé figures wishing for new sensations, windbags, swindlers, verbose poseurs, murderers and perverts?

On a more concrete and scientific level, what are these characters like who desire an "almost divine leading role"?

Among hysterics and schizophrenics the prolonged and abundant symptoms of psychological puberty can be observed, and to some extent the remnants of the particularities of puberty distorted by the adult personality.

The characteristics of the pubescent age often live on in schizophrenics and schizoid psychopaths, not only in repressed sexual instincts, but also in other parts of the personality, in the difficulties and confusions of skills involving emotional expression such as psychomotility, in autistic daydreaming, and most of all in the phenomena of intense sublimation: a tendency to pathos, to life-alien idealism, and senseless metaphysical contemplation.[6]

As shown later *Mein Kampf* and even more the so-called cultural speeches [*Kulturrede*] serve to provide an abundance of such examples.

This characterization of the situation is from those good old days of civil conformity which viewed so-called modernity with alien eyes. I am not sure just how closely my father followed Kretschmer. I assume that he shared the aforementioned view. He certainly vehemently protested at all times, orally and in writing, when ingenuity and mental illness were brought into positive relation with one another, when people supposed and preached that madness was a constituent part of its ally, ingenuity. Sometimes my father laughed, a little at himself as well, when he occasionally went out for a beer with some friends and went to the pub in Munich where the Beer Hall Putsch, the first big trial of power was organized (something that at the time was viewed as a descent into farce). He did not have any fixed ideas about front-line solidarity, probably due to the fact—or rather despite the fact—that he had fought through the First World War and had been awarded for bravery. He had a concept of the nature of heroism. He did not have a high opinion of the Führer's rhetoric talents, and he had his own opinion concerning the fantasies of the masses and the potential for their being led in their fantasizing. Although his mother tongue was Hungarian, he was familiar with the nuances of the German language, and he translated Ramon y Cajal's work on the duties of science and scientists from Spanish to German (this book is now in its eighth edition). He also published a book in German together with his Hungarian mentor Károly Schaffer. In brief, he did not think that Hitler was even talented, let alone ingenious; he rather considered him to be a nondescript figure, and he talked about his emotionless face with the same irony he used when describing Stalin's low forehead.

Thus I entered Hitler's library with the same grain of morbid curiosity that seized me upon stepping into the locked ward of the Psychiatric Hospital in Marosvásárhely (Tîrgu Mureş, present day Romania). My father, as the director, allowed me in after much nagging, and he showed me a few lovable old men: soon I realized that there is no need to visit a loony bin, to use an old street term, if one wants to see lunatics…

But was Hitler indeed mad? Or was he sane? This is the great dilemma. If he was mad—as John Lukacs argues—then he was not responsible for his deeds. In fact, he was not responsible on a state or public legislative level. Miksa Fenyő, who had already caught the scent of tragedy in 1934, indicated in despair that "It is exactly the issues of responsibility and guarantee that make the Führer theory so frightening." He was, after all, a democratically elected dictator, and "the Germans in their millions put him at the head of the Third Reich, and as for the question of responsibility, well, perhaps that is not the right word to use, as people trust blindly in his actions."[7] However, the question at stake is *fundamentally* one of human responsibility. If we consider Hitler to be an everyday or even talented person, as Lukacs supposes, then we establish and emphasize the fact of his responsibility.[8] In this case the problem is that—on the basis of our own humanity—we have to assume some sort of community with him, albeit a severely uncomfortable and uneasy community. Perhaps the refusal of this idea guided Mária Ormos, Hitler's Hungarian biographer, in her thoughts:

> I believe that Hitler's fanaticism grew to be the peril that the world came to know through two further characteristics. The first one is that his fanaticism was built upon an anti-humane and, in that sense, evil credo. The absence of positive emotions gave place to this evil and anti-humane system of beliefs. It is all the same as to what we trace this back to, because the psychological attitude that allows a person to view millions of individuals as lice, bedbugs, worms, a plague, or bacterium, and to then declare this and eliminate them—well this attitude is impossible to "learn" or to acquire through intellectual means. It requires a distorted personality, a programmed self. Taking the general behavioral forms of the large majority of people into consideration, including most criminals, we can arrive at the conclusion that Hitler, in his fanaticism built upon his evil principles, was a rarity, a practically unique phenomenon. In other words he was abnormal.[9]

The only trouble here is that the real dirty work was not done by the Führer. He never appeared at the sites of human eradication. He "only" gave the commands. And he ordained the holocaust without leaving any written proof behind. At the same time, in January 1939, before putting the death factories into operation, he openly announced in the Reichstag what he was about to do: "Today I want to make another prediction. If the Jewish bankers [...] again succeed in dragging the people of Europe into a world war, then the result will be [...] the eradication of the Jewish race in Europe." Hannah Arendt reflected on this as follows: "Translated into non-totalitarian language, this meant: I intend to make war and I intend to kill the Jews of Europe."[10] This is how the people who applauded him understood it. Still, Himmler, the servant who playacted faithfulness almost to the very end, was horrified when he received the command. But then the petit bourgeois carried out the work as routinely as they did their everyday chores. Did the great man who had been programmed program them? Who knows? What we do know is that Hitler covertly and overtly assumed responsibility for what happened in accordance with Nazi dialectics regarding proclamation and secrecy. His responsibility lies exactly in that he ensured the guiltlessness of those who perpetrated deeds of evil beyond human means of measurement.

Here, I believe, lurks our greatest problem: Hitler is our contemporary—as Joachim Fest, the author of the best Hitler biography to date (written in 1973) said in his foreword to the new edition of his work in

December 1995. John Lukacs continued with the same thread in his aforementioned work *The Hitler of History*. Fest wrote:

> What is attached to Hitler's name is unique, that is: his unchanged presence. Fifty years after he perished he is still our contemporary, and his shadow is growing increasingly dark. It manifests itself in our repeatedly recurring anxiety and loss of emotional balance and exorcism, no matter how much of which is a ritual and clearly reflex-like action; beyond that it leads towards the making of certain issues and queries taboo, and adds to the ever-swelling mass of writings and studies, even if the picture is barely enriched with new insight; thus all that happens is that his already established characteristics gain ghostly outlines. Although Hitler has become anachronistic, a phenomenon from a time falling far beyond the horizon, the newsreel, film and voice recordings from the twenties and thirties exemplify just what the ideological obsessions that ruled over him were.

Yet according to Fest he did not become a historical figure. Instead, he grew into a myth of which there was little trace even in 1973.[11] This was not only due to the upswing in racist subculture, but due to the fact that Hitler's career, rocketing to prominence from nowhere, was possibly an example to be followed for some. Fest also argued that dilettantism broke into politics with Hitler, who became a genius of demagogy in a world where the "great democratic demagogues," like Clemenceau and Lloyd George, redrew the borders of Europe[12] (Hitler and Lloyd George mutually admired each other, each in accordance with their own temperament).[13]

The boom in Hitler books on bookstore shelves is something of an illusion. A young German historian who has recently written a book on Hitler's worldview was warned several times by his older colleagues that he ought to know that he was walking on thin ice. What they meant was that he should not write about Hitler while he is still the topic of constant heated discussions—not just in private conversation,[14] but in the press too, if we recall the 1986 historians' debate. True enough, the debate was centered less around Hitler's personality than the evaluation of the relationship between Nazism and Bolshevism, or more precisely between Auschwitz and the Gulag.[15] However, at the same time the forged Hitler "diaries" cropped up in Switzerland and were on the market for four million dollars…[16]

Ernst Jünger was a classical writer, and "one of the many intellectual misleaders of the Germans."[17] As we shall see, he dedicated one of his books to the Führer. He considered Hitler's face to be an ideal dictator-image because of its emotionlessness—people could see what they wanted to in it.[18] The professional literature on Hitler often substantiates this claim indirectly, as followers of the most varied psychological trends used the Führer as an example to demonstrate the evil effects of the most varied of complexes.[19] Hitler was presented to us as a nihilist, a Muslim, a Gnostic, a ruler of the physiocratic philosopher type, as Nietzsche's descendent and as Wagner's spiritual offspring. Meanwhile the director of the documentary *Shoah* protested against Hitler's historical representation stating that it intends to make the incomprehensible comprehensible. This is what Fest referred to as some kind of "anti-myth"[20] with a pedagogical character. John Lukacs' *The Hitler of History* rose from the tension between myth and anti-myth, and is a fascinating enumeration of the various Hitler-representations and problematiques.

Can we gain new insights into Hitler and the issues surrounding him by taking his books, or what remains of them, into our hands and leafing through them for about a month and a half? What could be at all new after all those substantial Hitler monographs? The odd segment of data and the until recently unknown sources—placing Soviet politics into a fundamentally different light—concerning Stalin's preventive war plans might be considered new, because through them the strategies for evaluating Hitlerian politics could be modified. Of course, all this could be in part biased exaggeration, as fundamentally Hitlerology repels me with its (perhaps inevitable) grayness. It is a bit like the anatomy of nothing, since the sole achievement of Hitlerian politics was devastation: the annihilation or intention to annihilate people and their surroundings. He became the ruler of an empire of nothing, at least in the sense that it seems he has temporarily taken the world of evil instinct—or at least a part of it—with him into oblivion, evil which he succeeded in setting into motion, of which he was the carrier.

As we talk about this nothingness, we inadvertently try to push the Nazi world into oblivion and free ourselves from its memory, usage of words, and gestures. Yet at the same time we are all fascinated by the inner dynamics of this subculture, even today. How and why did such rabble obtain such immense power? How did that "self-centered bitterness" take form and have an effect? How did this all result in, to cite Hannah Arendt's grand work, "self-centeredness" going "hand in hand with a decisive weakening of the instinct for self-preservation?"[21] In other words, how did the cult of the self and cult of the individual became indivisibly intertwined with an exalted death cult and fear of death simultaneously? Intellectuals who could be called proto-existentialists often voiced the unity or coincidence of opposites as a characterization of their age and state of mind, i.e. the *coincidentia oppositorum*, because it sounded better and seemed more heuristic. Ernst Nolte portrayed the period between 1917 and 1945 as the "European civil war." He also saw the great contradiction in Hitler's intention to raze everything to the ground before the Russians, whilst at the same time accepting that the future belonged to the eastern people he detested (he even nodded in approval of this, as to some extent he admired soviet totalitarianism as a total system) and simultaneously being repelled by parliamentarian democracy. As Nolte put it, "Paradoxes and contradictions permeated the era, and they were stronger in Hitler and his National Socialism than in any other figure or phenomenon of the twentieth century."[22] At the same time he was an expressly empty personality who chattered a lot simply to forget the vacuum within. He belongs to that list of figures from world history who had great influence but left no single witty remark behind. His humor was the humor of trivial brutality.

But what is his library like? People are in many ways like their library. What is "attractive" about Hitler's library is its documentary character. It is the mirror of an era. The dark depths of this era, which are startling even to this day, open up to allow a glance into the darkness of the subculture from which Nazism, in its organized form, arose. Nonetheless, as we shall see, it has its highlights in the documents on the defeat of the Nazi disease.

Still, I cannot claim that it is uplifting to study Hitler. When the possibility arose for me to undertake this work I began leafing through some American character analyses of Hitler from the forties (with some, I think quite rightly, healthy disheartenment). Excellent psychologists, those respected within the profession, put these character analyses together in well-organized professional workshops. For example, one such workshop was lead by Margaret Mead, and the psychologist and psychiatrist Erik H. Erikson was among the members who offered an analysis on the determining role of the Führer's childhood based on *Mein Kampf*,[23] something which he then transferred into his book on Luther.[24] I could only feel despair that no such work could be carried out in Hungary at that time. After 1945–49 a different type of silence followed in that country…

"The Führer is Reading"

"The Führer is Reading." With this script under the photograph, Heinrich Hofmann, the Nazi court photographer, immortalized his ruler.[25] The photograph was published in 1932 in the album that presented the famous election campaign tour by airplane. The representation must have conveyed the meaning that the Führer was happy to deeply immerse himself in a book—even between two speeches in the midst of a whirlwind journey. But then the question arises: did Adolf Hitler stop reading after this long journey? Or did Nazi hype have no further need for this image, since the Führer had to act once the period of preparation was over? In Hofmann's picture book from 1936 Hitler appears as if he is just leafing through a book. He is certainly reading, but it is a newspaper, not a book, that he holds in his hands (and as a good local patriot he is reading a local paper from Berchtesgaden).[26] Thus the motif of Adolf Hitler reading gradually disappears from his iconography, and we are left with the following question: just what was it that the dictator read after all?

The far-reaching nature of the question is revealed by the fact that many consider the readings of his youth to have been a determining factor in his development. It is almost commonplace to attribute responsibility to Karl May.[27] The Führer himself declared that May "opened his eyes unto the world."[28] Yet Karl May had an expressly humane viewpoint, and we may well recall that Old Shatterhand—whose figure was modelled on a Hungarian person—would only strike with his weapon as a last resort, and that his sympathy for the Apaches could hardly be qualified as racism. After Hitler had taken the reigns of power he reportedly re-read the favorite author of his adolescent years,[29] and established a Karl May museum. It is as if he forgot that Karl May ever held a pacifist lecture in 1912 in Vienna, and that his heroes were opposed to violence.[30] Old Shatterhand could be termed mad in as much as Werther could, someone who, quoting Nietzsche, was beyond "good and evil." In contrast to this, in his work published in 1937, Stephen H. Roberts revealed that Hitler's "secret" lay in his mimicking of Wagner.[31] Joachim Fest, Hitler's excellent biographer also considers Wagner's influence to be of definitive importance, and suggests that without the grand operas Hitler could not have been what he became: at the end of the day he was a victim of the Romantic ideal of the genius embodied by the composer.[32] Moreover, *Wagner's Hitler*, the monograph which examines the relationship between Hitler and Wagner, discusses the Führer's egregious hatred for Jews and suggests that "this kernel of Hitler's existence" was simply a "Wagnerian heritage."[33] In fact, as others have stressed, Hitler was only interested in theatricality without understanding the depth of Wagner's thoughts.[34] Even so, when the Führer acted out his own Wagnerian play in his own way, he did it under the influence of the originals. *Ostara* and Lanz von Liebenfels, the occult magazine and its editor in chief, are also commonly referred to in terms of their influence on Hitler. Perhaps it was Liebenfels who was Hitler's maestro in Vienna early in the century; perhaps it was this exalted, obscure and racist parvenu with an assumed noble title who was the one who delivered his ideals to Hitler.[35] On the other hand most historians highlight the role that Dietrich Eckart—the wayward, morphine-addicted poet—played during the years Hitler spent in Munich after the First World War. Furthermore, after rereading *Mein Kampf*, C. C. Mann—in his excellent extended essay[36]—recognized or rather sought the combat of the German spirit in Hitler's internal battles.[37]

Thus we have good reason to highlight that how and what Hitler read is of interest. How could the Führer have connected with the German spirit if not primarily through his readings? What library-goer could resist the temptation of curiosity if given the chance to browse through the Führer's books (especially when there are only two larger studies and a few articles published on the subject of his library)?[38] Meanwhile the library has become a legend in itself that calls for research. The questions central to this library are very simple: how many books did Hitler have? What were those books? What do we know about the Führer's erudition and reading habits? What can or could this library tell us about these issues? Not only do such anecdotal questions as these come to mind, but also the question as to whether Lawrence Birken was right in reaching the following conclusion after pondering the sources of the Hitlerian world of ideals: "The tawdry character of Hitlerism is supposed to derive from its roots in the half-baked fantasies of Lanz von Liebenfels or H. S. Chamberlain. It is unlikely, however, that biographers will ever be able to determine for sure what books Hitler read, or, assuming he read them, what books actually 'influenced' him."[39] The Führer as reader was left out of Hitler's *Psychogram*, although its author refers to a few texts and stresses that "Hitler, as an autodidact, had boundless respect for books—something which he never admitted to."[40] Perhaps it was left out because one could only know so much about Hitler's readings and reading habits, and it probably appeared too risky to entertain the issue. However, this work, giving due consideration to the aforementioned details, attempts in some measure to fill the gap in our knowledge concerning these issues.

I would like to express my gratitude to the Fulbright Foundation which sponsored my research in Washington for three months. I also thank the librarians of the Library of Congress for their kind assistance. Special appreciation goes for Joseph Agyenmang for encouraging me to write this little book, and many thanks for the support I have received from John Lukacs and Zoltán Szász.

Abbreviations

NARA: National Archives and Record Administration, Maryland
NSDAP: Nationalsozialistische Deutsche Arbeiterpartei
LC CMD: Library of Congress, Collection of the Manuscript Division
w. y. without year
w. l. without location

Notes

1. Joachim C. Fest, *Hitler: Eine Biographie* [Hitler: A biography]. Berlin: 1998, p. 693.

2. A. J. P. Taylor, *The Origins of the Second World War*. New York: 1987, p. 72.

3. Marlis Steinert, *Hitler*. Paris: 1991, p. 203.

4. Jehuda L. Wallach, "Adolf Hitlers Privatbibliothek" [Adolf Hitler's private library]. *Zeitgeschichte*, 1992. No. 1–2, p. 46.

5. Iván Horváh, "Gondolatok a könyvtárról" [Thoughts on the library]. *2000*, Part I: 1997. December, pp. 46–61; Part II: 1998. January, pp 45–60.

6. Edgar Alexander, *Der Mythus Hitler* [The Hitler myth]. Zurich: 1937, pp. 17–20.

7. Miksa Fenyö, *Hitler.* Budapest: 1934, pp. 37, 39.

8. John Lukacs, *The Hitler of History.* New York: 1997; John Lukacs, *Hitler. Geschichte und Geschichtsschreibung* [Hitler. History and history writing]. Munich: 1997; John Lukacs, *A történelmi Hitler* [The Hitler of history]. Budapest: 1998.

9. Mária Ormos, "Betegek és betegségek a történelemben" [The ill and illnesses in history]. *Korunk,* 1997. No. 7, p. 25.

10. Hannah Arendt, *The Origins of Totalitarianism.* Cleveland, New York: 1962, p. 349.

11. Fest, *Hitler.* 1998, p. 13.

12. Ibid., p. 759.

13. Ibid., p. 16. See also Max Domarus, *Hitler. Reden und Proklamationen I.* [Hitler. Speeches and proclamations I]. Munich: 1965, p. 46.

14. Enrico Syring, *Hitler. Seine politische Utopie* [Hitler. His political utopia]. Berlin: 1994, p. 11.

15. *"Historikerstreit." Die Dokumentation der Kontroverse um die Einzigartigkeit der nationalsozialistischen Judenvernichtung* [Historians' debate. The documentation of the controversy about the uniqueness of National Socialist genocide against the Jews]. Munich: 1987.

16. Robert Harris, *Selling Hitler: The Story of the Hitler Diaries.* London: 1986.

17. Wilhelm von Sternburg, *Fall und Aufstieg der deutschen Nation* [Fall and rise of the German nation]. Frankfurt am Main: 1993, p. 191.

18. Ernst Jünger, *Werke. Tagebücher III.* [Works. Diaries III]. Stuttgart: 1963, p. 633.

19. Helm Stierlin, *Adolf Hitler: Familienperspektiven* [Adolf Hitler: Family perspectives]. Frankfurt am Main: 1997.

20. Fest, *Hitler.* 1998, p. 22.

21. Arendt, *The Origins of Totalitarianism,* p. 315.

22. Ernst Nolte, *Der Europäische Bürgerkrieg 1917–1945: Nationalsozialismus und Bolschewismus* [The European civil war 1917–1945: National Socialism and Bolshevism]. Frankfurt am Main, Berlin: 1989, p. 532.

23. Erik H. Erikson, "Hitler's Imagery and German Youth." Institute of Child Welfare, University of California, Berkeley. Prepared for the Committee for National Morale and the Council on Intercultural Relations. Library of Congress, The Papers of Margaret Mead, M33.

24. Erik H. Erikson, *Luther avant Luther* [Luther before Luther]. Paris: 1968, pp. 120–23.

25. Joseph Berchtold, Heinrich Hoffmann, *Hitler über Deutschland* [Hitler over Germany]. Munich: 1932, p. 55.

26. *Adolf Hitler: Bilder aus dem Leben des Führers* [Adolf Hitler: Pictures from the Führer's life]. Altona-Bahrenfeld: 1936, p. 16, 40.

27. Robert Payne, *The Life and Death of Adolf Hitler.* New York, Washington: 1973, pp. 26–27.

28. Ernst Nolte, *Der Faschismus in seiner Epoche* [Fascism in its era]. Munich: 1963, p. 359.

29. Alan Bullock, *Hitler and Stalin: Parallel Lives*. New York: 1992, p. 8.

30. Brigitte Hamann, *Hitlers Wien: Lehrjahre eines Diktators* [Hitler's Vienna: Study years of a dictator]. Munich: 1996, p. 545; George L. Mosse, *The Nationalization of the Masses*. New York: 1975, p. 196,

31. Stephen H. Roberts, *The House that Hitler Built*. London: 1938.

32. Joachim C. Fest, *Hitler*. New York: 1973, p. 48.; Fest, *Hitler*. 1998, p. 21.

33. Joachim Köhler, *Wagners Hitler: Der Prophet und sein Vollstrecker* [Wagner's Hitler: The prophet and his executor]. Munich: 1997, p. 384.

34. Ken Anderson, *Hitler and the Occult*. New York: 1995, p. 104.

35. Wilfried Daim, *Der Mann, der Hitler die Ideen gab: Jörg Lanz von Liebenfels* [The man that gave Hitler his ideas: Jörg Lanz von Liebenfels]. Vienna: 1994.

36. Cuthbert Carson Mann, *Hitler's Three Struggles: The Neo-Pagan Revenge*. Chicago: 1995.

37. Ambrus Miskolczy, "Hitler három harca" [Hitler's three struggles]. *Holmi*, 1998. No. 4, pp. 599–602; Mann, *Hitler's Three Struggles* 1995.

38. Reginald H. Phelps, "Die Hitler-Bibliothek" [The Hitler library]. *Deutsche Rundschau*, 1954. September, pp. 923–31; Jehuda L. Wallach, "Adolf Hitlers Privat-bibliothek" [Adolf Hitler's private library]. *Zeitgeschichte*, 1992. No. 1–2, pp. 29–50; After having finished the present study the remarkable volume was published: Philipp Gassert, Daniel S. Mattern, *The Hitler Library: A Bibliography*. Connecticut, London: 2001.

39. Lawrence Birken, *Hitler as Philosopher: Remnants of the Enlightenment in National Socialism*. Westport: 1995, pp. 5–6; and a review on this volume: Ambrus Miskolczy, "Hitlerről másként" [About Hitler in another way]. *Rubicon*, 1999. No. 1–2. pp. 62–63.

40. Hans-Jürgen Eitner, *Hitler: Das Psychogramm* [Hitler: The psychogram]. Frankfurt am Main, Berlin: 1994. p. 52, 91.

Chapter 1

Hitler's Erudition and Reading Habits

"Apparently [writes one of the best contemporary analysts of the Hitler myth] he never reads very much beyond official papers. He would never open a book, not even on the most tempestuous of days. His personal room at the Braun House had no books, and none of the pictures taken at his chalet show any. It is doubtful that he has ever made a serious attempt to study any historical or philosophical works."[1] This opinion, however, was formed in the heat of counter-propaganda, and was mostly based on personal impressions, because, as we shall see, Hitler also wrote studies on reading in his own way. Moreover, we are examining an era where books held prestige.

So, let us open an album from the Hitler library! The leader of the *Hitlerjugend* (Hitler Youth), Baldur von Schirach, took up his leader's defense against all the "gossip and lies spread about his private pastimes" with the following words: "His great pleasure is his library, which contains about 6000 volumes, all of which he has not only leafed through but also read. The majority of this library contains works on architecture and history."[2]

We do not know the exact number of books Hitler had because no account is left behind, unlike in the case of his record and picture collections. The only books that survived were those that the Americans found in a salt mine near Obersalzberg. Some of the Führer's personal possessions were obviously concealed there, and this was also where he weathered the storm whilst his house, the famous Berghof, was bombed. We do not know how many books remained or were destroyed along with the building of the Reich Chancellery in Berlin. Reputedly, he kept few books there, or at least any he did keep were not on display. Nevertheless, let us now enter this giant edifice, and set off towards his study with one of his Hungarian admirers as our guide. Our guide describes the path that leads there as just one stage in a ritual of initiation, and as we go along we indeed witness Hitler's forbidding, power-drunk, nouveau riche delusions of grandeur:

> The heart of the building is the Führer's vast study which looks out onto the garden. From the main entrance a stretch of over three hundred meters has to be covered by the visitor through halls glittering with mosaics and marble before he can reach the leader of the German people. The splendor and solemnity of the new palace of the chancellery reaches its peak in the Führer's study. It is impossible to imagine the masculine grandeur that the interior halls emit when looking at the external facade of the palace, which lacks ornamentation. Adolf Hitler's artistic taste, rich imagination, and rare talent for bringing old tapestries and paintings into harmony with works of art praising contemporary German aesthetic taste reveal themselves in his study. When looking at the interior architectural design of the halls, the furniture, and the bronze and crystal chandeliers, one is struck by the effort made to achieve proportion and balance, and by the avoidance of that artistic spontaneity and loosening of linear rhythm deriving from personal frivolity that lends baroque and especially rococo interior architecture its charm. The lines here run smoothly, with almost geometrical precision, evoking a sensation of disciplined order. The beauty of the various materials ensure that despite this order, the lines fail to become tiresome or trite; in fact, they are the source of a series of fresh experiences. The walls and the floors are covered with marble with the most ravishing veins and colors from Germany's numerous marble and stone quarries. Their sheen is a worthy rival to the fire of the warm-toned glass and golden mosaics. The wood of the furniture, the artistic ornamentation of the marquetry, the noble patterns of the covers and the pastel tones of their colors enhance the beauty of the overall effect, just as the murals, tapestries, pictures, statues, and vases of noble form do. The long series of halls command respect, and offer an especially enticing spectacle in the evening lighting. Speer is a master at exploiting the effects of hidden lights with the powerful illumination offered by chandeliers, candelabras, and wall lamps.
>
> All this noble glamour culminates in the Führer's study, with its coffered wooden ceiling and walls covered with lustrously polished red-brown marble. The hall is already staggering in size: 15 meters wide, 27 meters long, and 10 meters high. Above the doors are gold-plated shields, and amongst them the Reich's insignia, the eagle holding the swastika, stands proud. Kaspar Hermann planned the classical motifs of the marquetry on the enormous writing desk. On the table there are a few books, writing implements, a telephone, and some flowers in a vase.
>
> I looked at the Führer's study desk with curiosity: this is from where he rules the Reich, and from where his decisions come with dazzling repercussions for countries and continents. I was most puzzled by what books he might have read at his desk. Yet I cannot deny that the books that were there were a disappointment

to me, just as they would have evoked a similar feeling in all those who have a romantic image of the lives of the leaders of peoples. The books that rested on the Führer's desk when I was there were acts, regulations, and outlines of the structures of various organizations. I felt a certain sense of pity, and could empathize with the Führer's frequent visits to art galleries to immerse himself in the true source of beauty, in art that is. A commode bearing an old clock stands behind the desk next to the wall, above which a tapestry from the Baroque era breaks the sheen of the marble wall. Opposite the desk, above an open fireplace at the other end of the hall, we can see Chancellor Bismarck's portrait, while there are blue and yellow armchairs and seats around the fireplace next to a low round table. The Führer seats his visitors there, and the political meetings of great significance that decide the fate of millions of people are also held here.

An old clock, a two-cluster lamp, and some flowers are placed under a glass sheet on a marble table in front of the vast windows. The Führer's favorite old pictures, a huge globe, lamps, a carpet covering the entire hall, and flowers resplendent in large colorful flower vases placed on the floor all lend an arresting splendor to the furnishings of the room. The study is the reflection of Adolf Hitler's personality, just as the Pope's suites or Napoleon's halls radiate the personality of great rulers. To those understanding the language of art, these rooms reveal the characteristic features of their constructors in much more honest and true depths than portraits or photographs.[3]

This description, as we shall see, was also valid for his library. However, what remained of Hitler's library possibly ended up in the hideout in the salt mine. From there it was transported to Munich where a German assistant was entrusted with overseeing it. He enthusiastically showed the material to every person that passed by, and became so lost in this joy that it became vitally important, for the protection of the collection, to transfer the books to America. Today, Hitler's library, or rather the remnants of it, can be found in a special collection labeled "Third Reich" in the Rare Book Division of the Library of Congress (odd parts of the libraries of Goering, Goebbels, Himmler, and Rosenberg can also be discovered there, although we know nothing of their history or how they came to be there. Perhaps they lent these books to the Führer, or perhaps they were simply taken by accident with the rest when the Americans took a whole series of other documents). The cataloguing of the Third Reich special collection is slowly coming to completion, and this is fortunate for library-goers who can, after all, enter the storehouse. The sight of the collection is notably different to that of the catalogue cards. Large decorated volumes, many of which are bound in white parchment, catch the visitor's eye immediately. The reader happily recognizes the symbolism of these books of fine workmanship. The largest book bound in white skin, impossible to miss, is written on the subject of the colonies.[4] In it there is a dedication to Hitler printed in red letters with an illegible signature. The book encourages the re-acquisition of the colonies, or to be more precise, it states it as having already been accomplished in its greeting the Führer as the champion of the re-acquisition of the colonies: *"Dem Führer und Reichskanzler / des deutschen Volkes / Adolf Hitler / dem Kämpfer / für die / Wiedergewinnung / der deutschen Kolonien / in / Verehrung und Dankbarkeit / zugeeignet."* [Offered / to the Führer and Reich Chancellor / of the German people / Adolf Hitler / the champion / of the re-acquisition / of the German colonies / with respect and gratitude.] However, we know that the hegemonical endeavors for world domination show a far more complex picture than this dedication would suppose.[5]

The history of "the Jewish question" is somewhat smaller, but has gold letters on the cover. Only ten copies of this book were fastened together with such splendid bindings. (This volume is not the first, but the eighth with such decorations.[6] The author dedicated it to a party comrade, Karl Holz, who evidently offered it as a gift to Hitler since the Führer's *ex libris* can be found in it.)

The library, of course, is not a good one. No feeling of envy is aroused in its visitors. It is a disappointment for those who hope to come across Nazi classics, or perhaps for those who trusted in the owner's snobbery, and thought that the works of esteemed writers—or even the works of those whose books were burnt—would fill the shelves. However, the book-burner was consistent for once, as he was not interested in any form of counter-opinion.

Goebbels seems once again to have exaggerated a little when, in his writing *The Führer and the Arts*, he mused that "Hitler is the sworn enemy of dilettantism; he follows the proud view that it is worthier to read, see or listen to the great and the good ten times, rather than ten times change it for some average or below average product."[7] In actual fact, Hitler was a kind of cultural omnivore on a strict and one-sided diet. He ritually enjoyed Wagner in Bayreuth while he had the time for it, and he was a fan of Ferenc Lehár's *Merry Widow*. Also, he possessed the song entitled "*In meiner Badewanne bin ich Kapitän*" (In my bathtub I am the captain). It is possible that

Hitler said something to his minister of propaganda along these lines so that the word would spread. According to August Kubizek, a friend of Hitler's during his youth, Hitler had read almost every German classic, and his volume of Schopenhauer (presumably *The World as Will and Idea*) and later his copy of Nietzsche were always with him.[8] As Kubizek emphasizes: "Books were his world." He arrived in Vienna with two chests that were largely filled with books. On the other hand, the latest major Hitler monograph states that "it is not to be taken for granted" that the Führer would have been steeped in the classics.[9] Whatever the truth may be, there is no sign of Goethe, Schiller, Dante, Schopenhauer or Nietzsche in his library. It is, however, possible that he kept books by these authors in Berlin where the building of the Chancellery was bombed. Perhaps he kept some of them in the safe in the Berghof, too. Yet in April 1944 he left Berlin, and the contents of the safe, including any books, were burnt.[10] An obscure subculture and the result of semi-education are the two things that left the most significant mark on Hitler's library.[11] Nonetheless, it is unfair to say that it contains nothing of worth,[12] even though there is perhaps not very much. His female acquaintances frequently made him gifts of fine books. Leni Riefenstahl—the film producer who put the Nuremberg party day military parades onto the cinema screen and thus added an almost transcendental edge to Nazi dynamism and self-perpetuation[13]—surprised Hitler with a series of books by Fichte. The widow of the number one architect Paul Ludwig, Gerdy Troost—who was the only person to dare to contradict Hitler without fear of retribution[14]—presented him with a truly beautiful selection of nineteenth-century artistic correspondences for Christmas in 1942, perhaps because she had no fear of the Führer ever leafing through the compilation and taking note of the representatives of "non-Aryan art."[15] The only outstanding classical literary text found in his library today is the collected writings of Kleist, which also came from one of his woman admirers. Hitler, when reaching the peak of his power, complained (as he often did to his secretary) that he had no time for fine literature, as he read only scholarly works.[16] He reputedly had read a great deal whilst he was in prison, although this is doubtful given that he would hardly have had time to do so in the midst of dictating *Mein Kampf*.[17]

It has actually been posited that Hitler's mental regression can be explained by his reading too much at night, which, moreover, he did whilst lying down (this is apparently unhealthy). His doctor's diary makes no reference to this, and neither does the foreword by Hitler's rehabilitator.[18]

Certainly, Hitler was reported to have read a lot, and quickly too. An American neurologist who was once summoned to Nuremberg was one of a number of people to characterize him in this way.[19] Perhaps influenced by this characterization, Alan Bullock presented the Führer's personality as being reflected in his reading habits:

> Everyone who knew him was struck by the combination of ambition, energy and indolence in Hitler. Hitler was not only desperately anxious to impress people, but was full of clever ideas for making his fortune and fame—from water-divining to designing an airplane. He would talk enthusiastically and begin to spend the fortune he was going to make in anticipation, yet he was incapable of the application and hard work needed to carry his projects through to the end. His enthusiasm would flag, and he would relapse into moodiness and disappear until he again began to hare off after some new trick or short cut to success. His intellectual interests followed the same pattern. He spent much time in the public library, but his reading was indiscriminate and unsystematic. Ancient Rome, eastern religions, yoga, occultism, hypnotism, astrology, Protestantism: in turn each subject excited his interest for a moment.[20]

One of the most noted representatives of the recently flourishing Hitler revisionism vehemently reacted against this view. Of course, it should not be misunderstood that this revisionism is intended to rehabilitate Hitler, as it in fact intends to explain him. The "rehabilitating" author seeks the Führer's "ultimate secret," and finds it in the "applied philosophy" that lead Hitler when selecting his books: "The working hypothesis of this work is that the ultimate secret of Hitler's powers, and perhaps the unifying theme behind the books he chose to read, was an applied philosophy."[21] Before following up this diversion, let us remark that Hitler's reading technique and erudition was described in the most incisive detail by Joachim Fest: "We know about Hitler's reading matter only through what others have reported, for he himself very seldom spoke of books or favorite writers; like so many self-educated people, he was afraid of being considered derivative in his ideas. The only writer he mentioned fairly often and in various connections was Schopenhauer, whose works he claimed to have taken to the front with him, and from whom he could quote longish passages."

Indeed, Hitler's secretary once commented to the Führer, who was becoming entangled in some philosophical elaboration, that what he was saying could be found in Schopenhauer. Unmasked, Hitler thus responded: "Do not forget, my child, that all knowledge originates from others, and that each human being can contribute only a tiny piece more to that knowledge."[22] Fest characterizes Hitler's sources of knowledge as follows: "He went on extracting the elements of his world view from pseudoscientific secondary works: tracts on race theory, anti-Semitic pamphlets, treatises on the Teutonic peoples, on racial mysticism and eugenics, as well as popular treatments of Darwinism and the philosophy of history."[23] Sebastian Haffner's portrayal also rings true in a fundamental sense: "Strange though it may sound, his frontline experience was probably his only education. For the rest, he remained the typical half-educated man all his life—one who always knew better and tossed about picked-up pieces of wrong knowledge and misguided fact, preferably before an audience whom he could impress by doing so because it knew nothing at all."[24] Nonetheless—no matter how difficult it may seem to believe—Hitler and Wittgenstein were childhood, or rather teenage friends due to their passionate admiration of Schopenhauer and Wagner. Of course their paths soon separated. At school in Linz the Führer-to-be insulted the philosopher-to-be by calling him a Jew. Also, a young Jew from Linz who supposedly betrayed Hitler crops up in *Mein Kampf*, and this is apparently where the source of his anti-Semitism is to be sought. However, in their own ways, both of them later solved the subject-object dichotomy which so agonized romanticists. Wittgenstein resolved the question in the universal spirit and mind, while Hitler's solution lay in race. The source for both solutions is Schopenhauer's so-called Aryan philosophy. Hitlerism is a perverted form of this philosophy, and is one which engages in constant dialogue with a despised rival.[25] In Linz on March 12, 1938 the victorious Führer presumably referred to Wittgenstein once more when he expressed his sorrow that the "searcher of truth" could not be present to learn from history (in fact the literature to date would suggest that this supposed friendship and break up was Hitler's only negative personal experience with the Jewish people). Meanwhile, the Cambridge philosopher was busy spying for Stalin—and his observation, more precisely his seventh (!) Tractatus, "Whereof one cannot speak, thereof one must be silent" could now well be considered as the golden rule of spies.[26] Furthermore, Wittgenstein's hypotheses shed light on the torrent of words that poured out of Hitler, the man who evaluated and practiced reading and writing with such destructive power. What Wittgenstein states is that "What can be said at all can be said clearly; and whereof one cannot speak thereof one must be silent." Thus "The limit..." between what can be thought, and what cannot be thought can "...therefore, only be drawn in language, and what lies on the other side of the limit will be simply nonsense."[27] Hitler, as we shall see, stepped over this limit several times when orating about art. However, the way the supposed friend of his youth's following axiom fits the Führer's absurd strivings for world domination is eerie: "The thought contains the possibility of the state of affairs which it thinks. What is thinkable is also possible."[28]

It was not without reason that Hitler considered himself a *Baumeister* (master builder), although he called himself a writer as well. He selected (from the materials he read, amongst other things) what he could build into his own "work of art"—that he did not deny. When summarizing his whole worldview in *Mein Kampf* for the umpteenth time he stated:

> Naturally, I understand by "reading" something other than that which the average member of the so-called "intelligentsia" understands.
>
> I know people who "read" an endless amount, who go from book to book, from letter to letter, yet I would not want to call them "well-read." They possess an abundance of "knowledge," only their brain does not understand how to process and organize the material it has taken on board. They lack the art of being able to divide the valuable from the valueless in a book: that which ought to be kept in the head forever, and that which, if possible, ought not to be seen at all, let alone carried as purposeless ballast. Also, reading is not something we carry out for its own sake, but an instrument used for a purpose. In the first place it should help to fill in the frame which is formed by the individual's talent and ability; within that it should serve as a tool and a building material that one needs for one's calling in life, quite independent of whether that should be the simple act of bread-winning, or the realization of a higher predestination; in the second place it should broadcast a general worldview. However, in both cases it is necessary that the contents of what one reads should not be passed on for storage according to the structure of the book or the chronology of one's memory; instead it should be fitted like a piece in a mosaic into its orderly place in the general worldview: it is precisely in this way that it will help the reader to form a picture in his head. Otherwise a confused mass emerges from the memorized material, which is on the one hand

worthless, and on the other hand makes the poor reader conceited. In the end he thinks he really knows all that is serious, thinks he understands something from life, and is in possession of knowledge. Yet with each new addition he becomes increasingly alienated from the world, until he ends up either in a sanatorium, or in parliament as a "politician." [29]

Hitler, as indicated in this disclosure, held intellectuals in contempt. Nevertheless, it is easy to discover the confusion of self-perception and obsessive competitiveness which lies behind this contempt. Still, he borrowed some intellectual formalities in his reading habits. For example, he began reading a book from the back.[30] *Nota Bene*: unsurprisingly we may notice an eerie parallel between certain passages of Schopenhauer's *Parerga* and Hitler's *Mein Kampf*, and by way of example we can cite the great philosopher when he wrote that "When we read, someone else thinks for us: we repeat merely his mental process" and this is the downfall of many erudite people: they read themselves into stupidity. Important books need to be read twice because "when we know the end do we really understand the beginning."[31]

The problem is hardly following Schopenhauer. The problem, which is something interwoven through Hitler's lines, but does not feature in Schopenhauer, is "gnosis"—something that we shall come back to later.

The Führer thought that he was creating, and at the same time he believed that what he created would fit into some eternal order, with only him in possession of supreme knowledge. Reading for him was not a dialogue, and he never denied it either:

Such a person never succeeds in turning his knowledge to practical account when the opportune moment arrives, for his mental equipment is not ordered with a view to meeting the demands of everyday life. His knowledge is stored in his brain as a literal transcript of the books he has read and the order of succession in which he has read them. If Fate should one day call upon him to use some of his bookish knowledge for certain practical ends in life, then that very call will have to name the book and give the number of the page, for the poor unfortunate himself would never be able to find the spot where he gathered the information now called for. If the page is not mentioned at the critical moment, the widely-read intellectual will find himself in a state of hopeless embarrassment. In a high state of agitation he searches for analogous cases and it is almost a dead certainty that he will finally deliver the wrong prescription.

If this were not a correct description, then we would be at a loss to explain the political achievements of our parliamentary heroes who hold the highest positions in the government of the country, and we would have to attribute the deeds of such political leaders, not to pathological conditions, but simply to malice and chicanery.

On the other hand, one who has cultivated the art of reading will instantly discern in a book, journal or pamphlet that which ought to be remembered because it meets one's personal needs or is of value as general knowledge. What he thus learns is incorporated into his mental analogue of this or that problem or thing, further correcting the mental picture or enlarging it so that it becomes more exact and precise. Should some practical problem suddenly demand examination or solution, memory will immediately select the necessary information from the mass that has been acquired through years of reading, and will place this information at the service of one's powers of judgment so as to get a new and clearer view of the problem in question or produce a definitive solution.

Only thus can reading have any meaning or be worthwhile.[32]

Perhaps the remnants of Hitler's library can give a picture of what "meaning(ful)" and "worthwhile" reading meant to him, first and foremost by our leafing through and observing the books that he read.

Hitler had a specific technique for reading. In March 1942, whilst chatting to his table companions, he said that "he always reads a book in a way that first he looks at the end of the book, then he reads into it in a few places in the middle, and only if he gained a positive impression would he then work through the whole book."[33] Fortunately there are definite traces of this. When reading, the Führer had the good habit of marking those sections he considered important with a pencil, and here and there he even jotted the odd note down (hereafter sections that Hitler underlined or marked in the margin will be printed in italics).

Notes

1. Roberts, *The House*, p. 20.

2. Heinrich Hoffmann, ed., *Hitler wie ihn keiner kennt: 100 Bild-Dokumente aus dem Leben des Führers* [Hitler, as no one knows him: 100 picture documents from the Führer's life]. "Foreword" by Baldur von Schirach. Berlin: w. y., p. xiv.

3. László Balás-Piry, *Hitler művészei* [Hitler's artists]. Budapest: 1942, p. 63.

4. Kurd Schwabe, Paul Leutwein, eds., *"Die deutschen Kolonien"* [The German colonies]. Berlin: 1936. Dedication: *"Dem Führer und Reichskanzler / des deutschen Volkes / Adolf Hitler / dem Kämpfer / für die / Wiedergewinnung / der deutschen Kolonien / in / Verehrung und Dankbarkeit / zugeeignet / Berlin: November 1936."*

5. Pál Pritz, *Pax Germanica*. Német elképzelések Európa jövőjéről a második világháborúban [Pax Germanica: German ideas on the future of Europe during the second World War]. Budapest: 1999.

6. Richard Wilhelm Stock, *Die Judenfrage durch fünf Jahrhunderte* [The question of the Jews over five centuries]. Nuremberg: 1939.

7. *Adolf Hitler: Bilder aus dem Leben des Führers* [Adolf Hitler: Pictures from the Führer's life], p. 68.

8. August Kubizek, *Young Hitler. The Story of Our Friendship*. Maidstone: 1973, p. 131–35.

9. Ian Kershaw, *Hitler 1889–1936*. Stuttgart: 1998, p. 75.

10. Christa Schroeder, *Er war mein Chef* [He was my boss]. Ed. Anton Joachimsthaler. Munich: 1985, p. 213.

11. Phelps, *"Die Hitler-Bibliothek"* [The Hitler library], p. 929.

12. Robert G. L. Waite, *The Psychopatic God*. New York: 1977, p. 73.

13. Hilmar Hoffmann, *"Und die Fahne führt uns in die Ewigkeit"*: *Propaganda im NS-Film* ["And the banner leads us into eternity": Propaganda in NS-film]. Frankfurt am Main: 1991, pp. 11–12, 42–43, 142–145.

14. Jochen Thies, "Nazi Architecture: A Blueprint for World Domination: The Last Aims of Adolf Hitler" In *Nazi Propaganda. The Power and the Limitations*. Ed. David Welch. London, Canberra: 1983, p. 49.

15. *Künstlerbriefe aus dem 19 Jahrhundert* [Art letters from the nineteenth century]. Berlin: 1914.

16. Albert Zoller, *Hitler Privat: Erlebnisbericht seiner Geheimsekretärin* [Private Hitler: An account of his private secretary]. Düsseldorf: 1949, p. 50.

17. Mária Ormos, *Hitler*. Budapest: 1997, pp. 95–96.

18. David Irving, *The Secret Diaries of Hitler's Doctor*. London: 1990.

19. Douglas M. Kelley, *22 Männer um Hitler* [22 men around Hitler]. Olten-Bern: 1947, p. 222, 246.

20. Alan Bullock, *Hitler: A Study in Tyranny*. New York: 1964, pp 35–36.

21. Kimberley Cornish, *The Jew of Linz: Wittgenstein, Hitler and their Secret Battle for the Mind*. London: 1998, p. 154.

22. Zoller, *Hitler Privat* [Private Hitler], p. 41.

23. Fest, *Hitler*. 1973, pp. 200–201.

24. Sebastian Haffner, *The Meaning of Hitler*. London: 1978, p. 5.

25. Cornish, *The Jew of Linz*, pp. 113–137.

26. Roland Jaccard, "Wittgenstein, philosophe de classe d'Hitler et espion soviétique" [Wittgenstein, class philosopher of Hitler and Soviet spy]. *Le Monde*, 1988. April 21, p. 1.

27. Ludwig Wittgenstein, *Tractatus Logico-philosophicus*. London, New York: 1922, p. 27.

28. Ibid., p. 43.

29. Adolf Hitler, *Mein Kampf* [My Struggle]. Munich: 1941, pp. 36–37.

30. Percy Ernst Schramm, *Hitler: The Man and the Military Leader*. Chicago: 1971, p. 73.

31. Arthur Schopenhauer, *Parerga und Paralipomena*. Trans. by E. F. I. Payne. Vol. 2. Ch. 26. Oxford: 1974, p. 233, 241.

32. Hitler, *Mein Kampf*, pp. 37–38.

33. Henry Picker, *Hitlers Tischgespräche im Führerhauptquartier 1941–1942* [Hitler's roundtable talks at the Führer's headquarters 1941–1942]. Stuttgart: 1963, p. 200.

Chapter 2

Books That Hitler Read: Penciled Notes Attest

I.et us examine how and to what the penciled notes attest.

There is obviously a question as to whether it was always Hitler who wrote into these books. However, our impressions and experiences indicate that both the fine graphite pencil lines and the rough blue or red underlinings originate from his hand. In any case, who would have dared to defile his books apart from the authors themselves who might have wished to draw his attention to something in this way? True enough, there are some books, as we understand it, that he obtained second hand in his youth, and his handwriting is also hard to recognize, since, whether calligraphic or scrawled, it is as plain as his face—the plain, empty face to which he could partly thank his political career, according to Jünger's aforementioned view.

Reflections on Ernst Jünger's "Magic Realism"

Perhaps the veteran writer from the trenches was taken in by Hitler's medium-like lack of personality when he characterized the Hitler cult. He sought a central figure for his nationalism, and recognized it in Hitler, to whom he dedicated his book in 1926 with the simple words "To the national Leader"—an act which he was later taken to task for on numerous occasions.

Jünger's work *Fire and Blood* is perhaps the best piece in the Hitler Library.[1] This small volume is a confession about the war, and is a diagnosis of the human killing machine. It is a frightening product of his oft-mentioned "magical realism." It does not agonize over or self-indulgently re-live memories, but prepares for the future; it is the flowering of the "modern nationalism" of 1919: "The men for whom I write know that it is not about past but about future things." Hitler seemed to have at most only leafed through the several dozen war books dedicated to him, but he argued with the contents of this one. He put a question mark in the margin beside the following paragraph:

> Battle is a frightening measure of the opponents' production, and victory is the success of the business rival who was able to produce more cheaply, more purposefully and faster. [Hitler's question mark in pencil in the margin] It is in this that the era from which we come reveals its other face. The reign of machines over humans, and of servants over lords, together with a deeper contradiction that had already begun to shake the economic and social orders during peacetime, is breaking through murderously in the battles of the current era. It is here that the style of a materialist generation reveals itself, and technology celebrates a bloody victory. (25)

It seems likely that the Führer would not have approved of this passage because in laying claim to what he announced as the one single redeeming worldview he had proclaimed the reign of humans over technology. I doubt that he agreed with the following train of thought either, but here he only drew a line along the margin: "We come from an era in which post offices *were built like Romanesque palaces, railway stations like Gothic castles, and power stations like small urban mansions; an era in which new forms are hidden behind old facades, and in which spiritually we have yet to mature to the extent of our technical development. If only this iron-interlude* [that is, battle] would serve us in our coming to terms with ourselves." (41)

Hitler could also have taken ideas from here. At the height of his power, in a long speech he gave about art on the Nazi Party Day, he disapproved of historicizing styles, and dismissed so-called Teutomania in general. He even expressed himself in the following way when he bid his final farewell to Hindenburg, who was lying in state in a historicizing type of memorial in Tannenberg: "Now leave for Valhalla!"[2] This was a symptom of the psychopathology of everyday life, since it also meant that he wanted to be completely rid of everything to do with Hindenburg, even his shadow. He must have quickly realized that what he said was sacrilegious and distasteful, and the historicizing environment of the monumental memorial must have oppressed him. Thus the well-known representation of Hitler as a knight in armor is misleading, and it could hardly have appealed to him either. A parvenu generally feels apprehensive of past heritage with which he has little connection, yet still he seeks it. Thus, unsurprisingly, the suit of armor did not fit in with the "Hitler myth" in which he appeared "as a simple soldier from the front who came from among the people" as the new savior. For him the front line was a school for National Socialist "democracy."

The solidarity displayed fighting on the front meant that each man felt he was equal to his peers. Hitler did not underline Jünger's thought (but would surely have agreed with it) that the frontier's "bed is the battlefield." Here, in Jünger's vision, everything gains a new meaning, and becomes a source of fresh perception: "To hold life and death in one's hands is a grand feeling for a person, and in battle there are no laws other than the eternal laws of nature." Here "Wild animals are beautiful."(51–52) Interestingly, Hitler saw himself as a wolf and named his general headquarters after a wolf, because he served as an army dispatcher in the war with the code name "Wolf." "With wolf-like instincts he recognized how the masses can be best captured"[3] (in fact the word Adolf derives from *Adalwolf* or "noble wolf,"[4] but whether or not Hitler paid any attention to the etymology of his first name is uncertain as he was averse to the nobility).

Jünger dressed up something in a literary form that Nazi propaganda was only able to express with primitive racist tones. The Führer either chattered or bellowed about the melody of life, but he was unable to suggest it in whispers whilst retaining definite contours: "We do not want a peaceful and constructed world; we want the world with the full range of its possibilities, with its whole scale of colors and sounds, with its all-embracing melody and the pulsing tensions of its contrasts. For us it is just fine as it is." (52) What is war good for? It is good for offering meaning. Hitler marked the following in pencil along the margin, again with a line: "And while we are murdering ourselves, we must surely be serving *something more important than if we were poured into some large pot of porridge. We are creating, and our common workshop is the battlefield. All truth and all artwork emerges from the controversy, from the abraded peaks of contrasts and from the sparks which splash from clifftops.*" (51–52) One can imagine just how much Hitler must have liked the passage where

Jünger writes about the dignity of the soldier who not long before had been afraid of the schoolmaster. Unsurprisingly, he marked it in the margin, just as he marked the following: "*The world flows in a terrible and cruel manner. And if we want to get over this while keeping our roots alive then we must keep a great distance from it. What we have to swallow here, some are incapable of digesting in a whole lifetime.*" (88) Hitler either did not understand the next section, or disagreed with it, as the question mark jotted in the margin informs us: "A mother could never understand what is happening to us here and now. And nor would I wish for my mother to be one of those heroic women that dramatists put on stage in their plays, who accept that their son becomes the victim of an ideal. A father might accept that, but for a mother it is incomprehensible." (89) The question mark indicates Hitler's frequently mentioned inability to make connections, and may also indicate his growing emotional emptiness. He was practically idolized by his mother after she had lost several of her children, and vice versa. His poetry, published by the contemporary press, testifies to that: in it he wonders what will be when his mother dies. When she did in fact die the doctor reported that he had never seen a more distressed person than the mourning son. He was so deeply traumatized by the event that some interpret his deeds as acts of revenge on the world for his mother's sufferings.[5] These explanations with their psychological element suggest that Hitler became a hard, severe man after his mother's death, and that he became empty and insensitive, especially towards the bond between mothers and their children. When he was taken to court after the Beer Hall Putsch, he declared in his legal right of reply that the movement, the Nazi movement that is, "would have gone awry [...] if a mother had come up to me and said: 'Herr Hitler, my child's blood is on your hands.' But I can assure everybody that no mother has come to me yet!"[6] At least this is how the chronicle of the Nazi movement revived the case in the spirit of faithfulness.

Returning to Jünger's work, we cannot know what the Führer was thinking when he marked the continuation of Jünger's aforementioned line of thought in the margin: "And when on the day after tomorrow, no, early tomorrow morning, we set out to attack, the earth will be stained with blood that we shall spill with our own hands. *Then on the other side, in a family milieu perhaps similar to those depicted in*

*Dickens novels, the same scenario will repeat itself. With the raising
of the powerful question, something that connects us with the enemy,
the dark and suffering mother sways back and forth. We have a lot to
learn if we want to rid ourselves of this war, to bring everything into
harmony."* (90)

As for Hitler, he would do everything in his power to do so. And
he even felt that he had re-phrased Jünger's following thought (which
he had again marked) better in *Mein Kampf*: "Everything is simply an
expression, and the hardness and mercilessness of the forces that drive
life can express themselves in the weapons of men. With our grenades
we do what the strongest in the animal world does with its claws and
teeth to the living body." (94) Then we see the contrasting image that
flashes up in Jünger's memories of survivors making small parcels of
their comrade's belongings and then purposefully discussing inconse-
quential things on their bunks. The "Reader" underlined this, too:
*"Like children we lay in our warm beds in the early morning hours
threatened by the petty adversities of school. And in the same way,
existence seeks to burrow into the nest of dreams, always gently and
with care, as opposed to harsh, vigilant reality."* (95) Then comes the
nighttime march before the attack is launched, which the "Reader"
also marked: *"We rise and feel as if the last safe piece of ground is
sinking under our feet."* The "orgy of life" begins. Here are our last
two characterizations, singled out in pencil from among the many:
*"The will to live radiates from the individual to the nation, and the
individual stands ready for action; furtively the irresistible strength of
an electric charge encircles every fiber of his being. This is why it is
that at such moments—uplifting and horrifying, creative and destructive, like life itself—one can be nothing but a hero. The last merchant
spirit starts to billow and surrenders to the sense of both higher existence and nonexistence."* (111)

It is impossible and unnecessary to think any longer, because
"There are things towards which one must allow oneself to be driven,
things that can only be understood in themselves." (120) Nevertheless,
it is hard to know what Hitler managed to grasp from this elevated,
feverish talk. The fortune or misfortune of tyrants is that those people
who either praise them or undermine them attribute them with far
more than what they deserve in reality. People see more of what we
call human essence in them, while that is exactly the thing tyrants

want to annihilate, even if only in order to sustain themselves. This is what happened to Heidegger, Carl Schmitt, and Jünger whilst dealing with Hitler. While the philosopher and the scholar of law did not dare to oppose the dangerous idol, the writer created a novel of opposition (albeit with Stalin as the declared central figure). He did not participate in the July 20 conspiracy, perhaps because he believed that things had to be left to take their course, and that artificial intervention is pointless. Even though he could have been summoned to court, Hitler pardoned him. But Jünger, unlike his aforementioned friends, practiced self-criticism, and then described the survivor of his former-self in *Der Waldgang* [*The Forest Walk*]. He is perhaps the only great writer to have lived beyond his hundredth year.

It is not only books that have their own destiny, but their authors, too. Happy is he who lived in the nineteenth century—we might think. But is that indeed so?

Arndt's "Catechism"

Chronologically, that is in terms of the dates of publication, Ernst Moritz Arndt's *Catechism* opens the series of books in which Hitler scribbled.[7] The author's great-grandchild gave this work by the most popular German pamphlet-writer of the Napoleonic era as a gift to his leader. The "Reader" remained uninterested in the poems, but fascinated by the relationships between humans, animals, and God. He underlined: "*God created animals for the use of humans.*" Then he marked the following in the margin in pencil: "*Free is he who acts according to God's will, does what God inscribed into his heart; but he who trembles with fear is a slave, and he who acts out of fear is a lowly animal.*" Also: "God lives only in the brave heart, and heavens are too high for the simple mind." (7) The thesis is tempting: the Hitlerian phenomenon is an organic continuation of the distinct German path. The continuity of the thought of self-serving nationalism is indisputable. But the theory of races and its application, i.e. that humans could be categorized into races and methodologically eliminated, is an original, twentieth-century phenomenon. Arndt had to be radically reinterpreted in order to pass exemplary legislation for animal rights in Nuremberg simultaneously with the Anti-Jewish Law. Thus it is not surprising that the aforementioned decoratively bound book *The Question of the Jews over Five Centuries* attempted to find the precursors to the theory of races not in biology but in both the superstitious obscurity of the Middle Ages and some confused nineteenth-century brochures. It disapproved of the Reformation and of Luther in particular because with the responsibility of leading an individual religious life "the barrier between Jewish-ness and German-ness practically collapsed."[8] Hitler was also aware of just how incompatible Christianity and the theory of races were, more aware than those who tried to connect the origins of the Hitlerian conceptual world with Christ or Luther. As he said at his general headquarters on a long January night in 1942: "Rome was broken by Christianity and not by the Germanic tribes or the Huns." Without Christianity "Rome would have conquered the whole of Europe."[9]

It is a big question as to when Hitler read what. He read Arndt's *Catechism* after taking power. At that point he referred less often to the gods than he did in *Mein Kampf* and more to God and divine Providence—probably because, amongst other things, he did not want to irritate his audience with his polytheism. At times, however, forgetting himself and fulfilling the spirit of Romanticism, he assumed God's place and boasted of self-realization on the basis of one's own strength. Perhaps he even took King David's words seriously when he marked them in Arndt's book: "God is our strength [...] and we have no fear even if the world collapses."(8) It is safe to say that it was no accident that this "Catechism" was republished in 1942. However, it is difficult to fathom out how, and to what purpose, various people might have interpreted it. For example, it could even be the case that Hitler's military opponents believed the same things that Hitler marked out: "He who fights for the tyrant, and draws the murderous sword against truth shall have his name cursed among the people, and his memory shall never be cherished." (9)

Lagarde's Rages

Thus Arndt cannot be considered as the vanguard of Nazism, unlike Paul de Lagarde. We could say with a little exaggeration that Lagarde is in need of "rehabilitation"—in a negative sense. This angry little pseudo-noble, like Lanz von Liebenfels and Guido von List, is a representative example of the hatred inherent in nineteenth-century conservative thinking.[10] His significance is beyond doubt,[11] and his oeuvre has been widely held to have prophesied "cultural despair;"[12] even though he is less frequently dealt with than Chamberlain, and is hardly mentioned[13] or completely dismissed[14] in this context. Even Joachim Fest, who referred to him as a purveyor of the mood of crisis, left him off the list of those whose thoughts contributed to the composition of Hitler's worldview (however, it is also true that Fest also forgot to add Chamberlain to this list, naming Wagner, Lenin, Gobineau, Nietzsche, Le Bon, Ludendorff, Northcliffe, Schopenhauer and Lueger).[15] This is the same Joachim Fest who found Hitler's subjection of reality to his categorical principles to be characteristically German,[16] who described alienation from reality with Lagarde's expression "books and dreams"[17] (although the following paraphrase is perhaps more fitting: "warped books and nightmares"). The author of Hitler's *Psychogram* remarked that it was Lagarde who compared the Jews to bacterium and strychnine.[18]

Lagarde's main work is a collection of articles first published in 1885 under the title *German Writings*. Two editions of the work occupy prime position in Hitler's library.[19] The publisher of Nazi writings, J. F. Lehmann, published them in 1934, and both are inscribed with a dedication. One of these reads: "To the prophet of the Third Reich, to its creator," and the other one: "From the old prophet of the German people to his successor." It is evident whom the first dedication is intended for. The second, however, could also have been intended for Alfred Rosenberg, some of whose books became muddled up with Hitler's. The "trouble" is that the various markings in the book with the second dedication are in blue pencil, and Rosenberg, too, used this color for making notes in his own books. Still, the arguments for the volume belonging to the Führer are stronger. The publisher might have had enough tact not to elevate Rosenberg to such heights as he did in the dedication, since that would have meant that he placed his main work *The Myth of the Twentieth Century* above *Mein Kampf*. However, the book was still of great importance, as it was reportedly bricked into the Nuremberg sports' hall along with *Mein Kampf* when the foundation stone was laid. The marked sections could be attributed to either Hitler or Rosenberg, although there are some details in the sections underlined or delineated along the margin that could have appealed more to Hitler. For example: "The perverted misunderstanding of *Edda* is the result of the forcing of an erudite, symbolic language upon the German people." Also, it would be more typical of Hitler to put a question mark next to the passage referring to the wish for a single religion for the entire German nation. However, we could say that for power political reasons the Führer was a supporter of denominative religious peace and pluralism. He did not want denominative religious disputes and debates about religion to distract attention from his main goal. In contrast to this, Rosenberg wanted to establish a new worldview as a substitute for religion with the term "myth." While Hitler represented Nazi atheism by misusing God's name—bringing up the subject of his own will as an argument—Rosenberg, with his "myth"-ology, compiled a kind of private theology on the pattern of the Christian credo, where human beings and the world are not God's creations, but form an eternal entity equal to the essence of God. To the great amusement of Goebbels he attempted to make this viewpoint official, and his ideological zeal might have been the reason why Hitler humiliatingly neglected him in the Reich's central administration.[20] The Führer was against bestowing a "party-papal quality" upon *The Myth of the Twentieth Century*. He also disagreed with the title because "[...] it is impossible to say that we contrast the myth of the twentieth century, something mystical, with the intellectual movements of the nineteenth century, for as National Socialists we have to say that we contrast the belief and knowledge of the twentieth century with the myth of the nineteenth century."[21] Nonetheless, it was Rosenberg who was considered the foremost ideologist, and during the war he was given great power in the eastern territories.

When Rosenberg called Saint Paul an "epileptic Jew" on whose subjective experiences the Christian Church founded itself[22] he was perhaps hinting at Hitler, too. Let us remember how much he rebuked the Führer (whom he also idolized) and ascribed the defeat of National Socialism to him—even though he thought that this defeat would be transitory.[23] Also he was probably well aware that Hitler held the apostle and prophet in high esteem.[24] Even so, either the Leader or the Ideologist could have underlined the anti-Semite commonplace, also maintained by Lagarde, that Paulus—his name was spelled in Latin to lend it a sense of distance—had brought the Old Testament to the

Church. Similarly, both readers might have highlighted the notion of the Jews being foreign, and that "*an alien particle causes pus in an organism.*" Thus argued: "*Each Jew is evidence for the weakness of our national life, and proves the worthlessness of what we call Christian religion.*" (30) However, we do come across some sections that are marked with the distinctive fine pencil lines that indicate Hitler's hand. For example, he marked the following with a small line leaning to the writing: "*He who makes no internal revolution out of his free will shall not escape an external one: the external revolution is punishment for the absence of an internal one, instead of a persistent illness. [...] every revolution evokes degeneration.*" (43) Lagarde was of the opinion that the French revolution divided the "organism" into individuals, and that a cast ruling system had begun in England in 1688. However, if there were to be a German revolution (and the "Reader" marked this, too) then "*All the power of Germany shall be expressed in state actions, and the state that ought only to be the nation's servant, shall become the lord of the nation's surrogates.*"(44) This is the Hitlerian theory of revolution and state: social mobility instead of social change, with economic life as the executor of state commands. Indeed, later on Hitler's pragmatism used war to prolong the life of an economic dynamism that was based on extensive growth.[25]

Lagarde offers advice in this respect as well, and the "Reader" duly underlined it. Above all, he advised that Germany should colonize the Hapsburg Empire, in other words it should be amalgamated. In any event, the Hungarians lacked talent and would disappear "before our very eyes" like the Celts: "*For three centuries young Hungarians came in their masses to Protestant universities in Germany and Holland: never has one of them risen out of mediocrity.* [reads as: Hitler did not go to university, only pretended to be a student in Vienna. He had all reason to take this argument further and to build it into his political philosophy.] *No Hungarian has ever been of any importance in any of the intellectual fields.*" (32) Lagarde had some hopes for the Czechs (he even learnt the language) but then he realized (again the following section is underlined) that the Czechs are just the same as the Hungarians: "Hungarians, Czechs, and similar nations living under the dominion of Austria represent a burden to history."(33) And while "*we are currently at war on the one side against Russia and on the other England and France,*"(38) the unity of Central Europe has to be established by relocating the Austrian and Polish Jews into Palestine. Intellectuals, "who are swimming on the surface of the new German empire" are a "[…] cursed weed that has to be cleared from our lakes and rivers." Also: "[...] *all we need is a grand, strong, and clear-willed person.*"(286) Hitler underlined all this and made himself believe that he would realize Lagarde's Kaiser-ideal. Indeed, the angry little professor wanted a powerful Kaiser "who has no one beside him, only his subjects below him, and only God and the Last Judgment above him."(481) However, the latter thought—which is after all a practice in the stylistics of nihilism—could hardly have been taken at all seriously by either the writer or the "Reader."

Chamberlain and Wagner

Another book containing many of Hitler's scrawls is Chamberlain's biography of Wagner.[26] However, the word "scrawl" is not precise. The text is not colored with scribbled blue lines, but with fine, dotted pencil lines that skip over conjunctions. Our impression of the person who read the Lagarde book was of one who enthusiastically and fervently gobbled up its "truths." This is in contrast to Chamberlain's "Reader," who seems to have proceeded with caution as if weighing up the words.

Unlike Lagarde, Houston Stewart Chamberlain needs no "rehabilitation." His influence is highlighted universally throughout writings on history. One often hears of the work that provided the intellectual foundations for the theory of races, *The Foundations of the Nineteenth Century,* but to the author's credit he at least did not consider the work to be scholarly, but rather a product of his intuition.[27] Those features of his work that are more positive, at least when compared to Lagarde and his Nazi followers, are duly promoted. Chamberlain thought it preposterous that the Nazis wanted to make the Jews "general scapegoats," and he had deep respect for Saint Paul. He was a good citizen and more or less liberal.[28] He wrote serious works on Kant, Goethe, and Wagner.[29] Chamberlain was more important for Hitler as a man than for his work, although Hitler did mention it once in *Mein Kampf.*

The son of an English general became German by proclaiming German superiority, superiority for which he gave special thanks to

God. Nonetheless, what might have been even more significant for Hitler is that Chamberlain took Wagner's daughter as his wife. Thus he became a symbol, a symbol of the great composer, who gave the Führer his quasi-blessing when addressing a letter to him before the Beer Hall Putsch.[30] It is well known that Eva Wagner wrote this letter, because the maestro was bedridden with illness by then, and only the letter's signature was authentic.[31]

Chamberlain's message was clear: the parliamentarian system had to be obliterated. Nevertheless, his glorification of Hitler had some ironic undertones. The use of irony is a habit of the old and the new amongst those intellectuals who—to use Plato's expression—give advice to tyrants (just like Carl Schmitt who could be said to have ideologized this approach in a manner of speaking).[32] How fitting his characterization was in an atmosphere characterized by the awaiting of the German messiah, and how much Hitler sensed this (who knew very well that he had talked himself into power) is a different matter: "the real awakener brings tranquility," and while "the fanatic wants to persuade, you want to convince," wrote or rather announced Chamberlain to his "disciple." [33]

We do not know whether Hitler read Chamberlain's drama *The Vintner*, or whether he tossed it aside because the somewhat disagreeable waiter is called Adolf (interestingly, Hitler himself he was once dubbed as the "chief waiter with a stigma," although this title is only to be found in the diary of one of Hitler's desperate contemporaries).[34] However, the same hand wrote the dedication in the book sent for Christmas 1924, Chamberlain's collected volume of *Dramatic Poetry*, as did the following letter: "Would H. S. Chamberlain's attempts at drama remain unknown to Adolf Hitler? With hearty Christmas greetings we recommend them (especially *The Vintner*!)."[35] (The story of *The Vintner* is simple: The greedy landlord Seugnié wants to confiscate the lead character, Jan's land, who of course resolutely fights because he knows every single vine, and argues that the work is his even if it brings no profit. In the end he dies when the usurer comes.) It is even less likely that the Führer would have got deeply involved in the humoresque entitled *Mr. Hinkebein's Skull*, offered to him as a supplementary Christmas present, also with a dedication.[36] Chamberlain wanted to give an impression of how a philosophical contemplation "becomes further cogitated" in a particular "autodidactic" and semi-erudite environment through a Svejk-like half-educated figure who reads a lot even after his A-levels; and how petit-bourgeois philistines exchange deep philosophical and intuitive thoughts for small change. The work is compiled from Hinkebein's monologues which are interrupted by some comments or questions from the note-taker and the doctor, only to be lost in the flow of pontification. Our hero is so proud of his head that he wants his skull to be exhibited in a museum after his death (as we know, Hitler also thought a lot of his own head and took measurements of it). What Hinkebein actually says could be poking fun of the Nazi death cult and the eternity cult: "Death is my hope, the dawn of the most beautiful day... When Hinkebein is dead he will want to be totally dead—so that he could live in his totality. Hence my brain is to be preserved in spirits and my skull to be exhibited behind glass in a museum." (67) The doctor's judgement is fitting as well: "What I do not get is that this man reveals the symptoms of all the different psychological disorders, and yet he is quite a sane and unimputable chap." (71) Thomas Mann's comment on "brother Hitler" fits Hinkebein, too: "This chap is a catastrophe; but that is no reason not to find him and his fate interesting."[37] Hitler might have glanced through Chamberlain's *Words of Christ* which he received from a source other than the author. He was not impressed by the attempt to prove that Jesus' followers talked in the Aramaic language, that only a few of those who witnessed his life understood Hebrew, and that the evangelists spoke only Greek. Therefore he would be the one to reconstruct the meaning of Christ's message.[38] Hitler was not especially taken by Chamberlain's Biblical criticism either: "Whether it's the Old or the New Testament or simply the sayings of Jesus, as Houston Stewart Chamberlain would have it—it's all the same old Jewish swindle. It will not make us free," said the Führer to Rauschning.[39] Evidently, Hitler told the Wagner family that he accepted the Master's view according to which Jesus was an Aryan (in fact Wotan's son), and the Führer also said that "his Christian feelings" dictated that he see the fighter in the Savior.[40] At the same time Hitler frequently used quasi biblical phrases; he expressed his relationship to his party comrades in January 1936 as follows: "I know: all that you are, you are through me, what I am, I am only through you."[41]

The most personal piece in Hitler's library is Chamberlain's Wagner volume (see note 26, Chapter 2). An unnamed female Wagner fan from Leipzig made a gift of it to the Reich Chancellor on March 20, 1933 for his forty-fourth birthday, a good month before the actual event. The significance of the present is that it underpins Joachim Fest's Wagner thesis mentioned earlier,[42] which John Toland's work, the other grand Hitler biography, also discusses.[43] The Führer considered Wagner to be his only forerunner. However, their relationship cannot be reduced to being one that was simply based on anti-Semitism alone, as Fest emphasized. Hitler simply saw, with reason, a mood in Wagner's anti-Semitism that sprang from resentment. This was unlike his own racism, which he viewed as scientific. The Führer's attachment to Wagner was more deeply rooted. When he was sixteen he saw *Rienzi* in Linz, and was practically transported into ecstasy. Afterwards he gave a speech to his friend August Kubizek about the endangerment of his own mission and "Germanness." Thirty years later he invited Kubizek to Bayreuth, and when the subject of the aforementioned performance was raised, he declared that "It all began in that hour." He was reputed to have known *The Mastersingers of Nuremberg* by heart:

> And still I don't succeed.
> I feel it and yet I cannot understand it.
> I can't retain it, nor forget it.
> And if I grasp it, I cannot measure it.

Wagner's theory of genius offered comfort to Hitler in moments of failure in his life. The vision of the battle between Wagnerian heroes and the evil outside world justified his opposition to the world, and strengthened him in his primitive life philosophy of "all or nothing;" it strengthened his resolve in waiting for a miracle, and strengthened him in his belief that one day something astoundingly grand would happen, and that he would be rewarded for everything that afflicted him and his people. Wagner's operas provided him with the experience of seeing enormous crowds being moved, or at least revealed to him that enormous crowds could be moved. Subsequently, art for Hitler also became the art of moving crowds. Wagner believed that the unity of nature and man existed in the Greek *polis*. Without preaching a return to the ancestral states he declared war on decay. He proclaimed that the Greeks were Aryan, and viewed Greek art as the example to follow, targeting its further development as a program—in the name of eternity. He wanted to substitute monumentality for thought. As he stated in an open Letter to the Reich Chancellor von Papen on October 16, 1932, "divine order" is the reign of the wisest and cleverest, while "there is only one proof of divine vocation, and that is achievement,"[44] or rather: monumentality. This is life itself, because "no people lives longer than the documents of its culture!" and, as he elaborated in Nuremberg, on November 5, 1934, referring to the pyramids as examples: "what would the Egyptians be without their pyramids and temples...?"[45]

It is not Wagner's fault that he uncovered "the myth of blood" for the Führer. It proved to be simply gossip that Hitler intended to marry Wagner's English daughter-in-law.[46] Yet Nazi destruction and decay were accompanied by reminiscences of Wagner: "Perhaps the passivity of the Germans [...] has something to do with the catastrophic cultural heritage which they inherited not least from Wagner," writes Fest, indicating how scenes from the war and Wagnerian metaphors correlate with one another, such as *Twilight of the Gods* taking place in a bunker, or the Capitolium in flames in *Rienzi*.[47] Hitler's secretary's diary states that *Twilight of the Gods* was the last performance that Hitler watched in Bayreuth in July 1940. Also, the radio broadcasted an excerpt from it after his suicide.[48] Before that the last opera that he saw was *Turandot* by Puccini with his Spanish guests in January 1943.[49] Yet he continued with Wagner in real life—in his own melodrama. He announced to those people around him in words inspired by Wagner that he would wed Eva Braun and then choose death with his wife. In a peculiarly ironic twist of fate the witness to the wedding, found with some difficulty, was also called Wagner, but he signed his name with a double "a" in his nervousness.[50] As Thomas Mann put it: "The whole thing is Wagnerian in its messed-up state, and this was noticed a long while ago; also well known is the well-founded, albeit slightly forbidden degree of respect that the political wonder-man shows towards Europe's artistic magician, someone whom Gottfried Keller called 'a friseur and a charlatan.'"[51]

What message did Chamberlain's Wagner biography—a book which a sharp-eyed American journalist once discovered on Hitler's bookshelf, despite its small size—convey?[52] Had the journalist leafed through it, he might have noticed clues that the person who had underlined sections of the book may well have drawn inspiration from it for his annual speech on culture at the autumn Nuremberg Party Rally, in which the orator roused his audience—whose attention had slackened during the course of an expansive elaboration of eternal ideals—to applaud by promising to sweep away the Neanderthals, the Futurists, the Cubists, the Dadaists, and the Impressionists. Hitler's vocal range went from a croaky whisper to a bellow, and it was compared to the structure of the Wagnerian tune. The Führer could only have thought of himself when reading and underlining the following passage: "*The soul* of this art *is music*, its most perfect form is drama. If only the German, thanks to his geographical position and intellectual potential for acquisition, would accept the different artistic impressions. [...] He had to create *his own* art that *had never existed before, an art born from the innermost need and richest talent,* an art which reflects his *soul* clearly and perfectly." (47)

Naturally Wagner created this art:

> Since he was the *first* to *refer to the characteristic qualities of the German with fierce honesty and fanatic stamina*: the *ability*, that the entirely *Semitized*, so-called *Latin* world has lost, he wrote, the German tribes can regain if "*they go back to their roots.*" Besides this, he was the first to undertake the transformation of the *German ideal into reality, as a clearly artistic performance refusing any kind of speculation*: the establishment of the [Hitler's mark in the text] *festival performances in Bayreuth* stands alone in human history. [Hitler's second mark in the text alluding to the following remark at the bottom of the page: "And yet such a 'high price' has to be paid for the Bayreuth-experience, that it is impossible for a simple terrestrial being to bear."] In Greece the entire nation arranged festive performances for themselves; but did the state give vast sums for it? In Germany just one man, Wagner, achieved all that. (68)

Precisely when Hitler wrote the above observation in the margin is unknown. Presumably he had been preparing to—later—offer a similar experience of cheap festive performances by erecting enormous sports halls.[53] However, in the autumn of 1933 he suffered a great disappointment at the Nuremberg Party Rally. Apart from the fact that the party days generally exhausted him to the extent that he had to withdraw for a rest before and after them,[54] that year party members filled the pubs instead of going to the festival performance of *The Mastersingers of Nuremberg* at the opera house. They continued to have fun in the pubs even after the Führer sent for them. The following year they were given strict orders to be present. The Führer was again dissatisfied, because many of the party members fell asleep. In 1935 he exchanged the men in uniform for a civilian audience. The ticket cost a fortune but the atmosphere was just right.[55]

As Hitler was reading Chamberlain's Wagner biography his heartbeat must have indeed quickened upon recognizing one of his own earlier pearls of wisdom: "Essentially my movement is nothing but a process of regeneration emerging from the ancient powers of the German people," he said on October 13, 1932.[56] Chamberlain also believed that renewal was nothing else other than regeneration:

> Regeneration is *re-creation*, a *new-birth*, i.e. *reaching back to that given by nature*, to the *unadulterated ancient powers* of life—while *a real politician* (may he be from any party) *only* knows *reformation*, the *slow* and *progressive* change and improvement of the social and artificial order which is held as being *eternal* [here follows a question mark written by Hitler in pencil]—the Socialist only wants to *change* this order with his revolution to suit *his own* interests, in other words in the interests of a *new political order*.
>
> This concept of regeneration fundamentally differs from all the usual doctrines for world peace. Stretching back to the "eternally natural," to the "purely human," as the road to salvation is proclaimed, it brands the current state of the *claimed "progress,"* as a *state of fall*. Consequently we must see how this concept of the *fall of humanity* presupposes the *degeneration of humanity*...(81)

The "Reader" put an exclamation mark beside the following paragraph: "This idea of regeneration is found in the [Hitler's mark] *Christian religion* and in the thoughts of Jean-Jacques Rousseau. However, the Christian *Church gives* up *regeneration of human society in this* world, and is satisfied with leading each individual on the path of re-birth..."

However, for Rousseau "the *'eternally natural'* is an *unadulterated 'natural state'* that is the negation of *all culture* and all science."(32)

Chamberlain saw that the road to regeneration, "that can rightly be called *German*" was shown by Schiller and Wagner, and therefore: "[...] it was *not politicians, but these two poets* who *showed the way to the German people*, how it *must* be walked *if they wished to achieve their mission*... The *fundamental teachings* of these two men *are the same*, and as Schiller said: humanity *fell from nature* through being clever, and thus its return must also be through *rational intelligence*." Hitler also underlined that the poet's adoption of such roles is something peculiar to the German intellect, because "The poet is actually a *seer*; he 'creates what he sees.'" (83–84) Yet this was not the first time that Hitler had come across poets, as he had read Schiller in his youth.[57] In his speeches Hitler often praised poets, composers, singers, sculptors, skilled builders, and of course all creative people blessed with divine mercy. Yet he kept quiet about writers and painters, as before 1933 he used to stress that he was a writer, and he still had not given up painting. As for what Chamberlain wrote about Schiller, it was as if it cropped up in the Nuremberg speech of September 1, 1933, with race also appearing as a metaphor for the natural state—the classic mixed metaphor in its original form:

> The race that stamps its mark on the whole life of a people also sees the tasks of art with its own eyes. It creates works of art after its own sense, viewing all the circumstances and conditions of the purpose and material as sovereign. Meanwhile only the clearest human understanding and spirit can find the most uplifting beauty. The ultimate measure of this beauty however lies in the recognition of crystal clear purposefulness. This has nothing to do with supposed "objectivity" that does not want to understand that man should not mistake animalistic primitivism for harmonic beauty [crowd expresses approval].

As it is this racial beauty is given and eternal, or more precisely it is natural, if we correctly understand the "artist" who had earlier berated style as being the factor that prevents the emergence of ancient racial power. His pictures, especially those copied from postcards, cannot be accused of possessing any style. Style is unnecessary, pondered the Führer: "No: only instinct—because of the loss of their racial unity, uncertain people need rules in order not to loose the wonderful thread which the simple—through being natural—representatives of a merciful race once found [audience expresses approval]."[58] Besides inspiration Hitler found concrete guidance in Chamberlain's book, or rather confirmation that he was on the right path. In the citation of Wagner's speech on June 14, 1848 Hitler underlined the following with several lines: "*Omission* of all *noble privileges*." It was his desire to level Nazi democracy just as the Wagnerian cry was to "*win over* colonies," not to mention the "*establishment of a large general people's army*." But what might have inspired Hitler's imagination even more was the following train of thought from Chamberlain: "Neither *possession*, nor *ownership* give us '*laws*', as only the king's grace does; Wagner represents this *Old Germanic standpoint* and fights against the current *acceptance of Roman law which provides the grounds* for '*the ever deeper devaluation of humans.*'" (113) Nonetheless, he put a question mark by the Wagnerian quote which said that being liberated from the constitution meant that "the *republic* would become a *real republic,* and we must then demand that *the king be the first* ["?"—Hitler's pencil mark in the margin] and *foremost republican.*"(119) Did Hitler notice that Wagner used the term republican in the Roman sense? Or did he forget that "republic" could also simply mean "state"? Perhaps the reason he marked it was that the Wagnerian thought correlated with the *Führerprinzip,* the principle that the leader expresses the people and, on the basis of some communal agreement, has total power. Also, Hitler approved of Chamberlain's next summons so much that he not only underlined it, but also marked it with two vertical lines in the margin: "Let us follow the example of the great German Master, who teaches us things we see as true deep in our hearts, and knows that they are things we must stand for against the whole world and even our own selves! Let us turn our fundamental principles into clear beliefs—let us view our first and most important obligation as being the leading of others to these beliefs, and let us build upon God!" (129)

Wagner was more than a composer to Hitler. Of course, only to a certain extent, since the Führer was the only one able to feel that he had been gifted with perfect knowledge. On September 6, 1938 in his cultural speech at the Nuremberg Party Rally he delivered this thought by defining the essence of Nazism (and Nazi nihilism) more precisely than ever. Also, he highlighted the difference between Nazi mass protests, church rituals and the Wagnerian scene:

National Socialism is no cultic movement, but a folk-political doctrine [*völkisch-politische Lehre*] that grew solely out of racial recognition. Its essence is not that of some mystical cult, but that of caring for and leading a people defined by blood.

The characteristic common to all our meeting places is not the mystic dark obscurity of some cult location, but the beauty of a room or hall, bright and purposeful with its light. Thus no cultic event takes place here, just the spreading of information [*Volkskundgebung*] in the manner that we have learnt and become accustomed to in the course of long battles, something that we wish to stay as it is.

This is why no occult researcher of the otherworld with a mystical attitude is to be allowed to find his way into the movement. These people are not National Socialists, but something else, something that has absolutely nothing to do with us.

It is not secretive suggestion that stands at the forefront of our program, but clear recognition and with it, overt acknowledgement. If we place a divine creation into the focus of this recognition and acknowledgement, then we maintain the existence of a divine work, and fulfill divine will—not under the guise of mystical obscurity at some cultic location, but out in the open, out before the Lord.

There were times when obscurity was the precondition of certain doctrines, but today we live in an era when the precondition for the success of our actions is light. It is, however, painful if with the intrusion of some confused mystical element the movement or the state gives out unclear instructions. [...]

Our cult takes care of only natural things and of what God wants. [We shall later discuss Hitler's use of the name of God in his ideological Machiavellism.]

Our humility is—for us humans—unconditional obedience and respect for the known divine laws of existence.

Our prayer: to fulfill the duties imposed upon us in our acceptance of this. As for cultic acts, the churches are concerned with them, not us.

If, in spite of this, someone still thinks that these duties do not satisfy him or that he is unable to comply with them, then he has to prove that his God can do something better.

But such people cannot undertake tasks which art cannot fulfil. And artists cannot attempt to solve tasks which fall outside the creative forces of art. I consider this immensely important, because at any given moment the choice of the wrong path could render an entire century artistically unproductive.

Music, as absolute art, obeys unknown laws. We do not as yet know exactly what the basis is for something sounding good, just as we do not know what is responsible for making something sound bad. One thing is certain, that music can be seen as the greatest shaper of emotions and feelings which moves the mood and which is least suitable to satisfy rationale.

This is how it can so easily happen that rationale and a musical ear do not unite in the same body. Rationale uses language for utterance.

The world of feelings and moods, difficult to represent linguistically, reveals itself through music. Thus music can exist without language, although of course, through its followers it may help to deepen the impression of certain linguistically fixed things.

The more illustrative role music has, the more important it is that the underscored plot be visible. Then the ingenuity of a great artist is something supplementary to the clearly defined plot that ensures the general mood and effect achievable through the music itself.

This art of creating an elemental and general musical character as a mood found its peak in the works of the master of Bayreuth.[59]

Thus Wagner is merely a composer, he merely illustrates, because "It is completely impossible to express a worldview as science through music." This is the Führer's task; it is he who allocates further tasks:

Our poets' or thinkers' duty is to learn to control the language in a way that it will not just clearly reproduce the perceptions that flicker before us (as if in some engraving) or merely convey them to their fellow humans, but to make those perceptions into a work of art by controlling the tonal forms inherent in language.

Technical knowledge is the necessary external condition for the revelation of inner ability.

Whether we are discussing architecture or music, sculpture or painting, one thing must never be ignored: all true art must stamp the mark of beauty on its work, as for many of us the nursing of the healthy is the ideal. However, every healthy thing is correct and natural on its own. Thus every correct and natural thing is beautiful. Today courage is as important in finding beauty as it is in finding the truth. The world-enemy which we fight pinned the annihilation of the truth to its flag, along with the annihilation of beauty.

Our duty is to be courageous enough to find real beauty, and to withstand deception by the idiotic and shameless babble of decadent penmen who attempt to declare that all that is natural and beautiful is kitsch, that the ill and the unhealthy are as interesting and valuable, and as such, worthy of respect. If humanity should set off down this road and become distanced from eternal-beauty, then it shall soon loose the measure by which we evaluate human cultural achievements.[60]

The alpha and omega of this "argumentation" is race, because it is natural and therefore beautiful, and so on. This is how Wagner's music became the background noise (or rather some sort of psychotropic drug) used by the race cult.[61] In January 1942, from his principle wartime residence, Hitler stated the following: "When I hear Wagner it sounds to me like the rhythm of a future world."[62] On hearing this, the passage from Joseph Roth's 1938 article entitled "The Myth of the German Soul" inevitably springs to mind: "It is no wonder that Hitler likes Wagner's operas, or pretends to like them. I do not think that he appreciates their musical value. He likes their symbolism—false symbolism, it has to be said—and their poster-political character. Perhaps he does not like Wagner at all."[63] It is a great and irresolvable question as to whether he was at all capable of love. Yet there was one thing he certainly did love: his car. Hitler himself said in January 1942: "My love is automobiles. The car gave me the most beautiful hours of my life…"[64] In this way he spoke as if he were a member of the *nouveau riche*. We shall see that many saw him as one, and not by accident.

Readings on Economic Politics and Military Science

In the clear light of the horrible darkness, the Führer was obviously "learning" all the time. He underlined a few things in books about social and economic politics. Scholarly literature occasionally mentions a few of these as works where Hitler marked the odd line.[65] One such work was by the former Social Democrat Berthold Otto entitled *The Future State as a Socialist Monarchy*, in which Hitler even put his name. He did not just put marks in the book, but even corrected an error of word order in it.[66] It is a book in which Hitler must surely have agreed with the basic idea of the unity of state and people, but less so with the suggestion of the elimination of money. He marked it with a line along the margin: "The introduction of the work token [*Arbeitswährung*] would be the basis for the first—officially recommended—socialist institutions. *The state would then declare that from the day following the announcement it would accept no gold or exchange money as payment from any native citizens, so that never again, for all the treasure in the world would one receive a railway ticket* from Berlin to Potsdam or obtain stamps to put on a letter."

Goods would get from the producer to the consumer through the post. The purchaser, or rather comrade [*Volksgenosse*] would pay with a new ticket similar to a stamp, and would stamp it with his own personal stamp where his personal identification number is clear: "After receiving a bill one simply reports *the number printed on the bill* to the post office. Then—without having to dial a separate telephone number—after some further inquiry one is connected to the post officer in authority who will then say the number again to double check."[67] Otto thought that shareholding companies should be reformed. The members should elect their director. A new order should emerge, that is the "cooperative large enterprise," as *"Obviously, peasant small-holdings everywhere should be allowed to unite into large companies."* Small ventures pose the main problems. It is hard for a peasant to be equal to his servant as a cooperative member. Bankers also dislike work tokens:

> In fact it is a peculiar thing to talk about justice in the case of such comprehensive transformation. This is because *such grand transformations transform justice.* In the old view, the cessation of slavery was an infringement of the lawful rights of

the owner, causing him untold devastation. However, in the eyes of the reformer, slavery is an abuse of rights in itself. Therefore to end an injustice is an act of justice; the old right stops, and a new one comes in its place. Thus at the moment when a nation enters into an economy of accountancy from a monetary economy, all moves to acquire financial power become impossible, and thus all that is founded on the power of money is rendered unjust and immoral.

Hitler marked the next part with two small corner-marks, too:

There is no greater stupidity than the belief that the corner stone of civil society is freedom—much more so it is the enforcement of freedom. Through enforcement real freedom would emerge, and then everybody could handle economic matters morally or immorally, and it would come to light what faith and belief meant in the business sphere. What is called faith and belief now is usually the fear of the powers of enforcement. It is without doubt that the secession of the institutions that represent powers of enforcement would mean the upheaval of societal order for everyone. It is exactly the point that the civil system is not a natural system that developed through freedom, but an artificial system that was established over thousands of years with great effort, a system which is maintained through only the most horrible forces.

Then the "Reader" marked the following with a line along the margin: "In the Middle Ages only Jews were allowed to charge interest, even though old Jewish laws forbade that, too. Charging interest only became generally widespread with the development of monetary economy and trade spirit—the transactions that had been seen as immoral in the Middle Ages have now become moral." (73) In the new world there would be no sense in charging interest, as all monetary business will have come to an end.

Otto's speculation about organization also caught Hitler's attention: "Science first begins with 'wondering.' In our own self, things are either self-evident or wonderful and surprising. Yet each thing is simultaneously both. While something seems self-evident there is no need to make any effort, and nothing is done; it is only when we manage to wonder about the self-evident that we notice that we have not in the least understood it: it is then that a natural opportunity for effort opens up and leads to understanding."

The "Reader" again marked an example illustrating this train of thought along the margin:

The fact that this little seed will turn into an acacia tree over the years is so self-evident that everybody accepts it who knows about the acacia tree. But then

> where do we go from there? As long as this feeling is there, there is no chance for
> the establishment of the scientific field of botany. It is only when we ourselves
> decide to wonder at this great transformation, when we are surprised at seeing this
> process, and when we research these and other individual processes to understand
> what is happening, that science begins. Of course, he who progresses far enough
> in science grows accustomed to proceeding from wonder to wonder without ever
> completing anything; we however do not wish to get lost in such distant abstrac-
> tions at all.

Although Hitler did not underline any further, the following section is
more than informative:

> We are not interested in the seed and the tree, but in the normally developed Cen-
> tral-European human and in the larger system which develops for him and partly
> from him. This system seems to develop with his conscious and yet instinctive,
> free and yet necessary cooperation. We try and wonder about things like workers'
> unions, about everyday events like the establishing of some association, about
> trivial phenomena and natural necessities like the family. We try to wonder about
> all these and thus arrive at deeper recognition. Meanwhile of course we are talk-
> ing about very simple things, just like the physiology of plants which, despite all
> its complexity, is remarkably simple to those who understand it. (391)

It is a haunting work, and as we shall see, its logic left its mark on the
logic of *Mein Kampf*. Otto's monarchist-socialism was, so to say, the
scientific foundation of Hitlerian "epistemology."

The other work in the library dealing with economic issues considers
the possibilities of German emigration to Argentina. It approves of un-
selfish cultural exchange between the countries, and holds that the
achievements of science and technology constitute the public treasure of
all nations. This time the thick blue lines drawn along the margin indicate unambiguous disagreement. Red, on the other hand, marks identification with a thought.[68] The book must have interested Hitler because at
the time he read it he had not yet received his German citizenship, and
he had to prepare himself for possible emigration.[69] Perhaps it was the
Ukraine that floated in front of his eyes, instead of Argentina, when he
marked the section saying that "The poor, who are unproductive, should
be given a piece of land, which is just as unproductive, and thus both of
these forms of unemployed capital will be revived."

J. Bush dedicated his book on business calculations to Hitler in
1932,[70] and the Führer's color pencil marked the sections concerning
the absence of capital and the narrowness of the markets, as well as
those sections concerning decreasing production costs and state sup-

port of entrepreneurs.[71] Perhaps already thinking of taking over power, Hitler underlined the passage that followed the section in which the author emphasizes the determining character of daily work hours and arrives at the conclusion that poverty helps knowledge to victory:

> *Fundamental improvement is not to be expected until our governors have acknowledged that fixed state costs, like fixed business costs, have to be as low as possible to enable an economic upswing. Currently we are very far from achieving this due to internal and foreign political reasons.*
>
> *Our Governors should keep it in mind at all times that the private entrepreneur is the foundation of the state whether in small trade, industry, trade or agriculture. He ensures the possibility of income for workers and administrators, and through his taxes and the taxes of his employees, he enables the state and the community to carry out their duties and pay their office workers.* (66)

This might have been the handbook for Hitlerian economic political pragmatism, if we can entertain such a notion.

We know that war was close to the Führer's heart. Yet it seems that military science was less to his taste because there are few serious works of military science in his library, and there are few signs that indicate his having studied this field.[72] Obviously, it is possible that the great works of military science were exhibited in the building of the Reich Chancellery, and that the Führer engrossed himself in them there. There were a lot of voices that acknowledged his knowledge of military science, especially among his followers, servants, and those who were busy justifying themselves, while some other voices doubted it. These people saw the world differently, that the basis of Hitler's military erudition was the trenches and the dispatch service between military posts. This was just one more reason for him to dislike educated and rational military leaders. Still, it is surprising that we find only one work from the oft-cited Clausewitz, and that even that version is aimed at the general public rather than being a work of scholarly character.[73] The catalogue number of the Reich Chancellery can be found in it, yet this does not mean that he borrowed it from there, as the editor dedicated the work "to the Führer and savior of the German people."

Hitler cannot have been impressed by the grand book given to him by Fritz Thyssen that introduced the great military commanders and strategists,[74] as he must have found Cromwell, Napoleon, Washington and Clausewitz to be depressing, even though he happily used them as examples. He must have been even unhappier later on when the grand capitalist Thyssen turned against him. Still, the book is a fascinating documentary. There is a telegram in it from precisely the Thyssen family wishing him a happy birthday, although it appears to have been glued in at a later date. There are also a few newspaper cuttings about the seizure of Thyssen's assets, and excerpts from the millionaire Nazi supporter's letter of February 3, 1940, in which he regretted that he had reorganized the Nazi Party in 1932 with the help of von Papen, von Kirdorf and Krupp, and had consequently helped Hitler into power.

Two other books offer an interesting insight into the Führer's reading habits. They both concern First World War military operations against France.[75] One of them is a thoroughly professional work. Hitler's *ex libris* lurks within it, but not a single underlining can be found. In contrast to this, the Führer scribbled into an earlier popular work[76] written by Field Marshall Schlieffen's doctor who was a military strategist. It should be noted that he received this book in June 1940 from an admirer.

The Führer must have gladly marked the sections which elaborated on Belgium's occupation being commanded by the instinct of self-preservation. Such sections suggested that the English had been preparing to do the same—but in their case with the consent of the Belgian government. The "Reader" recognized that history may be repeating itself when he drew a line along the margin. In addition he double underlined a few sentences from the following passage: "This time it also has to be considered that Schlieffen first of all targeted France, the ally of England, with the realization of his plan in mind—this is because during that time the Russian army was unable to act because of the Japanese. *Thus shortly before his death at the end of 1912, he kept himself to this plan, according to which he set up the majority of the German army in the West. All he did was to expand upon this plan, as he knew that the whole Russian army would have to be accounted for later on as an enemy.*"

He wanted to create a *fait accompli* with a rapid and decisive strike on the western front: "*Political or emotional sentimentalities, such as the protection of Alsace, the safety of Baden, the protection of Prussia or Silesia from the Russian invasion, were alien to him* [Field

Marshall Schlieffen]. He had only goal in mind: the rapid destruction of the French and English armies." Hitler must have liked the fact that Schlieffen's plan was built on Frederick the Great's strategy. He marked the citation from the Prussian king as well:

> Most difficult is the drafting of those military plans where a much stronger and larger army has to be fought. Then shelter must be sought in politics, and one must strive to turn one's enemies against each other or to divide them by ensuring advantages for one side as opposed to the other. From a military point of view one has to know to loose at the right time (he who wants to protect all will protect nothing). A principle has to be sacrificed to the enemy, while the entire force has to be regrouped: then the enemy must be forced to enter into battle, and everything must be done to annihilate him.

At times we have the impression that the Führer felt it an honor to scribble into something. Indeed, his markings in general seem to be manifestations of his approval, and he usually underlined sections with a message value. Yet there are also a number of works without any markings, and we were also able to handle many such books that he had presumably read into or, as we know for a fact, he studied.

Notes

1. Ernst Jünger, *Feuer und Blut: Ein kleiner Ausschnitt aus einer grossen Schlacht* [Fire and blood: A small cut from a large battle]. Magdeburg: 1925. Dedication, in Latin script: *"Leipzig, Sebastien Bachstr. 18. / 9. 1. 1926 / Dem nationalen Führer Adolf Hitler! / Ernst Jünger."*

2. Kurt G. W. Ludecke, *I knew Hitler*. London: 1938, p. 688.

3. Guido Knopp, *Ne féljünk Hitlertől!* [Let's not be afraid of Hitler]. Budapest: 1997, p. 21; Guido Knopp, *Hitler, eine Bilanz* [Hitler, a measure of balance]. Berlin: 1995.

4. Eitner, *Hitler*, p. 13.

5. Rudolph Binion, *Hitler among the Germans*. New York, Oxford, Amsterdam: 1976, p. 35.

6. Philipp Bouhler, *Adolf Hitler, das Werden einer Volksbewegung* [Adolf Hitler, the birth of a people's movement]. Lübeck: 1932, p. 25. Dedication: *"Dem Führer in Verehrung / und Treue gewidmet / München: October 1932 Ph. Bouhler"*

7. E. M. Arndt, *Katechismus für den Teutschen Kriegs- und Wehrmann, worin gelehrt wird, wie ein christlicher Wehrmann seyn und mit Gott in den Streit gehen soll* [Catechism for the Teutonic war and soldiers, in which it is taught, how a Christian soldier should be and how he must go to war with God]. Köln: 1815.

8. Stock, *Die Judenfrage* [The question of the Jews], p. 511.

9. Picker, *Hitlers Tischgespräche* [Hitler's roundtable talks], p. 168.

10. Hans Kohn, *The Mind of Germany*. New York: 1960, p. 270.

11. George L. Mosse, *The Crisis of German Ideology*. New York: 1964, p. 31–39; Karl Dietrich Bracher, *The German Dictatorship*. New York: 1976, pp. 31–32.

12. Fritz Stern, *Kulturpessimismus als politische Gefahr* [Cultural pessimism as a political hazard]. Bern, Stuttgart, Vienna: 1963, pp. 25–126.

13. Nolte, *Der Faschismus*; Fest, *Hitler*. 1998.

14. Bullock, *Hitler*.

15. Fest, *Hitler*. 1998, p. 201.

16. Ibid., p. 550.

17. Ibid., p. 543.

18. Eitner, *Hitler*, p. 113.

19. Paul de Lagarde, *Deutsche Schriften* [German writings]. Munich: 1934.

20. Joachim C. Fest, *The Face of the Third Reich*. New York: 1970, pp. 163–74.

21. Picker, *Hitlers Tischgespräche* [Hitler's roundtable talks], p. 269.

22. *Lehrstoffsammlung und Grundplan für die weltanschauliche Schulung der Nationalsozialistischen Deutschen Arbeiterpartei* [Study pack and foundation plan for the schooling of the National Socialist German Workers' Party]. w. 1., w. y., p. 29.

23. Serge Lang, Ernst von Schenck eds., *Memoirs of Alfred Rosenberg*. Chicago, New York: 1949.

24. Eitner, *Hitler*, p. 117.

25. Paul R. Josephson, *Totalitarian Science and Technology*. New Jersey: 1996.

26. Houston Stewart Chamberlain, *Richard Wagner der Deutsche als Künstler, Denker und Politiker* [Richard Wagner, the German as artist, thinker and politician]. Leipzig: w. y. Dedication: "*Ich halte es für männlich und offen, / seinem Irrtum an- zuer- / kennen, aber nicht das halte / ich für männlich, dem einen / Vorwurf darüber zu machen, / der von seinem Irrtum / zurückgekommen ist. / v. Bismarck / Am Tage Ihres 44. Geburtstages / Ihnen, verehrter Herr Reichs- / kanzler, in Dankbarkeit / ergebenst / zugeeignet / von ein Wagnerverehrenin / Leipzig: 20. IV. 33.*"

27. Mária Ormos, *Nácizmus—fasizmus* [Nazism—fascism]. Budapest: 1987, pp. 110–11.

28. Nolte, *Der Faschismus* [Fascism], pp. 351–53.

29. Kohn, *The Mind of Germany*, p. 268.

30. Fest, *Hitler*. 1973, p. 55, 181.

31. National Archives and Record Administration, Maryland (NARA), Captured German Documents Microfilmed in Berlin, (Hoover Institution): NSDAP Hauptar- chiv [main archive]. T 581 Reel 52. No. 1210.

32. Carl Schmitt, *Ex captivitate salus*. Cologne: 1950, p. 21.

33. Paul Bülow, *Adolf Hitler und der Bayreuther Kulturkreis* [Adolf Hitler and the cultural circle of Bayreuth]. Leipzig, Hamburg: w. y., p. 9.

34. Friedrich P. Reck-Malleczewen, *Tagebuch eines Verzweifelten: Zeugnis einer innerer Emigration* [Diary of a skeptic: Witness to an internal emigration]. Stuttgart: 1966. Cited in Fest, *Hitler*. 1998, p. 89.

35. Houston Stewart Chamberlain, *Bühnendichtungen* [Dramas]. Munich: 1915. Dedication: "*H. S. Chamberlains dramatische Versuche / blieben Adolf Hitler wohl*

noch un- / bekannt? / Als herzlicher Weihnachtsgruss / sind sie ihm hier zugedacht / (ins besondere der Weinbauer!) / Bayreuth, Dec. 1924."

36. H. S. Chamberlain, *Herrn Hinkebein's Schädel: Gedankenhumoreske* [Mr Hinkebein's skull: humorous deliberations]. Munich: 1922. Dedication: "*Adolf Hitler, / noch diese kleine / heiter – ernste Zugabe – / unter vielen stillen, / tiefen Wünschen über / reicht / von / Eva Chamberlain / Bayreuth, Weihnachten / 1924.*"

37. Thomas Mann, *Reden und Aufsätze 4.* [Speeches and writings 4]. Frankfurt am Main: 1974, p. 846.

38. H. S. Chamberlain, *Worte Christi.* Munich: w. y. Dedication: "*Unserem geliebten Führer / in Dankbarkeit u. Verehrung / Clara von Behl / Weihnachten: 1935.*"

39. Hermann Rauschning, *Hitler Speaks.* London: 1940, p. 57.

40. Köhler, *Wagners Hitler,* pp. 325–26.

41. Domarus, *Hitler,* p. 570.

42. Fest, *Hitler.* 1973, pp. 48–56; Joachim C. Fest, "Um einen Wagner von aussen bittend: Richard Wagner" [Of a Wagner from the outside]. In *Der Ring von Niebelungen: Ansichten des Mythos* [The Niebelung circle: Views of the myth]. Eds. Udo Bermbach, Dieter Borchmeyer. Stuttgart, Weimar: 1995, pp. 182–88.

43. John Toland, *Adolf Hitler.* New York: 1976, pp. 34–37, 142–45, 996–97.

44. Adolf Hitler, *Die Reden, Aufrufe und Kundgebungen des Führers III.* [The Führer's Speeches, appeals, and declarations III]. Type written manuscript. Library of Congress, Rare Books and Special Collections.

45. Adolf Hitler, *Die Reden, Aufrufe und Kundgebungen des Führers V.* [The Führer's speeches, appeals, and declarations V]. Type written manuscript. Library of Congress, Rare Books and Special Collections.

46. Walter C. Langer, *The Mind of Adolf Hitler.* New York: 1972, p. 95.

47. Fest, "Um einen Wagner" [Of a Wagner], p. 186.

48. Eitner, *Hitler,* p. 90.

49. Library of Congress, Collection of the Manuscript Division (LC CMD), German Captured Documents, Rehse Collection, Reel 163.

50. Toland, *Adolf Hitler,* p. 997.

51. Mann, *Reden* [Speeches], p. 848.

52. Toland, *Adolf Hitler,* p. 139.

53. Berthold Hinz, *Die Malerei im deutschen Faschismus: Kunst und Konterrevolution* [Painting in German fascism: Art and counterrevolution]. Munich: 1974, p. 181.

54. Eitner, *Hitler,* p. 118.

55. Albert Speer, *Erinnerungen* [Recollections]. Frankfurt am Main, Berlin, Vienna: 1969, pp. 73–74.

56. Hitler, *Die Reden, Aufrufe V.* [Speeches, appeals V], p. 8.

57. Kubizek, *Young Hitler,* p. 131.

58. Hitler, *Die Reden, Aufrufe V.* [Speeches, appeals V], p. 8.

59. Ibid., pp. 184–86.

60. Ibid., pp. 190–91.

61. Eitner, *Hitler,* p. 137.

62. Picker, *Hitlers Tischgespräche* [Hitler's roundtable talks], p. 68; *Adolf Hitler: Monologe im Führerhauptquartier 1941–1944* [Adolf Hitler: Monologues in the Führer's headquarters]. Eds. Heinrich Heim, Werner Jochmann. Hamburg: 1980, p. 234.

63. Wolf R. Marchand, *Joseph Roth und völkisch-nationalistische Wertbegriffe* [Joseph Roth and folk-national concepts of value]. Bonn: 1974, p. 366.

64. Eitner, *Hitler*, p. 152.

65. Phelps, "Die Hitler-Bibliothek" [The Hitler-library]; Wallach, "Adolf Hitlers Privatbibliothek" [Adolf Hitler's private library].

66. Berthold Otto, *Der Zukunftstaat als sozialistische Monarchie* [The future state as a socialist monarchy]. Berlin: 1910, p. 62. *"Der Quittungsempfänger meldete seinem Postamt einfach die aufgedruckte Nummer der Quittung; er würde daraufhin – ohne noch besondere Telephonnummer zu brauchen – ohne weiteres mit dem suchen zuständigen Postbeamten verbunden, der zur Kontrolle die Nummer zurücksagt."* [Hitler's correction of word order: *"ohne weiteres suchen mit dem zuständigen Postbeamten."*]

67. Ibid., p. 62.

68. Hermann Lamm, *Auswanderungsmöglickeiten in Argentinien* [Emigration possibilities in Argentina]. Dresden: 1929.

69. Wallach, "Adolf Hitlers Privatbibliothek" [Adolf Hitler's private library], p. 37.

70. Eitner, *Hitler*, p. 137.

71. John Bush, *Die Geschäftskalkulation: Ein Handbuch für Geschäftsleiter in Industrie, Gewerbe, Handel und Landwirtschaft* [Business calculations: A handbook for managers in industry, handicrafts trade and agriculture]. Halberstadt: 1926. Dedication: *"Dem Hochverehrter Führer unserer / Bewegung Herrn Adolf Hitler / überreicht vom Verfasser / Pinneberg, d. 8. Nov. 1932."*

72. Wallach, "Adolf Hitlers Privatbibliothek" [Adolf Hitler's private library], p. 41.

73. Carl von Clausewitz, *Krieg und Staat: Eine Auswahl aus den kriegsphilosophischen und politischen Schriften* [War and state: A selection from war philosophical and political writings]. Ed. Hans Nieman. Potsdam: 1936. Dedication: *"Dem Führer und Retter / des deutschen Volkes / als geringes Zeichen / der Dankbarkeit zur / Erinnerung an seine / Worte beim Schluß des / Parteikongresses 1936 / in Verehrung zugeeignet. / Dessau, den 14. 9. 1936. / Hans Niemann."*

74. *Führertum: 25 Lebensbilder von Feldherren aller Zeiten* [Führer-dom—leadership: 25 cameos of field heros from all times]. *Auf Veranlassung des Reichswehrminister Dr. Groener bearbeitet von Offizieren des Reichsheeres und der Reichsmarine und zusammengestellt von Generalmajor von Cochenhausen.* Berlin: 1930. Dedication: *"Dem Führer Adolf Hitler zur / Erinnerung an seinen Besuch in / dem Düsseldorfer Industriebetrieb / Januar 32 / Fritz Thyssen."*

75. Karl Justrow, *Feldherr und Kriegstechnik: Studien über den Operationsplan des Grafen Schlieffen und Lehren für unseren Wehraufbau und Landesverteidigung* [Field commander and war technique: Studies on the operational plan of Grafen Schlieffen and teaching for the home defence armoury]. Oldenburg: 1933. Dedica-

tion: "*Dem Reichskanzler / des deutschen Reiches / Herrn Adolf Hitler / in großer Verehrung überreicht / Justrow.*"

76. Hugo Rochs, *Schlieffen: Ein Leben- und Charakterbild für das deutsche Volk* [Schlieffen: A life and character description for the German people]. Berlin: 1921. Dedication: "*Meinem Führer / gewidmet. / Motto: 'so oder so' / Sieg Heil! / Stannenberg / 19. 5. 1940.*" Cited and analyzed in Wallach, "Adolf Hitlers Privatbibliothek" [Adolf Hitler's private library], pp. 40–42.

Chapter 3

Books That Hitler Read Into

Perhaps the only common feature of the books dedicated to Hitler was that their authors, as we shall see, represented points of view that directly conflicted with one another. Obviously, Nazis wrote the majority of these books. Indeed, an intellectual and moral low point is marked by Nazi belles-lettres, if this pile of books can be referred to in that way at all. But why their belles-lettres?

On Nazi Belles-Lettres

The answer to the question of why belles-lettres mark such a low point is based on impressions and to some extent on our astonishment. It is no use denying that there is a certain amount of "amusement" to be gleaned from Nazi "scholarship" since it is like caricature, resembling something similar to that which we might personally experience. The effect of the title *Hitler is Alive!* is one of comic *déjà vu*.[1] The representation of the philosophy of the theory of races at literary fiction level provides the perfect "realism"—at least for the target audience of readers: believers of the cause, or rather initiated accomplices. A realistic image is depicted of the way in which the Nazi subculture thought, and about its likely absurdities. Moreover, the means in which images are represented lend a stronger emphasis to the absurdity of the Nazi worldview dubbed the "theory of races."

The construction of "the Jew" in theoretical works transports the reader into a peculiar fantasy world with abstract concepts and formulaic curses. It is no accident that many failed to take *Mein Kampf* seriously, and it is evident the Jewish readers themselves felt that the special characteristics of "the Jew" were not applicable to them at all. According to Stefan Zweig's original memoirs in their manuscript form: "Our mistake was—and it was made all over the place—that we oriented ourselves from the wrong papers, those written for erudite people which spoke with the old liberal conceit about the self-important agitator; none of us then thought of glancing through *Mein Kampf* before it was too late. Only a few journalists mocked the oppressive and staccato prose, instead of dealing with the content."

They thought that Nazism "[…] was not aimed against freedom, peace, erudition, capital, nor culture or religion, nor even against the Jews, but only against Bolshevism and the 'Marxist' Jews [the author added religion retrospectively, in red]."[2] They did not think that such a half-schooled figure might walk in Bismarck's footsteps in the country of culture where learning had the power to create societal classes and erudition was idolized.[3] In any case, as Stefan Zweig believes, Freud, who as a person was deeply shocked by what happened while remaining unsurprised as a thinker, declared that "There are just as few hundred percent truths as there is hundred percent alcohol."[4] This actually crops up in Nazi "literary works" as well. Had Stefan Zweig looked through a couple of these works he might well have looked through *Mein Kampf* as well.

Literary versions of history render certain things palpable that are hardly possible to transfer to the reader with convincing power in an essay. For example, the aforementioned *Hitler is Alive!* includes a short story where the fate of a Jewish rag and bone man could well be an application of the paradigm of contradictory racist and anti-Semitic clichés embellished with aristo-phobia and anti-Western, or rather anti-Parisian feeling. More precisely, to use Hannah Arendt's expression, it might be the paradigm of "the banality of evil."

The story is as horrific as it is simple. A poor old huckster grows rich, but only his daughter knows his secret. In accordance with anti-Semitic mythology the old man's dream is typically Jewish: he wishes to marry his daughter off and then vanish, so that he does not get in anyone's way. Meanwhile, we are informed that the Jews do not consider people from other races as humans. Yet it is the Jews who are on their way to extinction, but manage to stay alive by living as parasites on other races. They caused the starvation and death of 28 million people in Bolshevik Russia. Even the rag and bone man made his dog suffer from hunger until the local priest bought it from him. However, the Nazi-style happy ending has yet to come: the girl's suitor, a pseudo-earl, kills the merchant's daughter in Paris. Vigilante SA lads catch the old man who tries to escape from Germany, and because he tries to smuggle gold and silver out of the country they justly lock him up because, as the author implies, Germany is a nation of law. Then, whilst in prison the captured "criminal" commits suicide. However, before he does, he scratches something onto the wall: "Hitler is stronger than Judah. So Jehovah has to accept his sacrifice! Jehovah, the Jewish God, Avenge your children!" However: "We Germans wish to serve our people and God, and thus we shall not fall, but strive upwards and onwards with Adolf Hitler into the Third Reich! To the salvation of our people and the whole world."[5] In the book's dedication the author commits himself to the fight. While this book expresses Nazi "universalism" to a certain extent, Artur Dinter's novel, *Crime Against the Blood* is clearly a book of self-serving racist nonsense with, of course, plenty of "scientific" pontification. It is no wonder then, that in 1917 the company that was to become the Lehmann Verlag Publishing Company did not want to undertake the publication of this book. It was printed in a run of only a thousand copies, but in 1918 it reached four thousand issues, in 1921 170,000, in 1927 235,000 and by 1934 260,000 volumes were issued.[6]

Hermann, the main hero, knows everything that Hitler has not yet realized. The mixing of blood is nothing but an affliction: the death of the race. The poison: Jewish and Negro blood. Thus it is no surprise that the main hero's wife, who had a Jewish ancestor who strove to undermine the German race, gives birth to an Afro-Judeo monkey. She then dies during her second birth. Afterwards Hermann establishes a race-hygiene research institute. He wants to remarry. But his fiancée was once seduced by a Jew, and so she kills her child and then herself. Our main hero kills the paramour. The court exonerates him.

Did Hitler like this work? Perhaps he did, to some extent. The notion of the Jew afflicting the Germans crops up in *Mein Kampf*, the book with which Hitler intended to supersede every participant of Nazi discourse. However, he could not have approved of Dinter saying that the German people are compounded from Celts, Slavs and Germans: "the German people is not full-blooded [*rassenrein*], but a racially clean [*rassisch rein*] people."[7] Then, after Trotsky's removal, Dinter propagated an alliance with the Communists, and as a result of his catechism of the religion of races entitled *197 Theses* Hitler expelled him from the party (this was to the author's great surprise as he had dedicated that work to the Führer "with faith," just as he had his novel).

As indicated earlier on, Hitler recognized with an excellent feel for tactics that the issue of religion should not be agitated. Meanwhile, his anti-Semitism also covered anti-Christianity. When he brought his "new-pagan" revenge down upon the Jews, he wanted to eliminate the "mystical Israel" which symbolized Christianity—as it has been again pointed out in recent times.[8] It is typical of his demagogy: he denounced the Jewish people as being incapable of creation, yet—in a paradoxical way, whilst remaining faithful to his viewpoint on the theory of races—he also respected the Jews (or more accurately "the Jew," as he used the singular consistently). By announcing the German people as the chosen people, he wanted to occupy precisely the place of the Jews. It was in fact praise that "the Jew" was even capable of poisoning the excellent German people.

The author of Hitler's *Psychogram* also assumes that Hitler had an inferiority complex in relation to the Jews because he talked with admiration about the way they survive through everything, that they are still there even at the end of the world; he even said something along the lines that the Jews and the Germans are like brothers. Thus "the eternal Cain" could not protect himself from the thought that Arminius and Abraham had the same ancestors, although he did say something about the Jews being created from another God.[9] The master builder [*Baumeister*] held the Greeks and the Romans in higher esteem than the ancient Germans; he toyed with the idea that he was completing Jesus Christ's work in his opposition to the Jews, and he reached back to early Jewish tradition when he made the Christian God into a "Nazi War God" [*NS-Kriegsgott*].[10]

We are often struck by the impression that Hitler viewed the Germans as "a race on its own," while the Jews were "a race for its own." Hitler, who happily chattered, or rather bellowed about the gods, did not want to simply cover up his new paganism—it was as if he wanted to ally with the Jewish God against the Jews: "Eternal nature takes merciless revenge on trespasses against its orders. So I believe today I am acting in accordance with the mind of the almighty Creator: in being aware of the Jews I fight for the Lord's work."[11] Wickham Steed, a journalist who contributed to the division of the Hapsburg Empire, and thus—unintentionally—helped clear the Führer's path, believed that the above citation from *Mein Kampf* was "psychologically [...] one of the most interesting passages in Hitler's autobiography," in that it is the manifestation of his persecution complex.[12]

The above passage is interesting from the perspective of Hitler's Machiavellianism. He occasionally stated that it is not the Jewish, but the German people who are the chosen ones, and he wanted to validate this idea in an alliance with the Jewish God. At the same time he subordinated the Judeo-Christian God to "eternal nature," because he denied that nature was a divine creation. The politician's artful speculation seemed contradictory in the ideological sphere and seemed to belittle ideology itself. Even so, these commentaries could not resolve the contradiction between Hitlerian and Nazi images of the Jews.

Rosenberg had obviously recognized this inherent incongruity of Nazi anti-Semitism, i.e. that it simultaneously abuses and praises the enemy. Thus—working in his role as ideologist—he denied that the Jews were a race at all, and as we shall see, he did this by adjusting to the Führer's views. In the meantime Nazi hawks could hardly wait to deal with the Catholic Church either. Among those hawks was Martin Bormann, the secretary. The Führer's most faithful servant was a prime example of one of the terribly sly, stupid, and persistent functionaries in the paper war who were typical of life in the authorities.[13] In the end, Hitler resigned himself in spirit to taking openly drastic measures against the Catholic Church at some time in the future, while he continued to pay church tax and go to church services every now and then.

His relationship with freemasonry is similarly duplicitous. He depicted the figure of the freemason as being synonymous with the Jew—a public enemy. At the same time he elaborated to Rauschning the exact opposite of that which he proclaimed in his speeches:

In Germany they are just a harmless union for the mutual protection of interests. [...] All the supposed abominations, the skeletons and death's heads, the coffins and the mysteries, are mere bogeys for children. But there is one dangerous element, and that is the element I have copied from them. They form a sort of priestley nobility. They have developed an esoteric doctrine, not merely formulated, but imparted through the medium of symbols and mysterious rites in degrees of initiation. The hierarchical organisation and the initiation through symbolic rites are things that we can say do not burden the brains but work on the imagination through magic and cultic symbols—this is the dangerous element and the element that I have copied.[14]

Thus, while Hitler preached the rational character of his ideology he actively collaborated to make the symbolism of religion and freemasonry serve Nazi sorcery (or to use another phrase, "Nazi propaganda"). Transfiguration became secularized by transforming the Christian salvation story into a story of racial salvation. The phrase "Heil Hitler," as Hanns Johst, the writer and prophet put it, "expressed that a thousand years of complaining about the vale of tears will finally come to an end, and the Reich will become a heavenly empire."[15]

Bishop Hudal's Attempt at Conciliation

One fascinating item in the Hitler Library concerns the relation between Nazism and Christianity, namely *The Fundaments of National Socialism: a Study of the History of Ideas.*[16] Its author is Alois Hudal, a Roman Catholic Bishop. Just what was it precisely that he undertook with this work?

The author wrote a dedication in this unusual book in September 1937: "To the Führer of the German rise, to the Siegfried of German hope and greatness, to Adolf Hitler."

These lines have recently been used to deride him, emphasizing that he saved Nazi officers at the end of the War whilst conveniently forgetting the fact that he had also done the same for Jews earlier,[17] even though these days this fact is well known.[18] Nevertheless, the dictates of his heart undoubtedly drew him closer to the Nazis. In retrospect he reprimanded himself for not noticing that Hitler was, amongst other things, merely a follower of the obscure, anti-Catholic, pan-German movement of the Georg Schönerer type, which arose in half-schooled small towns and villages[19] and spread mostly in the Sudetenland region where anti-Semitism mixed with proclamations concerning the Slavic danger. Hudal, too, came from Bohemia, and his German nationalism was defined by his anxiety about national existence on the borders as well as the emotions surrounding the "metaphysical sins" of the Versailles Treaty. Hence we arrive at the sinful and naive illusion: Nazism can be transformed into a nationalism which could be the basis for the excellence of both the German nation and petit-bourgeois Christian values, while also fulfilling its universal historical mission against Communism. This inevitably points towards a kind of Biedermeier fascism. Yet its apostle cannot be claimed to be unequivocally anti-Slav, as in 1922 he encouraged rapprochement between Eastern and Western Christianity.[20]

In his infamous book written in 1937 he raised his voice against racism rather vehemently. Thus far no one had made any effort to unveil the ideological precursors and complexities of Nazism with such detailed analysis. His presentation of the French race cult, or his alternatives to the glorification of the nation and the social utopia of the class-free society give us a basis for viewing him as a precursor of Ernst Nolte's comparative phenomenological analysis. His main opponent was Rosenberg, on the subject of whose pseudo-philosophy and principle work, *The Twentieth-Century Myth*, it is perhaps only George Lukacs who also managed to write so exhaustively at the time—from the opposing camp, that is.[21] Rome placed the book on its Index of prohibited books at Hudal's suggestion.[22] This move, however created a huge demand for the work, and the number of its issues reached the two hundred thousand mark,[23] something which Hitler might have viewed with a certain amount of irritation, as well as gratification. He did not like Rosenberg's book, and developments concerning the work might have made him feel justified about his own Church policy, that is his feigned neutrality towards religion. This political lesson taught him to be careful.

If, however, Hudal had read *Mein Kampf* more attentively and not been mislead by Hitler's tactical allowances towards religion, he might have noticed how Hitler continued along the lines of the Schönerer movement. Hudal skimmed through Hitler's work to find only what he needed in the same way that bourgeois citizens, degraded to the rank of Communist, skimmed through Lenin's writings. But it has to be said for Hudal that at least he reprimanded Dinter for, amongst other things, his anti-Semitism. The Roman bishop was also the precursor of today's sly cunning when he emphasized that the history of anti-Semitism is the history of resolving the Jewish question. In connection with Rosenberg's views he also raised the issue of anti-Semitism being, to a large extent, part of the problem of the Eastern German frontier's absorption into the Reich, while racially prejudiced anti-Semitism was opposed to Christianity as well. Thus he made allowances for Nazism while distancing himself from it. Through categorizing the Jews (as being Eastern, Western, Communist, Zionist, frontier, Conservative, or loyal to the state) he did not actually support the Nuremberg regulations, but did not rally against them either, apparently in a manner similar to that of Stefan Zweig, who also tried to demonstrate the differentiated nature of the Jews when contemplating the irrationality of racism.

In fact Hudal did the same, but on theological grounds—he produced a contrived version of the myth of the "wandering Jew" against religious Jews. He suspected the first racist was amongst the Jews who lived after Christ, because he thought that the Jews considered divine mercy as a natural endowment, a given thing, *a priori*. At the same time, for Hudal they are "the eternal emigrants of world history, whose restlessness in foreign cultural spheres also goes back to the loss of a national center-point."[24] Yet he paid particular attention to highlight that the problem of the Jews is spiritual and not racial, i.e. that it is not of a materialistic and natural character. On the other hand, he emphasized that he saw no reason for the protection of Jewish Marxists, in which case he leant towards the acceptance of the vulgar-empirical racial position. However, he was against Nazism in his observation that a lot of Marxists became Nazis, and that their materialism contributed to this transformation. Indeed, we can find one example of a novel in the Hitler Library (also dedicated to the Führer) where the hero becomes a Nazi after having set out as a Marxist because he suddenly "saw through the Marxist lie."[25] A Nazi "moralist," who also dedicated his book to the Führer, justifiably asked in his poem:

> You "Communist," do you know
> that you are not a Communist? [26]

Hitler himself told Hermann Rauschning, the Mayor of Danzig that "there is more that binds us to Bolshevism than separates us from it."

The chief binding agent was "the revolutionary feeling." He gave permission for Communists to be instantly accepted into the Nazi party. He thought that "The petit bourgeois Social-Democrat and the trade-union boss will never make a National Socialist, but the Communist always will."[27] According to an authentic contemporary witness the Nazi leader arrived at the conclusion that "Stalinism represents the development of Bolshevism into a sort of Fascism, the Fascism, it is true, of a Genghis Khan."[28]

Retrospectively it was also read into Hudal's argumentation that he accepted the Nuremberg laws as, so to say, a rightful means of self-defense.[29] Contrary to this the German bishop in Rome definitively refuted the racial concepts of law which state that the will of the race is the law itself, and stressed with a deep sense of theoretical awareness that such concepts of law can be traced back to Carl Schmitt's formulas. Thus he dismissed Nietzsche and Lenin's ethics of convenience (however, it is also true that in the meantime Schmitt, with his long period of silence following his little anti-Semitic article, lay the foundations for the raising of his voice as the upholder of the subjugated German spirit in his small book later published in 1950, with its title proclaiming moral superiority, *Ex captivitate salus.*). Hudal allowed his own naïve ethics of convenience to talk when he said that if "National-Socialism is only a political-social problem," then Catholics could join. But if it is a dogma, worldview or even a myth then "*non-possumus.*"[30]

Hudal's book is a strange example of word-magic. It was published in Vienna partly because the opportunity presented itself there, and partly because its subject was a hot issue there at the time. Due to the threat of *Anschluss* the relationship between the Catholic Church and the Nazi leadership seemed to be an essential question for Austrian Catholics. Franz von Papen, onetime chancellor and eternal intriguer, gave the dedicated book to Hitler and remembered that "He accepted it with pleasure and undertook to read it with interest. What is more, he gave an order for it to be imported freely into Germany, where I hoped it would have a sobering effect." Nevertheless, Goebbels, and even more so Bormann, soon complained that it had had a bad effect on the party, and von Papen was unable to convince Hitler of the opposite.[31]

But how was this work received in Catholic circles? The Catholic press in Vienna criticized Hudal's work because of its terminology.

Rome also tacitly disapproved of it. Pius XIth indicated at the beginning of reading the book that one cannot speak of *spirit* in connection
with the Nazi Movement, as it represents "massive materialism." On
the other hand Innitzer, the Cardinal of Vienna, and Kurt Schusch-
nigg, the Chancellor, supported the author.[32] Yet Faulhaber, the Cardinal of Munich, called him "the main party theologian." Afterwards
Hudal found respite for his troubled conscience in this double rejec-
tion, thinking that it was still better than undermining the military
front and working against the ideal of German unity.[33] It is in this
spirit that he worked with an SS officer to make peace with the State,
Church, Reich and the Western powers as late as 1942/43. In March
1943 (in a scheme which in the end was left in the drawer of his desk),
he aimed to request amnesty not only for the Catholics, who had suffered for their beliefs, but for the Protestants, too, and also aimed to
call for "the immediate disruption of the murdering of Jews which
causes enormous damage to the Reich abroad." Furthermore he asked
for "humane treatment of the Jews, and their employment for useful
work in the interest of the Reich."[34] Then he advised the German
commander of the "free town" against the deportation of the Jews,
because he believed that the Pope would protest. However, Pius XIIth
acted differently,[35] and with some gratitude Hudal was later able to
report to Rolf Hochhuth about it. Hudal's experiences and perhaps
even his personal traits were incorporated into Hochhuth's drama *The
Deputy*.[36] Even though his ambiguous attitude is perhaps impossible to
capture through literary means alone, Hudal is certainly worth a novel,
let alone a drama. However, it is true that he could hardly have found
rehabilitators as Carl Schmitt or Heidegger did. His excuse is also
weaker than theirs, because as a bishop his role was greater than that
of someone who contemplated law or philosophized.

We can find other interesting things in the drabness of the Hitler
Library, including some things among the books dedicated to him.
These are first and foremost the works of the well-known American
journalist Hubert Renfro Knickerbocker, which are the products of a
particular brand of journalist-diplomacy on the one hand, and war on
the other.

Knickerbocker's Diplomacy and War

The simple dedications in Knickerbocker's books are a little misleading: "with regards"[37] and "with best wishes."[38] The writer of these books had no respect for the Führer, but he kept this fact to himself, and even managed to win Goebbels' favor for a while.[39] Reputedly: "After Hindenburg and Hitler, he was practically the best known man in the country. His *réclame* was fabulous, personally and politically. [...] Once a musical comedy was named after him—a supreme tribute!" Nonetheless "[...] he wrote a series exposing the Brown Terror that caused violent comment in New York, as well as Berlin. Presently he was excluded from the country. There are hate affairs as well as love affairs. The hate affair between Hitler and Knickerbocker is one of the most torrid in political history."[40] What is this attractive "new type of American journalism"[41] all about? It is a strange mix of straightforwardness and enigma, fact and theory—strange in the sense that as the Nazi system rejected democratic values we would expect sharp or sharper anti-Nazism from a Western democratic journalist. Knickerbocker studied psychiatry in Munich and Vienna. He viewed Germany, Italy and Europe like a patient, and he offered a diagnosis, describing the symptoms without comments that might have hindered healing. He did not call Nazism and Communism a cancer, even though what he described was precisely that. For example, in the *German Crisis* he depicts the scale of the civil war raging between the Fascists and the Communists through the image of forty injured and one dead every other day. Then he portrays a meeting which begins with cries of "Heil Moscow!" and "Heil Hitler!" which is soon broken up by the police at the point when the crowd is about to sing the *Internationale*, something of a red rag to Nazi bulls. Thus a fight is avoided. His diagnosis:

> In Germany the line between the left-wing radicals and the right-wing radicals is not straight, but an almost closed circle. Imagine a circle which is broken on the top. The gap in the circle between National Socialism and Communism represents the Russian control of Communism. The Nazi and Communist masses, not leaders, but masses, share few ideals but a great deal of emotion, and today, they are divided most of all by this gap. And the greatest paradox of German politics is: what makes both the Nazis and the Communists so very important for Germany as well as the rest of the world is not the two parties' hatred of one another, but the emotional similarity of their followers.[42]

The section giving voice to an unemployed Nazi teacher is equally successful. He states, without any tergiversation, that Hitler will wreck the Versailles peace agreement, retake the Polish Corridor, dismantle the Republic, end unemployment and chase out the Jews. Knickerbocker then stated that if Hitler gained power the Nazi leadership would "discard this simple Nazi's [the teacher's] program as idiocy or as provocation," yet his teacher is "neither a halfwit nor a provocateur, but quite simply a Nazi" and "these are the ultimate aims of the Nazi program."[43] His interview with Spengler is a good supplement to this story, because it shows that a Nazi teacher had understood more of history than a widely acknowledged philosopher of culture. At the same time the whole thing gives a sense of the elasticity of the judgement on the situation. According to Spengler "today [the Nazi party] is a party without a leader or a program. Their leaders are agitators, their program is a program of action." Of course that was true to a certain extent. However, Spengler's presumption that France could have occupied South China is somewhat surprising. Nonetheless, the fear of endeavors toward autarchy were not without substance, and neither was his prediction of the possibility of a hegemonic United States, although he was not the only person to think that at the time.[44]

Did Knickerbocker have any illusions about Hitler? Or was his belief rooted in the coercing power of reality when he granted a certain normality to the event of Hitler taking power? He never denied that he had his reservations. He qualified the rhetoric of Hitler in the arena of the circus in Munich as "the Billy Sunday of German politics" (Billy Sunday became popular as an evangelist). The audience of "eight thousand people were an instrument on which Hitler played the symphony of national passion." His outlining of the possibilities is no less ironic: "The evangelist Hitler could establish a new religion. The actor Hitler could grab a crowded theatre. The rhetorician Hitler could create a revolution." But the following was praise: "Hitler is an artist. The famous Brown House, [...] a palace with a hundred rooms [...] is his creation."[45] Even the German translation tones down the level of praise, as the English original speaks of the fact that "the building is in faultless taste."[46]

At that time the journalist and the Leader still granted mutual allowances to each other. Hitler gave a restrained interview, in which he considered the presence of General Motors to be advantageous. He did not rage against American-style shopping precincts, and he pretended to be the protector of the poor.[47] All these scenes and stories are interwoven with the suspense of a horrible catastrophe. As Knickerbocker's diagnosis concludes: "Like most European nations, the majority of Germans, together with Clausewitz, believe that war and politics are the same."[48] And even if the population of Germany cannot reach 250 million as Hitler predicted, Russia's population is growing ever faster. America "should be grateful for the Atlantic ocean. There is no ocean between Western Europe and the Soviet Union."[49]

But what fate awaited Europe? How was the fate of Europe and Germany connected? *Will Europe Rise Again?* asks Knickerbocker in the title of one of his books, and in it he deals with the Danube region, amongst other things. The work only tells us what at the time many thought they knew and hoped: that Germany would overcome the crisis and that "if it rose, Europe would rise, too." If von Papen's program were to be realized then the Nazis would fall: "The German recovery can only be delayed, if politics strangles the economy. [...] The fate of the Danube region depends on the fate of Europe." The Europeans expect both a reduction in its debt to, but at the same time new loans from, America: "I wonder if Europe will show a good example in helping the Danube region? If that happens than recovery will come within arm's reach for the peoples of the Danube countries. [...] Politics can only hold back the clock..."[50] Knickerbocker did not dedicate any of his works that surveyed expectable future progress to Hitler, even though they were also published in Berlin. The works are concerned with the arms race and Hitler's "preventive peace,"[51] the swing of the Soviet five-year plan of "military expedition," which cost the lives of several million kulaks, and the irrational attraction of Communism.[52] It was after these works that he wrote his most passionate work, in which he urged America to enter into the war with such vehemence that it was as if he had wanted to erase all his recently held illusions. As a follower of the Soviet alliance he emphasized that the Nazis had copied Bolshevik ethics, but that there was no other way out than to fight one disease along with the other—his former professor in Vienna had taught him that malaria is easier to treat once syphilis has been cured. In this case malaria symbolizes Communism and syphilis Fascism.[53] By then the American journalist made no secret of how he had laughed when he first saw Hitler in 1923. Nevertheless, he did not underestimate his role, because he believed that without him, "the most effective mob-master," the Nazi party would become fragmented. He added an authoritative undertone to his invocation to war with a Jung-interview that was a fascinating and insightful analysis of Hitler.

This interview is actually missing from the extensive Jung literature, even though it offers an excellent supplement to the facts regarding the debate on the Swiss psychologist's relation to Nazism.[54] Jung's opinion in brief: Hitler "is not an individual but a whole nation." "No nation keeps its word. A nation is a big, blind worm." The "collective intelligence of the crowd is like that of an alligator's." Jung told the American journalist that England and France would not help Bohemia five months before Munich, whilst reminding him that in 1934 Masaryk had predicted that the Nazis would also soon overcome the usual ecstasy of revolutionary movements and then all live in peace together...[55]

Hitler would have read Masaryk's "prediction" with great satisfaction, since he could have perceived it as being praise of the view he embraced: that of the effectiveness of a totalitarian system against the impotence of civil democracies. Had he spoken English we might assume that Hitler would have read through this book which Knickerbocker expressly directed against him, because he often delved into books which were explicitly opposed to his ideology. One such example is a book sent to him by Hans Hoppeler. The book contemplates the humane benevolence of Christianity, something that the dedication also suggested: "To you my Führer, in a quiet and foreboding hour." Hitler marked the section about the calcification of the coronary arteries and of the over-straining of the heart, since he himself suffered from such problems. He even underlined the author's explanation of Saint Paul's words calling for love: *"We feel much better if we think less about ourselves and more about our siblings; if we sacrifice more for the community, we feel better than before: the joy that we offer to others returns to our own hearts! This is not a big sacrifice, but a small one, moreover it is alms!"*[56] Hitler always studied medical books with great interest.[57] He also used certain auto-suggestive practices to calm his nerves.[58] However, in Hans Lungwitz's book on neurosis he only read as far as the section where it had to be cut open, just a few pages; yet in these few pages he possibly gained the knowledge that the neurosis of a highly-strung person only counts as an illness to the doctor and the patient himself, if the patient admits to his illness at all. He usually does not admit to it, preferring to suffer from some organic disease. But then Hitler closed the book where it reveals that this type of "illness" is simply infantilism. It would obviously have annoyed him to read that people suffering from communal neurosis identify themselves with a race or a class and then fit into the community without ever wishing to grow up.[59] Perhaps then Hitler was aware of what it was he did not read, and what his reasons were for doing so.

Notes

1. Alfred Wiehr, *Hitler lebt! Erzählungen um Führer und Volk* [Hitler lives! Stories on the Führer and the people]. Radolfzell: 1934.

2. Stefan Zweig, "Blick auf mein Leben" [A glance on my life]. In *Incipit Hitler.* Chap. 15, pp. 6–9. LC CMD; Comp. Stefan Zweig, *Die Welt von Gestern* [Yesterday's world]. Frankfurt am Main: 1977, p. 260.

3. George L. Mosse, "Jewish Emancipation." In *The Jewish Response to German Culture.* Eds. Jehuda Reinharz, Walter Schatzberg. Hannover, London: 1985, p. 16.

4. Zweig, *Blick* [Glance]. Chap. 16, pp. 13–17; Comp. Zweig, *Die Welt* [Yesterday's world], p. 304.

5. Wiehr, *Hitler lebt!* [Hitler lives!], pp. 84–89.

6. Günter Hartung, "Artur Dinter: A Successful Fascist Author in Pre-Fascist Germany." In *The Attractions of Fascism.* Ed. John Milfull, New York, Oxford, Munich: 1990, p. 116.

7. Artur Dinter, *Die Sünde wider das Blut* [Sin against the blood]. Leipzig: 1927, p. 207.

8. Mann, *Reden* [Speeches], p. 305.

9. Eitner, *Hitler*, pp. 109–13.

10. Eitner, *Hitler*, pp. 159–66.

11. Hitler, *Mein Kampf*, p. 70.

12. Wickham Steed, *Hitler. Whence and Whiter?* London: 1934, p. 59.

13. Jochen von Lang, *The Secretary. Martin Bormann: The Man Who Manipulated Hitler* Athens, Ohio: 1981, pp. 125–29.

14. Rauschning, *Hitler Speaks*, p. 237.

15. Klaus Vondung, *Magie und Manipulation* [Magic and manipulation]. Göttingen: 1971, p. 162.

16. Alois Hudal, *Die Grundlagen des Nationalsozialismus: Eine ideengeschichtliche Untersuchung* [The fundaments of national socialism: A research in the field of the history of ideas]. Leipzig, Vienna: 1937. Dedication: *"Dem Führer / der Deut-*

schen Erhebung / dem Siegfried / deutscher Hoffnung u. Grösse / Adolf Hitler / ge-widmet / vom Verfasser / Roma 3 / XI. 1937."

17. Hohn Weiss, *Ideology of Death: Why the Holocaust Happened in Germany.* Chicago: 1996, p. 390.

18. Hansjakob Stehle, "Bischof Hudal und SS-Führer Meyer" [Bishop Hudal and the SS-Leader Meyer]. *Vierteljahrshefte für Zeitgeschichte.* 1989. No. 2, pp. 307–22.

19. Alois Hudal, *Römische Tagebücher: Lebensbeichte eines alten Bischofs* [Roman diaries: Confessions of an old bishop about his life]. Graz, Stuttgart: 1976, p. 115.

20. Alois Hudal, *Die serbisch-orthodoxe Nationalkirche* [The Serb Orthodox National Chruch]. Graz, Leipzig: 1922, p. 120.

21. György Lukács, *Adalékok az esztétika történetéhez II.* [Adages to the history of esthetics II]. Budapest: 1972, pp. 419–23.

22. Hudal, *Römische Tagebücher* [Roman diaries], p. 117.

23. Picker, *Hitlers Tischgespräche* [Hitler's roundtable talks], p. 269.

24. Hudal, *Die Grundlagen* [The fundaments], p. 99.

25. Eugen Hadamovsky, *Hilfsarbeiter Nr. 50 000* [Unskilled worker No. 50 000]. Munich: 1938, p. 15.

26. Richard Euringer, *Chronik einer deutschen Wandlung 1925–1935* [Chronicle of a German transformation 1925–1935]. Hamburg: 1936, p. 141.

27. Rauschning, *Hitler,* p. 134.

28. Hermann Rauschning, *The Revolution of Nihilism.* New York: 1939, p. 57.

29. Bruce F. Pauley, *From Prejudice to Persecution: A History of Austrian Anti-Semitism.* Chapel Hill, London: 1991, p. 172; Guenter Lewy, *The Catholic Church and Nazi Germany.* New York, Toronto: 1968, p. 281.

30. Hudal, *Die Grundlagen* [The foundations], pp. 163–79, 253.

31. Franz von Papen, *Memoirs* [Memories]. Transl. Brian Connell. New York: 1953, p. 382.

32. Bruce F. Pauley, *From Pejudice to Persecution.* Chapel Hill, London: 1992, p. 172.

33. Hudal, *Römische Tagebücher* [Roman diaries], p. 118, pp. 148–49, 294.

34. Stehle, "Bischof Hudal und SS-Führer Meyer" [Bishop Hudal and the SS-Leader Meyer], p. 321.

35. Lewy, *The Catholic Church*, p. 301.

36. Stehle, "Bischof Hudal und SS-Führer Meyer." [Bishop Hudal and the SS-Leader Meyer], p. 316.

37. Hubert Renfro Knickerbocker, *Deutschland so oder so?* [Germany this or that?]. Berlin: 1932. Dedication: "To Adolf Hitler / with the regards of / H. R. Knick-erbocker / Berlin, March, 1932."

38. H. R. Knickerbocker, *Kommt Europa wieder hoch?* [Will Europe rise again?]. Berlin: 1932. Dedication: *"An Herrn Adolf Hitler / mit den besten Wünschen / von H. R. Knickenbocker / Berlin November 1932."*

39. William L. Shirer, *Berlin Diary: The Journal of a Foreign Correspondent 1934–1941.* New York: 1984, p. 14.

40. John Gunther, "Foreword." In H. R. Knickerbocker, *Is Tomorrow Hitler's?* New York: 1941, pp. xiii–xiv.

41. Ibid., p. XIV.

42. Knickerbocker, *Deutschland,* p. 33.

43. Ibid., pp. 80–81.

44. Ibid., pp. 202–204.

45. Ibid., pp. 206–209.

46. H. R. Knickerbocker, *German Crisis.* New York: 1932, p. 247; H. R. Knickerbocker, *Germany: Fascist or Soviet?* London: 1932.

47. Knickerbocker, *Deutschland* [Germany], p. 213.

48. Ibid., p. 225.

49. Ibid., p. 231.

50. Knickerbocker, *Kommt Europa wieder hoch?* [Will Europe rise again?], p. 73, 181, 208, 241.

51. H. R. Knickerbocker, *Kommt Krieg in Europa?* [Will there be a war in Europe?]. Berlin: 1934.

52. H. R. Knickerbocker, *Rote Wirtschaft und Weisser Wohlstand* [Red economy and white welfare]. Berlin: 1935.

53. H. R. Knickerbocker, *Is Tomorrow Hitler's?*, p. 103–104.

54. Aniela Jaffé, *Aus Leben und Werkstatt von C. G. Jung* [From the life and workshop of C. G. Jung]. Zurich: 1968; Margrit Burri, *Germanische Mythologie zwischen Verdrängung und Verfläschung* [German mythology between suppression and libertation]. Zurich: 1982; *Lingering Shadows. Jungians, Freudians, and Anti-Semitism.* Eds. Aryeh Maidenbaum, Stephen A. Martin. Boston, London: 1991.

55. Knickerbocker, *Is Tomorrow Hitler's?*, pp. 50–51.

56. Hans Hoppeler, *Die Predigt unseres Körpers* [The preaching of our body]. Stuttgart: w. y., p. 15, 35.

57. Fest, *Hitler.* 1998, p. 950.

58. Eitner, *Hitler*, p. 137.

59. Hans Lungwitz, *Erkenntnistherapie für Nervöse: Psychobiologie der Krankheit und der Genesung* [Cognizance therapy for neurotics: Psychobiology of the illness and recovery from it]. Kirchhain: 1932, p. 13, 25, 104–105.

Chapter 4

Books That Hitler Did Not Read (In Depth)

Books that were uncut or visibly untouched can be categorized as either valuable or rubbish. Not one book illustrates this fact better than Rabindranath Tagore's book on nationalism, together with its dedication. The book claims that "nationalism is a great danger," because the nation is becoming empty; "it diverts one's willingness to make sacrifices for one's real moral and live aim and directs it towards a mechanical and lifeless aim."[1] The dedication written in April 1921 by Babette Steininger is more ambiguous. She cited a runic script inscribed in a decorative fastener which has two readings, "Logapore, Wodan, Donar, help!", or "Marriage must conquer Wodan, and should help Donar."[2] The second part of the dedication—which is cited at the end of this chapter—clearly refers to the relation between racist occultism and Hitler. We shall look into that later. First let us look at the works on the shelves according to the language and nationality of the writers.

French Authors, Franco-German Relations

If we examine the proportion of works of value compared to the proportion of rubbish on the shelves, then the result is perhaps unsurprising: representing value, the greatest number of books are written in French or translated from French. At one end of the scale there are the vehicles of humanitarian ideals such as Gandhi and Romain Rolland, while at the other there are works of anti-Semitic "literature." Although Gandhi's name does not appear in *Mein Kampf,*

Hitler presumably knew about him and hated him. Thus it is unlikely he would have studied Romain Rolland's Gandhi selection and Gandhi biography,[3] books which were fondly suggested to him. At the most extreme end of the scale we find, of course, Édouard Drumont's anti-Semitic book entitled *Jewish France*. Perhaps he studied this, but the notes in pencil correcting the translation are possibly from a previous owner (the donor perhaps), as the Führer never learnt to speak French.[4] He did not even cut open a similar work by G. Saint-Bonnet. Maybe this was because he received only the 157th copy and only the first 25 were decoratively bound. Maybe a glance at the title *The Jew, or the Internationale of Parasitism* was enough, as he instantly saw that it would say nothing new to him. It might only have been interesting from the perspective that the author, who argued that Jews cannot assimilate, was of Jewish origin himself; in the dedication he promised that he would also devote a book to Hitler.[5]

The dedications in the French or French-related books are also interesting from another perspective. They differ in their lack of the usual dull expressions of German respect and convoluted cultic praises. At times they are almost ironic (especially when the content of the work is precisely opposed to the Führer's ideals), and at other times they rely on word magic to make Hitler believe that he basically was (or might have been) a good person. Maïa Charpentier's vegetarian cookbook is one such work, with its following dedication: "To the chancellor of the Reich, to Monsieur Hitler, the vegetarian, and thus to the man of peace, from a good French woman desiring Universal Peace, the soul condition for human progress."[6] The book has not even been cut open (although the Führer, as his propaganda proclaimed, was indeed vegetarian, though on the grounds of a phobia which led him to fear blood and infection through blood. He could devour an enormous amount of chocolate and cake, which is quite uncharacteristic of vegetarians, and also something that Hitler propaganda and his anti-vegetarian biographers kept quiet).

Charpentier's book was perhaps sent to the Führer as part of some harmonized peace offensive, because in the same year, in 1932 that is, Louis Artus published a novel entitled *Peace on Earth!* He had a complementary copy inscribed "Printed especially for Monsieur Adolf Hitler," and the pacifist foreword was addressed to him. The names of the main characters are also symbolic: Jacques Lancelot and Erna

Bohr, not to mention the plot (in which German scientists discover some magic gas, but thanks to Erna they do not apply it. The war is abandoned. Love prevails).[7] It is unlikely that Artus would have known Kossak-Raytenau's novel *Catastrophe, 1940*, published two years beforehand, in which Germany defeats France with a gas attack after the collapse of Bolshevism—all in 1940. The Führer seemed not to have bored himself with this work that the author dedicated to him in 1937 calling him "the establisher of German cleanliness," since contemporary advert-sheets continue to yellow in their original places.[8] So what reason do we have not to believe the Führer who made the following statement in 1942: "I never read novels and almost never feuilletons"?[9] The prediction of war in the year 1940 is oddly coincidental though, and might even have had an effect on him.

The third French book dates from 1932. It concerns economic politics, which it states are determined by technological development, and can ensure a more equal distribution of goods. *A World Commences*, proclaims the work with its title, reminding the reader that Communism also strives for capitalism based on the individual, or rather small-scale producers, and also strives to ensure private property (however, Hitler and Stalin soon arranged matters so that things would not stay like this for long). The author might already have annoyed the Führer with his dedication woven around the words of the capitalized title: "To Hitler, the chief of German National Socialism from an economic internationalist, who believes that A WORLD COMMENCES, the organization of which he would like to see."[10] The most interesting book in this series of French attempts to influence Hitler was written in Metz, France, by a German author called Gustav Gonder. It is in German and concerns Franco-German relations.[11] The routine dedication would not have irritated Hitler, whereas the contents would have done so much more, as the author expressed his desire for the synthesis of French democracy and dynamic German economy. He bitterly criticizes Germany's wounded individualism, as well as the problems of economics and mentality that counteract democracy. Evidently this was of no interest to the Führer.

An Eastern and Central European Intermezzo

The presence in Hitler's library of books and authors from Eastern and Central Europe sheds light on the transnational character of Fascism.

It is hardly an accident that Hitler received the most books from countries that had suffered a Communist revolution. To be more precise, we can say that he received most of his books from anti-Communist fanatics. Naturally the Russians were at the head of the queue. The most informative dedication of the entire collection is in the memoir-like work of the Russian emigrant Vladimir Orlov,[12] which was so anti-Semitic (this is already evident in the dedication) that even the publisher considered it excessive and edited it heavily. The foreword reveals that the author was a victim of the former white guard, Knickerbocker, who had "provoked" him. The American journalist had been seeking evidence as to whether the Soviets had bribed an American senator, and consequently Orlov produced, that is forged, a few "documents," but not, as he stressed, for selfish reasons or recompense.

Konstantin Sakharow, a former czarist lieutenant general, not only sent his book about the Siberian Czech legions, but also asked the Führer in a letter to give him the opportunity to meet him and talk about his experiences in person.[13] The encounter may even have taken place since the work was republished a year later, this time with the author's dedication.[14] A former Russian teacher sent his work on the Freemasons and the Jewish struggle for world domination which claimed that the most significant leaders of the 1848 revolution in Hungary were Freemasons.[15] With the hypocrisy characteristic of Nazi subculture, Lehmann Verlag also published Pitirim Sorokin's *The Sociology of Revolution*, which endeavors to establish the "science of altruism" and severely indicts unrestrained terror and dictatorship.[16] One of the owners of Verlag cynically dedicated this "contribution to the explanation of the Red danger" as if he was trying to give the impression that what happened in Russia in the autumn of 1917 and afterwards was both useful for propaganda purposes and an example to follow.[17]

An undedicated book by Albert Kaas, a Hungarian, is also about the Red danger.[18] The Führer was interested in the Hungarian Soviet Republic in general. He often mentioned Béla Kun, and a few works with Hungarian references are in his library, although most were written by dilettantes, and all were offered to him with a dedication. There is, for example, a nonsensical little story about King Matthias, written in Hungarian and bound in a luxurious cover,[19] and another story about Hannibal, written in German.[20] Hitler perhaps even took a revisionist essay into his hands which encouraged peace on the basis of economic interests rather than "emotional peace."[21] He must have derived little joy from the small book on Hungarian achievements at the Berlin Olympic Games, which were partly due to the high proportion of Hungarian champions of Jewish origin[22] (one representative in the 1938 debate on the anti-Jewish law, János Esztergályos, pointed out that "83 Hungarian Olympic champions won a golden medal. From these 31 were Hungarians of Jewish origin.").[23]

The only Eastern European author who dealt with the "Nazi Revolution" was Bulgarian.[24] Interestingly we find nothing from Romanian authors in spite of the fact that the Romanian Iron Guards movement was the strongest Fascist organization in the Carpathian-Danube-Balkan region. Only one book on Romania survived, which was an album of the German war cemeteries that can be found in the country.[25] Even though the Transylvanian Saxons had a prime place in Nazi mythology because of their preservation of traditions, and even though Heinrich Zillich's novel on Brasov was compulsory reading for SS soldiers during training, only one work by a Transylvanian Saxon author survived in Hitler's library.[26] Also, we are only told of the life of the Swabians of the Banat (who were considered highly important in the plans for neo-German colonization) by one solitary booklet on local history.[27]

Nazi Lyric

The genre of poetry was not held in high esteem in Hitler's library. Paradoxically, after 1933 the Führer gladly made references to poets whilst at the same time considering poetry to be superfluous.[28] He considered the German people to be "the people of thinkers." In March 1942 Hitler said, "We have no poets today." He did not think that they were suitable for the transformation of the language, as only "the greatest thinkers of a people are born for that! In the times ahead of us only one man is suitable for that task: Schopenhauer!"[29] Ironically Schopenhauer, too, was a pacifist, just like Hitler's other favorite, Karl May. He escaped being seen as the chief source of inspiration or intellectual predecessor to Hitler,[30] although he occupies prime place in George Lukacs's *The Dethronement of the Mind* (an example of just how merciless such "intellectual genealogy" can be is the latest monograph on the philosophical background of Hitlerism which, in examining Hitler's philosophical background, stresses the intellectual similarity between Hitler and Spinoza).[31] It seems that the Führer was not too partial to poetry. He did not cite poetry, even amongst his friends.

Thus there are not many volumes of poetry in Hitler's library. Hanns Johst wrote just one greeting verse as a foreword to his short book of aphoristic thoughts. The following is an example of the book's contents: "The demand for freedom is revolutionary. But it is not more revolutionary than a religious socialism that strives for bread and wine."[32] On the other hand, his dedication promising loyalty remains faithful to the aforementioned dedicatory verse that opens the volume. It stresses that

> To us your existence is the sign:
> the eternal path of your great life
> lies in our faith!
> The faithful, obedient and grateful Hanns Johst

The reason the Nazis honored Johst and rewarded him was because, as a note to Goebbels says, "Hanns Johst is one of the very few poets who […] saw Germany's regeneration in National Socialism." His play, the *Schlageter* is "the first great drama of the German transformation, which teaches us how to make the ego grand in service and sacrifice to the whole." With the acknowledgement of his merits he became the president of the Reich's Chamber of Writers [*Reichsschrifttumskammer*]. He motivated people even as late as the end of July 1944 with the words: " […] today every poet, just like every shoemaker, tailor, soldier or munitions worker, should become an Adolf Hitler-fanatic."[33]

As a writer Johst must have been grateful to the Führer for being one of his most devoted fans. At least one would expect that to be the case, as in 1923 the still novice politician told the writer that he had seen his drama, *The King*, seventeen times in the preceding year, and added that he feared that he, too, would end like the hero of the play: a revolutionary who committed suicide when reactionaries and the bourgeoisie betrayed him.[34]

War Nostalgia and the Conservative Revolution

This Eastern European and lyrical detour is not intended to divert attention from the main stock of the library, the building bricks that form the paper pyramid of Nazi mythology. The foundations of this pyramid are built out of war literature, mostly the recollections of soldiers on the front. They are reports of their experience of the senselessness that they had tried to make sense of. As we have seen, it was only Jünger's work that Hitler penciled into from among those books.

He must have simply been bored by these books. This is no surprise, even if there are some rather apt situation characterizations among them, for example, the one by the aforementioned Nazi moralist, which is a good follow-up to Jünger's comments on the World War's (de)forming effect on humans: "The World War was a revolution." "With the World War life stepped into the place of dialectics." "The War taught us life."[35] Or to be more precise: lifelessness.

There are several war albums in the collection. In one of these he could even see a photograph of Admiral Horthy (Hungary's Regent and former admiral of the Hapsburg Empire) whom he was not particularly fond of.[36] Another was dedicated to him by his former commanding officer at Christmas in 1932: "to the worthy army dispatcher."[37]

We assume that the Führer did not dive into these books because he was interested in the future. His own past represented a burden to him, since he had been a simple subordinate who wanted to command, and such figures dislike remembering such things unless they get to the top, above everyone. As we know, the memory of the war remained important for Hitler. In 1940, the triumphant parvenu did not miss the chance of visiting First World War battle fields[38] and, of course, Paris in order to finally be able to say at Napoleon's sarcophagus that "That was the greatest and most beautiful moment of my life."[39] At that point the Third Reich seemed invincible. I wonder if Hitler had thought about the inventor of the cloudy, and thus effective term "The Third Reich:" Arthur Moeller van den Bruck?[40]

At the base of the pyramid of Nazi mythology are books by Moeller van den Bruck. If Hitler is the architect of the Third Reich then van den Bruck is its prophet, and a mystical prophet at that.[41] Hans Kohn draws attention to the title of his most significant book, *Das Dritte Reich*, saying that "The title cannot be translated as *The Third Empire*. There have been many empires throughout history, but there is only one Reich."[42] Indeed: "German nationalism is the fighter for the final Reich, something that will always remain as just a promise: a promise that can never be fulfilled. It is perfection, which can only be achieved through imperfection." The Reich is a mystical utopia, a kind of refuge in an increasingly harsh world: "The German nationalist of our time remains, as a German person, a mystic, but as a political person he has become a skeptic. He has realized that the civilizations of those peoples who self-affectedly call themselves Western do not rise, but fall with this "civilization." In this falling world, which is today at its peak, he tries to save what is German: the two thousand year old Reich. The animal in man is winning. The shadow of Africa is looming over Europe. We must be the guardians of our own values."[43]

This Nazi salvation story (also mentioned earlier) is a story about race. The actually only one thousand year old empire is a horrid amalgam of calmness and eagerness to act.[44]

His other work is characterized by the portrayal of a stronger race cult. It is a tastefully published little book entitled *Armin*. It is about the size of a small catechism, and in content it is the forerunner to the clumsy creation story in later SS catechisms (it is, however, not written in quite such a harsh style). At times Moeller van den Bruck almost reminds the reader of Mickiewicz and his Slav Messianism and mysticism. However, God is absent from this biblical story. It begins thus: "The ancestral people of the Aryans descended victoriously from the glacier fields of the Ice Ages. They were grand, and grew to be immense, but remained pure amidst the dangers and horrors of the moorland domain." Naturally "the ancestral people of the Aryans are the born rulers of this Earth." They wandered to India, where "they reigned over the yellow masses," and soon "the white nobility" conquered the "black slave-herd." "While the other races created a culture of the senses the Aryans brought the culture of intellect with them." They did not have to create a culture, because culture was something almost innate to their being. "They sprang from battle. They discovered Reason. Battle makes life worth living and worthy of the human: they felt this. Reason makes the human and the human life worthy of God: they recognized this." Battle and Reason then remained the two poles between which Aryan history wavered, stresses the author, who had to think up some sort of reincarnation myth if he wanted to provide an explanation for both the rise and fall of cultures and, within that framework, the eternal nature of the Aryan race. "The Indian martial nobility became a priestly cast," while the people were destroyed. The Iranians rose to become the third great Aryan culture: the Hellenic/Latin culture. "The Greeks were thinking, creating and building for them, and the Romans fought for them." Evidently "the most combative people among the Aryans were perhaps the Germanic tribes." "Nature seemed to have trained them for that." Then came Armin, whose "name carried a symbol." "He, in fighting, is destiny himself. [...] If he had given up the fight or had not dared to act at all, we would not exist today." In that case the Germans would have shared the same fate as the Gauls. Thanks to Armin "the most individual people of the world were born here. In need and danger newer personalities always arose," but the masses kept holding them back: "No other people had to produce more geniuses than this. But somehow they always had to be geniuses who stood out against their own people." For this reason, in the thinking of the best, the "I" or the ego is in the foreground [*Ichgedanke*], and the history of the best is the history of the ego [*Ichgeschichte*]. "And only the greatest, the fathers and the men of power succeed in finding their way back to the people and, at least temporarily, in making peace between the individuals and the masses. Thus all those who wanted to make one entity out of German-ness [*Deutschtum*] had to experience that deep horror which is inherent in the recognition of the pre-destined nature of all that is German. Armin was the first who underwent this." Yet he was only able to wear the royal gown briefly. "The Germanic tribes could not yet choose between freedom and non-freedom." Armin ruled for just two years. He was stabbed in the back. Nevertheless: "The path to any future, our path, led and leads across his dead body."

There are no markings in the book. Even if Hitler did sometimes use the German tribal chief as an example, he held Alexander the Great or Augustus in higher esteem, as they left vast constructions behind them. Also, as he commented in early 1942: "Wars come and go. Only the values of a culture remain."[45] Arthur Moeller van den Bruck counts as one of the highest ranked representatives of the so-called "conservative revolution" along with Oswald Spengler and Ernst Jünger. During the post Second World War examination of conscience this trend was seen as the preparatory line for Nazism, even if their members distanced themselves from it.

Golo Mann found the expression "conservative revolution" contradictory in itself, as its meaning is "preservative upheaval" [*erhaltender Umsturz*].[46] Klemens von Klemperer connects this with the "degeneration" of German rational thinking,[47] and with what George Lukacs called the "dethroning of the mind." All that then of course was seen in a different light, and the demand for a more refined evaluation is growing stronger today as well. Conservative revolution was a sort of "charismatic nationalism" or "political religion," a compound of several trends,[48] not least because it was primarily the result of intellectual initiative (that of authors, scientists, and publicists, all of whom sooner or later found themselves in opposition to the Nazis).

Moeller van den Bruck's racism is less obsessive than Dinter's or Hitler's. Race for him is worthy if it represents an ideal. And yet some healthy internal skepticism encouraged him to say that such ideals are impossible to realize. In 1922 he met Hitler, who at the time sought some kind of intellectual father in him. Hitler said: "You have everything that is missing from me. You provide the intellectual tools for the regeneration of Germany. I am only a drummer and a collector." Moeller on the other hand was not impressed by Hitler: "This guy understands nothing," he said.[49]

In 1925 Moeller, "since he no longer saw any way out for his people, threw himself out of a window" and died.[50] Thus, intentionally or otherwise, he drew attention to the fact that his ideals lead to a political cul-de-sac. After his death Hitler could not find many reasons for looking into the works of the "prophet." Moeller's merits even earned him the honor of having Rosenberg suppressing any knowledge of his existence,[51] even though he was one of the inventors of what H. R. Trevor-Roper called "a vast system of bestial Nordic nonsense."[52]

His personal fate and attitude was part of the reason why the concept of the "Third Reich" failed to take a firm foothold, even though it had deep roots. The Nazis only used the expression for propaganda purposes, and in 1939 the official use of the term was banned, with the official name of the National Socialist state becoming "The Great German Reich" [*Das Grossdeutsche Reich*].[53]

Nazi Mythology I:
Sexuality, Bluestockings and Go-Getters

A large part of the Hitler Library consists of racist essays on art, history, the earth, and race itself. The Munich branch of Lehmann Verlag donated many books to the library, but authors also gave complimentary copies, and a few publications came from elsewhere, too. The Führer perhaps glanced through one or two of these books, but he probably tossed much material aside, as he did the booklet presenting the racial particularities of SA-lads in nude photographs, which he saw as some hateful documentary on the Röhm-harem.[54] In certain respects that work can be viewed as the forerunner of modern homosexual magazines, just as the Führer's festivities were the predecessors of today's noisy music shows. Hitler demonstrated a high tolerance of homosexuality practiced in the SA, saying that it was all the same to him "whether from the front or from behind..." Nevertheless he still made use of accusations of sexual perversion when disposing of his political opponents. Indeed, he would even present false evidence if needed,[55] emphasizing that homosexuality was the beginning of the end for a race of people, in spite of the fact that he quite possibly had inclinations in that direction himself.[56]

Hitler may well have enjoyed the albums on the history of erotica by Eduard Fuchs (who was in fact Jewish), and he reputedly had a number of these in his library, probably because of their illustrations.[57] However, no trace of these albums remains, but there could be other reasons for their disappearance other than their deliberate extraction because of the author's Jewish background. Sexuality qualified as a Jewish phenomenon in Nazi mythology. Some made the figure of the Jewish woman appear monstrous (as in Ezra Pound's *vagina dorsata* or "thorny vagina"). Although the Führer did not refer to Jewish women in this manner, the Jewish figure, enticing and contaminating German women, appears in *Mein Kampf* in the section set in Vienna. An author of a contemporary book on Hitler commented that Vienna was the locale of sexual anti-Semitism. He drew a parallel between Rathenau's murder and the assassination of Hugo Bettauer (who was also killed because he was Jewish), an author of erotic books: "In the North a Jew with the death penalty in sight must not deal with politics for the Reich. In the South he will be the victim of his desire for joy."[58]

Hitler's relationships with women were characterized by mawkish gallantry. He condemned women but he was affected by their attractive power. He had an aversion to clever women, but could bear unintelligent ones more easily, and we know that he had similar feelings about men and his work colleagues unless they were unconditionally loyal. Several of the women with whom he became involved committed suicide under suspicious circumstances. His partner Eva Braun also attempted to take her life several times, too. Of course, this could well have been due to the careful attention that the Führer paid to his own asexual image. He was aware that he could ensure the attraction and admiration of the female masses if he remained unwed. The psychoanalyst/Communist Wilhelm Reich drew attention to the small detail that it was precisely apolitical voters that Hitler mobilized to achieve success. Apparently it was primarily the character of Fascist ritual and symbolism that affected them like some sort of substitute for sex, for "the apolitical person is preoccupied with his or her sexual conflicts," and the opportunity for the sublimation of such impulses was ensured by Nazi political ecstasy. They somehow understood, or rather sensed, that the swastika, for example, symbolized sexual intercourse,[59] yet according to Nazi propaganda it expressed the closed unity of the people. It was also required to evoke "racial cleanliness," "space to live" [*Lebensraum*], and "life regenerating fertility," according to Rosenberg's plans.

The Nazi symbol was once primarily a symbol of light and the constant renewal of life that could be found at the most diverse points around the globe.[60] Reputedly there was a *swastika* in the church at Hitler's birthplace, and the little Adolf drew it into his notebook. Yet it was undoubtedly the obscure apostles of Nazi subculture who first used it as an emblem.[61] Lanz von Liebenfels' *Ostara* bore it, Epp's counter-revolutionary troops wore it in 1919, and the Thule Society used it, all in the same way, twisting it from its original meaning, turning it away from its original usage as a symbol of life and making it the symbol of death. János Honti, later a victim of Nazism, understandably wrote a limited explanation in his encyclopedia entry:

> Swastika: an ancient ornament, which was used alone or in a reef (called a meander) from the Stone Ages by practically every people from Africa through Europe to Asia. Mesopotamia is among the places of its earliest occurrence. The German National Socialists view it as the ancient symbol of the Indo-German peoples and use it as their party badge.[62]

This swastika found its place in the center of the red flag which lent a socialist edge to Nazism...

The love letters written to Hitler by his female fans also underpin Reich's thesis.[63] In many cases the authorities were strongly suspicious of these letters, and they checked whether their writers were indeed sane. The letters usually radiate the deep respect and frenzied admiration normally granted to a pop star. Also, in contrast to the contents of the masses of birthday wishes the Führer received, there is no trace of politics in these letters.

The Führer was aware of the magic of female attraction. He liked courting or rather flirting with a Viennese-style joviality. Erich Fromm said that he could put on the mask of a friendly person.[64] He liked to have a few pretty women in his company, and he was especially partial to his "mother's women friends," those elder women who allowed him into their salon.[65] For example, he vetoed the barring of women with shingled or bobbed hair from the party, and he was opposed to the introduction of a female uniform. Yet we could say that he almost detested *"politische Tanten"* [political nannies] as he called them.[66] The only joy he could find in them was the fact that they often quarrelled among themselves. Their works bear witness to precisely these quarrels.

The satisfaction of experiencing brawls between "political nannies" was granted to him by Lady Mathilde, the new wife of the great old soldier Ludendorff, and her woman friends. The chronicle of the Nazi movement attributes the diverging paths of the organizers of the Beer Hall Putsch to Lady Mathilde, as the Ludendorffs accused Hitler of servility to Rome, saying that in fact the Pope was bribing Hitler.[67]

The Lady must have been disappointed with her husband's former ally, because in 1923 she wrote the following admonitions in the dedication to her book entitled the *Triumph of the Will of Immortality*, actually quoting herself, and indicating the page number should her handwriting be illegible:

> Song V "The Sacred Secret" (58)
> Do not forget, you youngster, you blessed soul,
> That if you ever leave the otherworld,
> Then you are only a perfect God,
> For as long as you live.
>
> Song VII "Runes of Existence" (73)
> Walk the country's principalities
> And tell the poor,
> The tribe subjugated by the thirst for power,
> Of the true runes of existence!
> Tell the dear, the fatally ill people
> The comforting words of their mother:
> Never may the living subjugate the living,
> May only the prating dead subjugate the prating dead!
> You are alive, my people,
> And thus you are God and free!

These philosophical tenets are just as lofty and confused in their prose equivalents. Yet this is the source of the SS religion called "German Religion." Party Secretary Comrade Bormann also participated in this with something similar when he declared himself to be a German believer in God. Of course, he did not write like Lady Mathilde about "the relativity of the conscience, [which is] the enormous obstacle for all moral development of entire peoples and the individual person," probably because most people do not hear the "voice of God" calling them. The Ten Commandments, according to her ingenious declaration, are confused. In fact: "Our moral life shows new paths for fulfilling the ingenuity of feeling, and offers new stone-tablets to us of hatred and love, as it says to us: your love and hatred will be lead by the desires of ingenuity..." What this exactly means will be clear shortly: "Such love and such hatred forbids unselected altruistic and egoistic deeds."[68] Another "political nanny" who also represented the trend of "German Christians" was Guida Diehl. Her brochure is in the library.

It was dedicated to Hitler "under the sign of the common struggle," and actually opposed Mathilde Ludendorff. Hitler evidently could not accept the German Christians' thesis that Judaism and Christianity would be mortal foes. He surely knew what a mire he would get into if he insisted that it was precisely the ancestral Germanic people's example that would demonstrate to the German people that they were "predestined to follow Christ,"[69] and that his role would be similar to Christ's: "Hitler taught us to see God better!"[70] What was it that had to be seen more clearly? That "there is neither ethics nor dogmatism in God's empire."[71]

Hitler of course took no interest whatsoever in the books sent to him as warnings which were written in the spirit of Christianity,[72] nor did he browse through the works of Nazi priests.[73]

Our investigations also give a sense of why Hitler thought more of the members of the Confessional Church [*Bekennende Kirche*], who practiced the best Lutheran traditions, rejected Lutheran priests who were compromisers and accepted the Old Testament, than he did of the "German Christians."[74] However, Hitler could also have sensed that the dilettante, pseudo-mystical hogwash that attempted to nationalize Christian teachings and re-explain them in an infantile manner would inevitably encourage a desire to return to Christian "roots". The Catholic Church acted as if it had not realized this. Rome comforted itself by denying the existence of the war, whilst meanwhile politicizing and striving for its own survival. It did not deny, and even overtly admitted in some circulars, that Christianity is opposed to Nazism, but at the same time they never made any attempt to condemn it. Perhaps they overestimated the internal weakness of the Church, as Catholic priests frequently reported the indifference of youths towards religion.

A brief but rather telling train of thought survived in the SS archives from early 1940 entitled *The Political Force of Racial Thought*. In this archive, among documents concerning internal political affairs, there is a significant amount of space devoted to a report on the grammar school in Benshein. There, "the internally hostile" students showed the most interest in the sciences. The Nazi teachers and school inspectors were astonished by this and asked how it was that in 1940 eighty percent of A-Level students wanted to study Catholic theology, even though they were the best students in the fields of biology and the connected theory of race.[75] With deep insight John Lukacs stressed that although a radical move from the Pope would not have stopped the mechanized elimination of humans, and might even have increased the number of victims, it still may have had an effect: "Even if a clear Papal condemnation of Hitlerism may not have assuaged the sufferings of its victims (which is not certain), its potential influence in the long run could have been enormous, not only among Catholics but also among all kinds of Christians, agnostics, Jews in Europe, millions of people whom the experiences of the war made receptive to and even desirous for the kind of spiritual leadership that the traditional and universal Catholic Church could have given."[76] Thus it was the Swiss Reformed Church that most overtly and sharply opposed Nazism.

The constant comings and goings of ritualism could only divert attention from the nihilism of Nazi mythology for a short while. The manic demands placed on the notion of "motion," which Hannah Arendt considers to be a basic character of totalitarian movements, inevitably had to lead to war. War was something they were preparing for from the start. The grand parades were also a part of this preparation. At the same time, as Ralf Dahrendorf pointed out, "The contradiction between the ideology and practices of National Socialism is as astonishing as it is understandable."[77] The works of the Nazi paladins would have illustrated this well, had they survived.

Searching through the works of functionaries we find nothing from Goebbels. It is conceivable that he did not want to bore the Führer, and was crafty enough to know that the Führer might find something in his writing that would turn Hitler against him. There is something in the library from Goering, but there is no sign of a dedication or *ex libris* mark in it.[78] This serves to prove his fine awareness of tactics, as the small book he sent to the Führer praises his own role as a faithful servant.[79] There is only one work by Rosenberg, too. It is a collection of pamphlets attacking the leaders and suspected leaders of the revolution of November 1918. It was offered by Gregor Strasser, to serve as an indication of his faithfulness (even so, he was among the first that Hitler had slain on the "Night of Long Knives").[80] Gottfried Feder's case is similar. He surprised his friend with his book at Christmas in 1924, who at that time was only one of the seven mythical party founders (Hitler liked to call himself the seventh party founder, because no matter how much he fought against superstitions, he believed to some extent in the mysticism of numbers, or at least would happily exploit similar beliefs that other people held. In fact Hitler received the 555th party membership card on his entry, and was the last member of a committee of seven).[81] The receiver of the gift himself wrote a foreword to Feder's work, stressing that with this book "the literature of our movement has found its catechism."[82] The work sketches out the demand for a mixed economy that sets limits on capitalism. The Führer himself helped form the racist "metaphysics" of this work,[83] although he disliked this word and avoided using it.

From among the esteemed philosophers in the field of the theory of races, a whole series of books by Professor Hans Günther was displayed on the Führer's bookshelf. The Lehmann brothers sent them. There are two volumes without a dedication,[84] but in a volume printed in 1923 the dedication is addressed "to the successful vanguard of the German concept of race;"[85] in a volume printed in 1925 we only find "with great friendship" (without any indication of the donor's name);[86] in 1930 we find the dedication "to the pioneer of the concept of race with thanks,"[87] which is identical to the dedication found in the 1933 volume, save for the fact that the latter is addressed to the Chancellor.[88] Whether the recipient read these books or not remains a mystery, as he left no mark in them. They failed to offer much that was new to him. They are of more interest to us, who grew up in the milieu of class division, because they introduce us to what became the official theory of races. In this theory we can observe racial inevitability in the place of Marxist historical inevitability, as well as the emphasis of Nazi materialism on blood-determination instead of class mechanism. Nevertheless, its apotheosis directly links it with the potential for downfall. In that much it is faithful to its voluntarism.

Günther was attacked by his colleagues for his materialism. In university life the elder professors tried to keep pushy Nazi scholars away in the name of intellect, charging them with materialism.[89] Of course the professor was successfully protected. He made no particular blunders, although his work from 1941 that demonstrated what Hitler's victory meant to each individual American introduced him as the "chief priest" of the theory of races.[90] Still, he managed to avoid being held responsible, and was still allowed to publish after 1945. One American society of genetics even elected him as an honorary member.[91] According to De Gaulle, the soldier who refuses a command and the intellectual who lies are both traitors. Yet professor Günther was presumably honest even at the time when he had to adapt to the shift in his circumstances…

Nazi Mythology II:
Race Breeding, Occultism and Gnosticism

The best example of the ways in which one could both deviate from and adhere to party ideology in one's practices may be that of Walther Darré, the minister of agriculture. Although we cannot see any of his books on Hitler's shelves, he was likely to have donated him some as he had already taken the trouble to send some to Baldur von Schirach. Hitler would only have nodded in approval of the dedication he wrote for Schirach: "If we do not have the courage to answer all questions of blood and accept their consequences clearly and unambiguously, then the result of our work shall remain a giant on trembling legs.[92]" Perhaps no other Nazi leader tried to apply their experiences of animal husbandry to social politics as consistently as this former horse breeder. In his work *New Nobility from Blood and Soil* he classified women as one would animals for either selective breeding or sterilization. He presented the swine as a national animal, because he considered pork consumption a measure of racial superiority. He also claimed that the Semitic nomads did not consume pork due to their lifestyle, as opposed to the northern peoples who were not nomads, but wanderers (otherwise it would not have been possible for the Greeks to have been Aryan). He wrote a book with the title *Swine Murder*, which reveals that the First World War famine occurred because in 1915, under the flag of the international Jewish political worldview, Jewish professors had over a third of the 25 million swine stock slaughtered. The author had a sense of discretion (or rather a sense for the furthering of his career) and did not send this work to the vegetarian Führer (at least this would appear to be the case as Hitler's name was absent from his gift list).[93] Hitler would happily listen to Darré's insane plans[94] but brushed aside any concrete or sensible plans he might have had for the financial support of the peasantry.[95] On the other hand Hitler granted Darré a free hand as long as he did not interfere directly with his plans. Thus in many respects Darré's suggestions were enacted in legislation, as in the case of the "Law for sustaining the peasantry," which prescribed the blueprinting of family trees so that "genetic values" could be checked upon when choosing a partner.[96] More importantly the minimum size of land that a peasant could own was fixed, and inheritance was made in effect only possible for the firstborn.[97]

Darré was not against the racial mysticism of the peasantry,[98] and, to use an ideological buzzword, he banned what we currently call bio-agriculture. The indictment against those who wanted to practice bio-agriculture rested on the assumption that they were the followers of Rudolf Steiner's esoteric anthroposophy. The Nazis had detested Steiner for a long time because he rejected the black magic and theosophy that was connected to the Nazi "German religion."[99] In 1922 he narrowly escaped a beating while giving a lecture in Munich in which he talked about the nullification of national borders.[100] Steiner held Wilson responsible for smashing Central Europe into pieces, and he considered the federal politics conceptualized by Bismarck and Gyula Andrássy as the ideal. His work on this subject (a selection of related articles) can be found among Hitler's books with an *ex libris* stamp.[101] Of course, we have no reason to relate Steiner's esoteric views with Nazi barbarism.[102] The history of the banning of bio-agriculture provides us with no reason to do so either.

Naturally, Steiner opposed chemical fertilizers. Yet anti-chemical fertilizer propaganda would have disturbed the German military economy based upon the production of artificial fertilizer. Darré did not allow any debate on this matter for precisely this reason, and not because he felt that theoretical objections to this method were unsound. However, after the first military successes he felt it possible to loosen the ties and even experiment with other agricultural methods. In early June 1941 he wrote to W. Frick, the minister of internal affairs, and stated that chemical fertilization "is dangerous in that it could lead agriculture into a dead end," and "would lead to the destruction of the German landscape." Thus attempts should be made to practice bio-agriculture since it represents one of the possibilities for stopping the infliction of damage. He considered the results thus far achieved in the field to be sufficient. He agreed with Rosenberg that the ideologist should study those parts of the issue connected to Steiner, whilst he would deal with the agricultural perspective. Darré sent the same letter to thirty other Nazi leaders (earlier on he had renamed bio-agriculture from the "bio-dynamic agricultural method" to the "agriculture of the laws of life"). However, Party Secretary Bormann harbored closer interests in the chemical industry. Late in June 1941 he announced the Führer's command that any further propaganda against chemical fertilization was intolerable, and that Steiner's teachings and worldview were unacceptable. People involved in bio-agriculture were arrested in a move intended to show the superior power of the party secretary.[103] Meanwhile technocrat Nazis viewed their party comrade Darré with suspicion because of his so-called proto-ecological views—they were worried about the cleanliness of the national principle.[104] However, this distrust had more to do with the general suspicion inherent in totalitarian regimes than it did with the ideological infidelity of the swine cult prophet.

The Führer was not moved by peasant mysticism. He was unlikely to have dug deep into books on the particularities and superstitions of the northern race, even if the author or the publisher recommended the work to him,[105] even if it was printed on the title page that the work was dedicated to him,[106] and even if the given work had been sent to him by Himmler.[107] Indeed, the leader of the mystical Reich was not so much Hitler as it was the *Reichsführer*, Himmler.

Himmler established the SS, the largest empire within the Nazi state that can be viewed as a series of private empires.[108] The most colossal institution of pseudo-scientific obscurantism operated within the framework of the SS: it was the *Ahnenerbe*, and its workshops dealt with everything from folk story research to genealogy.[109] Himmler was enthroned as chief-priest or chief-master during séances that mimicked Teutonic ceremonies.

Albert Speer believed that Hitler laughed at SS ideology.[110] However, as Bormann's diary says, he overlooked Himmler's acts of "superstition." This is perhaps because the *Reichsführer* was entrusted with the most important task: the setting up and operation of the concentration camps. The results of science supported the completion of the task, yet a great deal of occultism might have been necessary to bear the psychological load. Himmler's "scientific" passion was characterized by morbidity. In April 1943, for example, he wanted to improve the care of the Gypsies carried off to Auschwitz for reasons complying with the theory of races. Party Secretary Bormann's letter of March 12, 1942 reveals that, obviously in accordance with Himmler's approval, the Gypsy question was opened to reexamination. He did not want to alter the fate of Romanies who had been denounced as racially inferior and sentenced to death, but wanted to aid the so-called "racially clean gypsies" [*reinrassige Zigeune*]. He wanted them to be allowed to serve in the Wehrmacht, and thus prescribed the nurturing of their "language, rituals and traditions." The following is an extract from Bormann's words to Hitler: "Their exceptional handling would be justified, because in general they have not behaved anti-socially, and they preserve valuable Germanic traditions in their cults."[111]

In his pseudo-scientific passion Himmler was allowed to consult astrologers as well. However, after Hess' escape Himmler spoke out strongly against astrologers. This is partly because his confused subsidiary listened to them, partly because astrology represented a different perspective from that of his "objectivity," and partly because it did not recognize racial differences. In addition to that, one astrologer had predicted his downfall as early as 1939, albeit the date that had been predicted was 1940, when he in fact reached the peak of his power.[112] Yet in spite of all this Himmler still managed to keep the persecuted astrologers at his side, even the one who foretold the assassination attempt of July 20 and read the Führer's failure in the stars. This came in handy for "the faithful Heinrich" when the question of how he could save his skin arose, although he already knew the answer: betrayal, something which he then committed himself to.[113]

Nonetheless, certain boundaries were not to be crossed, and certain formalities had to be maintained. The dedication in the aforementioned book by Tagore must definitely have irritated Hitler, which was addressed to him as follows after a runic citation: "to my dear Armanen-brother."[114] The *Armanen* expression is the lucubration of the prophet of occult obscurantism and pseudo-noble Guido von List. It means "superior ancient-Aryan." It reminds one of the other pseudo-noble prophet, Lanz von Liebenfels, and his super human whose ideology is based on anti-Semitism and who carries the flag of the "racial revolution" through to victory (according to Liebenfels' "philological" argumentation, anti-Semitism is "anti-monkeyism," because "*simia*" means "*Affe*," or "monkey").

Hitler had already been able to acquaint himself with the ideals of von List and von Liebenfels earlier on that century in Vienna. The occult subculture took residence there as part of the world of secessionism, representing another side to that movement. Karl Kraus sensed the tensions there when he spoke in 1909: "Soon in Europe they will make gloves out of human skin."[115] In this glittering and filthy Vienna the impotent citizen stood at the peak of a social hierarchy which realized its potentials through art. In the underworld of this Dostojevskijan city the impotent petit bourgeois either striving for or dreaming of power in their uncertain existences indulged in magical daydreaming. It was in this environment that Lanz von Liebenfels' paper *Ostara: A Magazine for Blondes* was published and flourished as it did until the thirties. There is no evidence that Hitler read this paper[116] even if the editor did consider him as "one of our students." Only one though, as the Viennese master also viewed Lenin as one of his students.[117]

In the Hitler library we find Lanz von Liebenfels' "translations" of psalms and no other such works.[118] It could be said that the "translator" strictly followed "tradition" when he provided a few initial lines in Latin before each of his verses on racial cleanliness. If the Führer ever leafed through this work, he must have felt annoyed. Unwittingly perhaps, but it was precisely the theory of races that Liebenfels portrayed in a ridiculous light before the Nazis. He made pseudo-science a laughing stock. Johannes Hering, the party expert on occultism, formulated the so-called "correct" standpoint: "Naturally, from a National Socialist, that is from a sober scientific perspective, many elements of his [Lanz von Liebenfels'] teachings have to be rejected, as do the fantasies of Guido von List whose Armanen concept came completely out of the blue; his attraction to astrology, to which Dinter fell victim, should also be rejected. We have to be pure willed-persons. We have to triumph over fate in compliance with God's will."[119]

Of course Hitler could deal with occultism. He had to, because it was deeply interwoven into the fabric of his party. Indeed, he may well even have said things that could have been interpreted as meaning that "he was convinced that humans are in a magic relationship with the universe."[120] Undoubtedly, the world of occult obscurantism affected him. His relation to occult literature, however, was fundamentally two-sided. The ideals of occultism may have intrigued him because of their holistic nature, if nothing else, as he believed in holism. Therefore it is possible that Hitler was simultaneously attracted to and repelled by the occult. It is hard to believe, but he even wrote a poem:

I often go on bitter nights
To Wotan's oak in the quiet glade
To weave a union with dark powers.[121]

However his magic, as indicated earlier, was anti-occult magic: it was manipulative propaganda interwoven with elements that induced magical effects.

There are on the other hand occult works in his library. There is even an eighteenth century manuscript on the techniques of treasure hunting.[122] Perhaps this was his favorite occult book, because the messages of all the other books—even if they were positively related to him or contained what was ostensibly good advice—always revealed some warning that could be interpreted as a bad omen. This is because occult authors weighed up those characters who sought and found the truth on such an absolute scale that it only served to terrify the mortal reader. Moreover, such books were often offered to him by women. Yet it is also true that the "Reader" was hardly likely to have had the temperament to follow the maze of convoluted argumentation that whirls about in these works. For example the Grail message of Abdruschin (his civil name was Oskar Ernst Bernhardt) is six hundred pages of Gnostic hogwash.[123] It is hard to follow it to the point where it becomes clear why exactly Immanuel is the new messiah. Typical of the type of occultism that it preaches is the way it distances itself from such facts. But the reader inevitably thinks of the Führer when he discovers that "he who seeks or brings the truth does it not in his person but in the form of his message."[124]

The re-publication of the alchemist's compendium is nothing but a pile of nonsensical drivel (for example the part that describes how to make an animal out of dust).[125] Yet could the inscription under the dedication summarizing the argumentation found on two marked pages be referring to the Führer? "Only he, who recognizes God in himself from the whole of nature, knows the truth." Would the Führer have read the commentary in agreement with the statement that riffraff and theologians are unable to acquaint themselves with God? Similar feelings may have been evoked in Hitler on looking through the work by the (still) popular esoteric author Bô Yin Râ entitled *The Prayer*, which was also dedicated to him.[126] The work similarly argues that divinity lives in man and that prayers can only request "what there is in eternity *a priori*, from the will of archaic existence." Whoever recommended this book to the Führer marked the following sentence: "Those able to shape the future are those able to 'pray.'"[127]

The question arises whether something like this might have encouraged the Führer to allude to God's will. Yet even if we can find elements that are common to both Hitler's verbal flow and occult and esoteric literature, we do not necessarily have to search for the effect these readings had on him. Such common elements may suggest more that he shared a similar way of thinking with the authors of these works. After all, when he did read into such works we find traces of retrospective agreement. It is typical that Hitler did not underline anything in Herman Wirth's book *What is German?* which the author dedicated to him in a tone of somewhat undue familiarity: "To Adolf Hitler, in firm belief of his destined mission, under the sign of ⟨⟩."[128] The sign is a vertical line with a circle at either end, called the "Odal Cross," and Wirth's view was that it symbolized something that Rome fought against. The German word comes from the Old Prussian word "*tauto*" meaning "soil," and thus it refers to the organic unity of people and soil. The year, i.e. the period of time in which the Sun travels around the Earth, "is a revelation of God via the son of the spirit of the universe." This is what the swastika refers to. "Odal" is equivalent to "Adel" meaning noble, and ultimately meaning "from God." God is light, and all that is German comes from God. The author continues by stating that discovery of the German ancestral religion could stop the advance of Rome, and also "the northern man must and will redeem himself." After the publication of this work Hitler received yet another copy from an anonymous fan. In that copy he marked sections attesting political pragmatism in a few places along the margin:

> Our northern awakening, our "German" movement is not anti-this or anti-that: it only demands its right of divine intention for self-regulation as an organism in the world. There is no point any more in trying to suffocate this northern movement by means of external violence, or by the use of external or internal state powers,

calumny or the suppression of intellectual and psychological recognition. No state regime's transient power or spiritual or religious authority can hold it back. The greater the pressure, the greater the slander and the hatred, the more powerful it shall become.[129]

The "cross" in the dedication did not appeal to Hitler, but what he could read about the swastika must have, since he put a mark by it: "This [*das Odalkreuz = Hakenkreuz = Swastika*] is the symbol of the 'German' or the national movement which is lead in a National Socialist way, and has never shown itself to be against religion or the Church like the close ally of the political middle ground: Marxism and its political organization, social democracy, which is the mass deception of workers and of all well-meaning followers."[130]

It is characteristic that Hitler marked the rational sections in this small, somewhat occult (due to its obscurantism) work. The Führer did not need a herd of occultist experts, and could not, after all, be the apprentice of someone called Abdruschin. The occult author as a competitor might have seemed worse to him than any *"politische Tante."* We saw that he publicly reprimanded the occultists. He would have had reason to feel that the occult, old-Germanizing Romanticism endangered the absolute power of his Lagarde-Wagner-Chamberlain based "Führerness." True, the aforementioned Thule Society was one of the workshops of Nazism. But Rudolf von Sebottendorf's book was banned in 1934 when he began to enumerate just how many party members began their careers there and pondered over just how much the party could thank the Thule for. According to the official view, National Socialism could not have been the brainchild of anyone apart from the Führer—any societal or conspiratorial model would have contradicted the Führer-principle.[131]

As one expert on occultist practices wrote: "The National Socialist party did not tolerate secret societies, because it was a secret society itself, with its great master, racist gnosis, rituals and initiations."[132]

The Nazi Party became the victorious sect wanting to absorb everything into itself. Its totalitarian character led it to simplify and then secularize its ceremonies. This lent them an extraordinary dynamism of which there was just one enduring feature: the Führer.

Hitler bathed in this Führer-centered state. A certain degree of taste seems to be revealed by the fact that he did not delve deeper into the many obscure books of his or other related movements. Nevertheless,

the way he devoured like cakes the various brochures and other forms
of rubbish that eulogized him is more shocking than surprising. He
was admiring his own dull simplicity whilst browsing through the
various panegyrics and works dedicated to him, highlighting everything he liked without reservation:

> What bestows Hitler's grandeur and significance? Nothing more than his per-
> sonality. His clear, great mind researched and examined the political, historical
> and current lives of different peoples. He read a lot about the teachings of state art
> of all different peoples and ages, scrutinized them, selected what is correct, good,
> and useful for the German people and homeland, and then added his own new
> thoughts to construct a new program. And that which he recognized as correct and
> necessary he turned into action, lifted into reality with his great personal intellec-
> tual power, courage and intrepidity. These are the most essential and decisive
> factors; this is what bestows Hitler grandeur and significance. Without his dy-
> namic, grand personality he would have failed to form the National Socialist
> movement in Germany, despite all his theories. He carries his spirit and strength
> through into every fellow-fighter and the entire movement; he takes them and
> leads them forward. His personality is the greatest reality in the entire National
> Socialist movement: it is its *raison d'être* and power source in one. National So-
> cialism is in essence Hitler's personality.[133]

Beyond this the "Reader" may have sat back and smiled, feeling that
he had managed to deceive the whole world. Even Nazi gnosis held
that the world is not God's creation, but something eternal. Yet here
his racism was connected to Christianity (naturally in contrast with the
true spirit of Christianity), along with some quotes from *Mein Kampf*.
This is something he marked out separately along the margin:

> God, who created humans with such diversity, wants them to stay that way, and
> so he planted within them the endeavor to sustain and foster ethnic and racial dif-
> ferences and characteristics. Whoever fights against this is insane, and sins
> against God and his will. Our Führer, Hitler, expressed this in his book *Mein
> Kampf*, p. 630, in a fitting and noteworthy manner: "God's will gave form and
> character and abilities to humans. He who destroys his creation assumes the fight
> against the Lord's creation and his divine will." In this struggle God, the lord and
> creator of all things, will be victorious against internationalist lunatics.

This author obviously belonged to the branch of the Lutheran denomi-
nation which accepted Nazism. Contrary to Hitler, after he had re-
proached the Ludendorffs and Lady Ludendorff's endeavors to establish a religion, he also labeled them as "Judeo-Marxists" (even though

husband and wife proved to be rampant anti-Semites) so that he may then sing in praise of Luther and try to lend some sort of transnational character to Nazism. This may have filled the "Reader," a successful hypocrite himself, with great satisfaction, and may well have served to strengthen the resolve of his insidious nature:

> Luther [...] who, as we know, never thought about being unfaithful to his Catholic Church despite the hostility of the ruling bodies of that Church, sought only what he thought was in its best interests. He only set off upon the path shown to him by God and his own German conscience when Rome excommunicated him, and he grew to be highly significant not only for his German people and homeland, but also for many other peoples. Why? Unfortunately most people never give this question second thought. It was because he only wanted to be a German, and wanted to affect, live, fight, and die for his beloved German people at a time when the German people and homeland was in a gruesome state, depreciated, conquered, and exploited by other peoples. In this respect—that is in his love for his people, the homeland, and his consciousness of the people and the homeland—there is a striking similarity between him and Hitler. He, too, as the faithful son of his Church wants only the best for it, and in the same way he, with our people and homeland in a similar state, and despite the hostility of many Church people, wants to live, affect, struggle and die for the beloved German people. Consequently we can now already be peremptorily convinced that his activities bring great blessings not only to the German people and homeland, but also to many other peoples, and that his name shall live on not only in German history, but also in world history, long after the names of his enemies have been forgotten.

It is an interesting example of human self-adulation that the "Reader," who received so many congratulating telegraphs and letters every year for his birthday, underlined his own name in three places in a small book abundant in eulogistic expressions describing the Führer. One example will suffice to illustrate this point: "Eternal Providence and Wisdom sent the real leader and guide *Adolf Hitler* to the German folk-soul [*Volksseele*] in this terrifyingly difficult time..."[134] Could it all have been that simple? Was there in fact no secret power in operation? Hitler's career does not leave human imagination to rest. Several scholars have tried to reveal Hitler's connections to the occult world, but all without success. They tried to discover the intention to realize some manic occult obsession that he kept hidden from others in his deeds. Such authors, however, have proved to be more the captives of their own fantasies than analysts of the Hitlerian world of fantasy.[135] But is it not just the whole Hitlerian worldview that is occult? To some extent, it is. Its foundation is gnosis. Hitler's own works are the best sources for examining this question.

Notes

1. Rabindranath Tagore, *Nationalismus* [Nationalism]. Leipzig: 1918, pp. 128–29.
2. Phelps, Die Hitler-Bibliothek [The Hitler-library], p. 925.
3. Mahatma Gandhi, *Jung Indien: Aufsätze aus den Jahren 1919 bis 1922* [Young Indians: Writings from years 1919 until 1922]. Selected by Romain Rolland, Madelaine Rolland. Foreword by John Haymes Holmes. Munich, Leipzig: 1924; Romain Rolland, *Mahatma Gandhi,* Munich, Leipzig: 1923. Dedication: "Dem treuen *Kämpfer / unseres heiligen Vaterlandes / Herrn Adolf Hitler / in tiefer Verehrung. / Irma Niehrenheim. / Bayreuth, Weinachten 1924*"; another dedication: "*Glücklich der Mann der / ein Volk ist—sein Volk / das im Grabe lag und wieder aufersteht / 17. 10. 24. / Stromenfels / geb. Broussart.*"
4. Édouard Drumont, *Das verjudete Franckreich: Versuch einer Tagesgeschichte I-II.* [Jewish France: Attempt for a contemporary history I-II]. Berlin: 1886, 1887.
5. Georges Saint-Bonnet, *Le Juif ou l'internationale du parasitisme* [The Jew or the *Internationale* of parasitism]. Paris: 1932. Dedication: "*A Adolf Hitler / A qui je dois consacrer / un très prochain libre / Hommage sincère / G. Saint-Bonnet.*"
6. Maïa Charpentier, *La bonne cuisine végétalienne: 500 recettes pratiques* [The vegetarian good cuisine: 500 practical recepies]. Paris: 1934. "*Au chancelier du Reich à / Monsieur Hitler végétarien, donc / par destination, homme de paix, ce / livre d'une bonne française désirant / la Paix Universelle seule condition / du progrès humain. / Maïa Charpentier.*"
7. Louis Artus, *Paix sur la terre!* [Peace on the Earth!]. Paris: 1932.
8. Karl L. Kossak-Raytenau, *Katastrophe, 1940* [Catastrophe, 1940]. Oldenburg: 1930. Dedication: "*Adolf Hitler, / dem / Schöpfer / Deutschen Reinheit, / Deutscher / Freiheit, / dem / Schöpfer und / Kanzler / des / Dritten Reiches / der / Deutschen / in / Dankbarkeit / Kossak-Raytenau / im / April 1937.*"
9. Picker, *Hitlers Tischgespräche* [Hitler's roundtable talks], p. 194.
10. René Bergerioux, *Un monde commence* [A world commences]. Paris: 1932. Dedication: "*A Hitler / chef du National Socialisme / Allemand, ce livre d'un / Internationaliste Economique, / qui croît qu' UN MONDE COMMENCE / qu'il souhaiterait de voir organiser / R. Bergerioux.*"
11. Gustav Gonder, *Armes Deutschland, armes Frankreich: Eine Kritik zur deutsch-französischen Annäherung* [Poor Germany, poor France: A critique to the German-French approach]. Metz: 1930. Dedication: "*Herrn Reichskanzler / Adolf Hitler / in Verehrung gewidmet / Gustav Gonder / Saarbrücken, den 20. X. 33.*"
12. Vladimir Orloff, *Mörder—Fälscher—Provokateure: Lebenskämpfe im unterirdischen Rußland* [Murder—forger—provocateur: Life struggles in underground Russia]. Translated from Russian and liberally amended. Berlin: 1929. Dedication: "*Herrn Adolf Hitler / Mörder—Fälscher—Provokateure— / —dass sind hauptsäch-*

lich Juden / die ich auf 860 Seiten geschil- / dert habe. / Leider hat der Verlag mein / Buch 'frei bearbeitet'—und / 267 Seiten tragen außer Namen / kein Judischer Spur. / Dem Führer der Partei an / dessen Kämpfe und Siege ich leider, / als / gast des Landes, nicht Teil- / nehmen kann. / 1/XII 29. Sandau / a. d. Elbe / Wladimir Orloff."

13. Konstantin Sakharow, *Die tschechischen Legionen in Siberien* [Czech legions in Siberia]. Berlin: 1930.

14. Ibid., 1931. D558, S24. Dedication: "*Adolf Hitler / gewidmet vom Verfasser / Konstantin Sakharow.*"

15. Gregor Schwartz-Bostunitsch, *Die Freimaurerei: Ihr Ursprung, ihre Geheimnisse, ihr Wirken* [The freemasons: Their origin, their secrets, their effect]. Weimar: 1928. Dedication: "*Unserem hochverehrten Führer / Herrn Adolf Hitler / in treuer Gefolgschaft / der Verfasser / Gregor Schwartz-Bostunitsch / u. Frau Frikka / 21. X. 31.*"

16. Erich Müller-Gangloff, *Horizonte der Nachmoderne* [Horizon of the postmodern]. Stuttgart: 1964, p. 232.

17. Pitirim Sorokin, *Die Soziologie der Revolution* [The sociology of the revolution]. Munich: 1928. Dedication: "*Ein Beitrag zur Erklärung / der roten Gefahr / J. F. Lehmann.*"

18. Albert Kaas, *Der Bolschewismus in Ungarn* [Bolshevism in Hungary]. Munich: 1930.

19. Aladár Jávorkay-Hehs, *Kormányzó fia: Történet* [The governor's son: Story]. Budapest: 1931. Dedication: "*Seines Hochwolgeboren / dem Herrn Adolf Hitler / dem Apostol des 'Grossen Gedankens' / in tiefster Ehrfurcht / gewidmet von / Aladár von Hehs / Schriftsteller / Bpest, 15. VIII. 932.*"

20. Béla von Kary, *Nach Rom! Hannibals Aufstieg, Liebe und Niedergang* [To Rome! Hannibal's rise, love and fall]. Karcag: w. y. Dedication: "*Zugeeignet / dem Führer und Reichskanzler / Adolf Hitler / in Hochverehrung und Be- / wunderung! / Budapest im Juli 1936 / der Autor: / Béla von Kary.*"

21. Géza Lukács, *Der Neuaufbau auf Grundlage der friedlichen Revision der Friedensverträge* [The reconstruction on the basis of the peaceful revision of the Peace Treaties]. Salzburg, Graz, Vienna, Leipzig, Berlin: 1936. Dedication: "*Dem Führer und Kanzler / des Deutschen Reiches / Seiner Exzellenz Herrn / Adolf Hitler / Verehrungsvollst.*"

22. Jenő Piday, *A berlini olimpia: Ahogy mi láttuk...* [The Olympics in Berlin: As we saw it...]. Budapest: 1936. Dedication: "*Seiner Exzellenz / Adolf Hitler / dem Führer und / Kanzler / des Deutschen Reiches / mit vorzüglichster Hochachtung / gewidmet / Eugen v. Piday.*"

23. László Karsai, ed., *Befogadók: Írások az antiszemitizmus ellen 1882–1993* [Acceptors: Writings against anti-Semitism 1882–1993]. Budapest: 1993, p. 94.

24. Kr. Krestew, *Das revolutionäre Deutschland 1918–1933* [The revolutionary Germany 1918–1933]. Sofia: 1939. Dedication: "*Dem Führer des deutschen Volkes / Adolf Hitler / mit dem Ausdruck aufrichtigster / Verehrung eines wahrheitsliebenden / Berichterstatter / Berlin: den 11 Januar 1939. / K. Krestew.*"

25. Karl Stauss, *Kriegergräber in Rumänien* [War memorials in Romania]. Hermannstadt: 1931.

26. Anna Schuller-Schullerus, *Heimaterde* [Homeland]. Hermannstadt: 1938. Dedication: *"Dem geehrten Führer, Adolf Hitler, / der so viele liebe deutsche "Erde" heim brachte, / zum 50. Geburtstage, / in tiefer Verehrung / Hermannstadt im April 1939 / Anna Schuller."*

27. E. Männer, *Odenwälder im Banat* [Oden forests in Banat]. Mennheim a. d. B.: 1934. Dedication: *"Dem Führer und Reichskanzler / Herrn Adolf Hitler / ergebenst überreicht vom Verfasser."*

28. Werner Maser, *Adolf Hitler: Legende, Mythos, Wirklichkeit* [Adolf Hitler: Legends, myth, reality]. Munich: 1989, p. 186.

29. Picker, *Hitlers Tischgespräche* [Hitler's roundtable], p. 192.

30. Barbro Eberan, *Luther? Friedrich 'der Große'? Wagner? Nietzsche...?...? wer war an Hitler Schuld?: Die Debatte um die Schuldfrage 1945–1949* [Luther? Frederick 'the Great'? Wagner? Nietzsche...? ...? who was to blame for Hitler?: The debate of the question of blame 1945–1949]. Munich: 1983, pp. 135–37.

31. Hermann Schmitz, *Adolf Hitler in der Geschichte* [Adolf Hitler in history]. Bonn: 1999, p. 370.

32. Hanns Johst, *Ruf des Reiches—Echo des Volkes! Eine Ostfahrt* [The Reich calls—The people echo! A journey to the East]. Munich: 1940. Dedication: *"Getreu, gehorsam und / dankbar / Hanns Johst."*

33. NARA, Captured German Documents Microfilmed in Berlin, Reichskulturkammer, Reel 966.

34. Lukacs, *A történelmi Hitler* [The Hitler of history], p. 95; Pritz, *Pax Germanica*, p. 37.

35. Euringer, *Chronik* [Chronicle], p. 81, 129.

36. Hugo Kerchnawe, ed., *Im Felde unbesiegt: Erlebnisse im Weltkrieg erzählt von Mitkämpfern III.* [Invincible in the field: Experiences in World War told by a fellow veteran III]. Munich: 1923.

37. Fridolin Solleder, *Vier Jahre Westfront: Geschichte des Regiments List R. J. R. 16.* [Four years western front: History of the regiment's list R. J. R. 16.]. Munich: 1932. Dedication: *"Seinem tapfern Meldeläufer / dem hochverdiensten ehem. Gefreiten / Herrn Ad. Hitler / zur Erinnerung an ernste aber große Zeiten / gewidmet von / M. v. Baligand / Weihnachten 1931 Oberst."*

38. John Lukacs, The Last European War. New York: 1976, p. 92.

39. Heinrich Hoffmann, *Hitler wie ich ihn sah* [Hitler as I saw him]. Munich: 1974, p. 188.

40. Peter Alter, *Nationalism*. London, New York: 1991, p. 52.

41. Klemens von Klemperer, *Germany's New Conservatism*. Princeton: 1968, p. 194.

42. Hans Kohn, *The Mind of Germany*. New York: 1960, p. 331.

43. Moeller van den Bruck, *Das Dritte Reich* [The Third Reich]. Berlin: 1923, p. 261.

44. Lutz Winckler, *Studie zur gesellschaftlichen Funktion faschistischer Sprache* [Study to the social function of fascistic language]. Frankfurt am Main: 1970, p. 55.

45. Picker, *Hitlers Tischgespräche* [Hitler's roundtable], p. 168.

46. Golo Mann, *Deutsche Geschichte des neunzehnten und zwanzigsten Jahrhunderts* [German history of the nineteenth and twentieth centuries]. Frankfurt am Main: 1959, p. 715.

47. Klemperer, *Germany's New Conservatism*, p. 231.

48. Stefan Breuer, *Anatomie der konservativen Revolution* [Anatomy of the conservative revolution]. Darmstadt: 1993, pp. 192–95.

49. Rudolf Pechel, *Deutsche Widerstand* [German opposition]. Zurich: 1947, p. 279.

50. Otto Strasser, *Mein Kampf: Eine politische Autobiographie* [My struggle: A political autobiography]. Frankfurt am Main: 1969, p. 20.

51. Klemperer, *Germany's New Conservatism*, p. 193.

52. H. R. Trevor-Roper, *The Last Days of Hitler*. New York: 1962, p. 65.

53. Gábor Hamza, "A 'Harmadik Birodalom' eszméje a német filozófiai és politikai gondolkodásban" [The concept of the 'Third Reich' in the German philosophical and political thinking]. *Magyar Tudomány*, 1999. No. 7, pp. 779–87.

54. Peter Sachse, *SA-Männer von Leipzig: Ein Beitrag zur Rassenkunde Deutschlands* [SA-men of Leipzig: A contribution to the race science of Germany]. Leipzig: 1934.

55. Mann, *Reden* [Speeches], p. 156.

56. Eitner, *Hitler*, p. 149.

57. Toland, *Adolf Hitler*, p. 140.

58. Rudolf Olden, *Hitler*. Amsterdam: 1935, p. 46.

59. Wilhelm Reich, *Massenpsychologie des Faschismus* [Mass psychology of fascism]. Kopenhagen: 1934, pp. 152, 272–275.

60. Friedrich W. Doucet, *Im Banne des Mythos: Die Psychologie des Dritten Reiches* [Under the spell of the myth: The psychology of the Third Reich]. Esslingen am Neckar, 1979, pp. 90–115.

61. Anderson, *Hitler and the Occult*, p. 42, 144; Hamann, *Hitlers Wien* [Hitler's Vienna], p 305; Maser, *Adolf Hitler: Legende* [Adolf Hitler: Legend], p. 195.

62. János Honti, *Lexikoncikkek* [Encyclopedic entries]. Magyar Tudományos Akadémia Kézirattára [Manuscript Archives of the Hungarian Academy of Science], Ms. 4281/46.

63. Helmut Ulshöfer, *Liebesbriefe an Adolf Hitler: Briefe in den Tod* [Love letters to Adolf Hitler: Letters into death]. Frankfurt am Main: 1994.

64. Eitner, *Hitler*, p. 121, 133, 138.

65. Ibid., p. 158.

66. Hoffmann, *Hitler*, p. 117, 123.

67. Bouhler, *Adolf Hitler*, p. 25.

68. Mathilde von Kemnitz, *Triumph des Unsterblichkeitwillens* [Triumph of the will for immortality]. Munich: 1922, pp. 3, 370–371.

69. Guida Diehl, *Die Erlösung vom Wirrwahn: Wider Dr. Mathilde Ludendorff und ihr Buch Erlösung vom Jesu Christo* [The liberation from madness: Counter to Dr. Mathilde Ludendorff and her book Liberation from Jesus Christ]. Eisenach: 1931, p. 74. Dedication: "*Unserem sehr verehrten / lieben Führer / Adolf Hitler / als Zeichen treuen / Mitkampfes / Guida Diehl / Aug. 31.*"

70. Gertrud Kahl-Furthmann, *Religiöse Erneuerung* [Religious renewal]. Bietigheim: 1937, p. 73, 76.

71. Johannes Müller, *Die Verwirklichung des Reiches Gottes: Die Reden Jesu verdeutscht und vergegenwärtigt IV.* [The realization of God's Empire: The speeches of Jesus, germanized and decontrarified IV]. Munich: 1933, p. 15.

72. E. Stanley Jones, *Christus auf der Bergkanzel* [Christ on the mount]. Transl. H. Fellmann, Bremen: 1933; E. G. White, *Das Leben Jesus unseres Heilandes* [The life of Jesus our redeemer]. Hamburg, Vienna, Zurich: 1934.

73. Martin Wagner, *Die Religion der Freude* [Religion of joy]. w. l.: 1930.

74. Lukacs, *The Last European War*, p. 474.

75. LC CMD, German Captured Documents, SS- und Polizeiakten [SS and Police Files], Reel 58, Die Politische Tragweite des Rassegedankens [The political aftereffect of the concept of race].

76. Lukacs, *The Last European War*, p. 473.

77. Ralf Dahrendorf, *Society and Democracy in Germany*. New York: 1967.

78. Hermann Göring, *Aufbau einer Nation* [Construction of a nation]. Berlin: 1934.

79. Martin H. Sommerfeldt, *Göring, was fällt Ihnen ein!* [Göring, what are you thinking of!]. Berlin: 1932. Dedication: *"Meinem Führer / in Treue und Verehrung. / Hermann Göring / 9. November 1932."*

80. Alfred Rosenberg, *Dreissig Novemberköpfe* [Thirty November heads]. Berlin: 1927. Dedication: *"Adolf Hitler / in treuer Gefolgschaft! / 18. XI. 27 / Gregor Strasser."*

81. Fest, *Hitler*. 1998, p. 186, 242.

82. Gottfried Feder, *Der deutsche Staat auf nationaler und sozialer Grundlage* [The German state on national and social foundations]. München: 1924. Dedication: *"Adolf Hitler gewidmet / Weihnachten 1924 Gottfr. Feder."*

83. Birken, *Hitler*, pp. 45–55.

84. Hans F. K. Günther, *Ritter, Tod und Teufel. Der heldische Gedanke* [Knight, death and devil: The heroic thought]. Munich: 1924; Hans F. K. Günther, *Rasse und Stil* [Race and style]. Munich: 1926.

85. Hans F. K. Günther, *Rassenkunde des deutschen Volkes* [Race science of the German people]. Munich: 1923. Dedication: *"Herrn Adolf Hitler / dem erfolgreichen Vorkämpfer / des deutschen Rassengedanke / dankbar zugeeignet / J. F. Lehmann."*

86. Hans F. K. Günther, *Der nordische Gedanke unter den Deutschen* [The Nordic thought under the Germans]. Munich: 1925. Dedication: *"Freundlichst zugeignet / vom Verleger."*

87. Günther, *Rassenkunde* [Race science]. 1930. Dedication: *"Herrn Adolf Hitler / dem Bahnbrecher des Rassengedankens / dankbar zugeeignet / J. Lehmann."*

88. Günther, *Rassenkunde* [Race science]. 1933. Dedication: *"Die fünfzigste Ausgabe von / Günthers Rassenkunde / dem Bahnbrecher des Rassengedankens / Reichskanzler A. Hitler / treulichs zugeeignet / J. Lehmann."*

89. Monika Leske, *Philosophen im 'Dritten Reich'* [Philosophers in the 'Third Reich']. Berlin: 1990, p. 56.

90. Douglas Miller, *You Can't Do Business with Hitler*. Boston: 1941, p. 23.

91. Leske, op. cit., p. 262.

92. Richard Walther Darré, *Neuadel aus Blut und Boden* [New nobility from blood and soil]. Munich: 1937.

93. NARA, Captured German Documents Microfilmed in Berlin, T 580. Darré Heritage, Reel 249.

94. Rauschning, *Hitler,* p. 41.

95. Ormos, *Hitler,* p. 148.

96. R. Walther Darré, *Um Blut und Boden: Reden und Aufsätze* [On blood and soil: Speeches and writings]. Munich: 1940.

97. Darré, *Neuadel* [New nobility], p. 229.

98. Richard Walther Darré, *Das Bauerntum als Lebensquelle der Nordischen Rasse* [Farming as the life source of the Nordic race]. Munich: 1937.

99. Louis Pauwels, Jacques Bergier, *Le matin des magiciens* [The dawn of magicians]. Paris: 1960, p. 287.

100. Colin Wilson, *Rudolf Steiner: The Man and His Vision.* Wellingborough: 1985, p. 151.

101. Roman Boos ed., *Rudolf Steiner während des Weltkrieges* [Rudolf Steiner during the World War]. Dornach: 1933.

102. Giorgio Galli, *Hitler e il nazismo magico* [Hitler and his nazi magic]. Milano: Rizzoli, 1989, p. 40.

103. NARA, Captured German Documents Microfilmed in Berlin, T 580. Darré Heritage, Reel 231.

104. Roger Eatwell, *Fascism: A History.* London: 1995, p. 126.

105. Ernst Bertram, *Das Nornenbuch.* Leipzig: 1925. Dedication: *"Adolf Hitler / dem Kanzler und Führer des / deutschen Volkes in tiefer / Dankbarkeit und Verehrung / München: am Tage der deutschen Kunst / 15. Oktober 1933 / Ernst Bertram"*; Richard Claussen, *Unter Sternen zu den Sternen* [Under stars to the stars]. Berlin, Leipzig: 1934. Dedication: *"Dem Führer / des deutschen Volkes / in Ehrfurcht / überreicht, / Richard Claussen. / Schleswig, den 11. August 1934"*; Rudolph John Gorsleben, *Hoch-Zeit der Menschheit* [High-time of humanity]. Leipzig: 1933; Ludwig Ferdinand Clauss, *Die Nordische Seele* [The Nordic soul]. Munich: 1932. Dedication: *"Als Beitrag aus Seelenkunde / unseres Volkes / treulichst zugeeignet / J. F. Lehman."*

106. Hans Wolfgang Behm, *Die kosmischen Mächte und wir: Der Schicksalsweg unserer Erde* [The comic powers and we: The destiny of our Earth]. Berlin: 1936.

107. K. Schrötter, W. Wüst, *Tod und Unsterblichkeit im Weltbild indogermanischer Denker* [Death and immortality in the worldview of the Indo-German thinker]. Berlin: 1938. Dedication: *"Dem Führer / zum Julfest 1938 / H. Himmler."*

108. Trevor-Roper, *The Last Days of Hitler,* p. 64.

109. Michael H. Kater, *Das 'Ahnenerbe' der SS 1935–1945: Ein Beitrag zur Kulturpolitik des Dritten Reiches* [The 'Ahnenerbe' of the SS 1935–1945: A contribution to cultural politics of the Third Reich]. Stuttgart: 1974.

110. Trevor-Roper, op. cit., p. 83.

111. LC CMD, German Captured Documents, Himler File, Box 404. Folder 91. (84).

112. Leonardo Blake, *Hitler's Last Year of Power*. London: 1939.

113. Wilhelm Wulff, *Zodiac and Swastika*. New York: 1973, p. 115.

114. Dedication: "*Herrn Adolf Hitler / meinem lieben Armanen- / bruder B. Steininger.*"

115. Ron Rosenbaum, *Explaining Hitler: The Search for the Origins of his Evil*. London: 1998, p. 305.

116. Mosse, *The Crisis*, p. 295.

117. Fest, *Hitler*. 1998, p. 1084.

118. J[örg] Lanz von Liebenfels, *Das Buch der Psalmen teutsch, das Gebetbuch der Ariosophen, Rassenmystiker und Antisemiten* [The book of teutic psalms, the prayerbook of ariosophs, race mystics and anti-Semites]. Düsseldorf: 1926. Dedication: "*Vom Verleger dem deutschen / Führer ergebenst / überreicht / Essen, 24. 4. 27. / zur Gautagung / d. N. S. D. A. P. Herbert Krichtsein.*"

119. NARA, Captured German Documents Microfilmed in Berlin (Hoover Institution), NSDAP Main Archives. T 581, No. 1229. Reel 52. Johannes Hering, "Dr. Jörg Linz von Liebenfels und sein Orden des neuen Tempels" [Dr. Jörg Linz von Liebenfels and his Order of the new temple].

120. Rauschning, *Hitler*, p. 248.

121. Toland, *Adolf Hitler*, p. 68.

122. Benedict Bonafoscari, *Seegenreiche Gottes-Gaben Edler Mineralischen-Schäze und andere Kostbahrkeiten an mancherley hierinnen mehrerntheils auf aigner Erfahr und Uebung beschribnen Orthen Teutschlants mit Muehe und Fleis in meinem sehr hohen Alter zusamen getragen sothann aber meinem lieben Vetter Abraham Musculus zu sein und seiner 4 Söhne Unterricht und nutzbahrem Gebrauch freundschaftlich verehret im Jahr Christi unsers Heyllandes Anno 1656 von mir Benedict Bonofascari in Venedig.*

123. Abdruschin, *Im Lichte der Wahrheit: Gralsbotschaft von Abdruschin* [In the light of truth: Grail society of Abdruschin]. Grosse Ausgabe [large edition]. Munich: 1931. Dedication: "*Dem Führer / des deutschen Reiches / Adolf Hitler z. 20. 4. a. 19. 8. 34 / In Treue und Dankbarkeit / Paula Hauer, Magdeburg / Möchten Segensströme / für Führer / und Volk / sich hieraus ergießen.*" (The 15th publication this work was in 1990 in Stuttgart, as the only authentic and authorized copy.)

124. Abdruschin, *Im Lichte der Wahrheit* [In the light of truth], p. 122.

125. Anton Joseph Kirchweger, ed., *Annulus Platonis (Aurea catena Homeri) oder physikalisch-chymische Erklärung der Natur nach ihrer Entstehung, Erhaltung und Zerstörung von einer Gesellschaft ächter Naturforscher aufs neue verbessert und mit vielen wichtigen Anmerkungen* herausgegeben von Anton Joseph Kirchweger. Zweite Auflage. Wort- und originaltreu nach der seltenen Rosenkreuzer-Ausgabe von 1781. Dedication: "*Man beachte, wie die Menschen hasten / und sich mühen und doch nur in ver- / gessenen Gräbern enden, während hier / und da eine wahrhaft große Seele / sich selbst vergißt und durch ihre / Selbstlosigkeit unsterblich wird.*" / R. V. Emerson. Dedication: "*Heil die Adolf! / Renkam [?] / Wer nur Gott in sich und aus / aller Natur außer sich erkennt, / der weiß die Wahrheit.*"

126. Bô Yin Râ, *Das Gebet* [The prayer]. Leipzig: 1926. Dedication: "*Aus meinem / Besitz / Heim 20. April 1936 / an / Adolf Hitler.*"

127. Ibid., p. 37, 101.

128. Herman Wirth, *Was heißt deutsch? Eine urgeistesgeschichtlicher Rückblick zur Selbstbesinnung und Selbsthestimmung* [What does 'German' mean? A look back of ancient historical spirit for self-interpretation and self-definition]. Jena: 1931. Dedication: "*Adolf Hitler / im festen Glauben an / seine Sendung geschrieben / Herman Wirth / Hannover 1930 / im Zeichen des*"

129. Wallach, *Adolf Hitlers Privatbibliothek* [Adolf Hitler's private library], p. 32.

130. Ibid., p. 33.

131. Reginald Phelps, "Before Hitler Came: Thule Society and Germanen Orden." *The Journal of Modern History*, 1993. No 3, pp. 245–60.

132. René Alleu, *Hitler et les sociétés secrètes: Enquête sur les sources occultes du nazisme* [Hitler and the secret society: An Inquiry into the occult sources of Nazism]. Paris: 1969, p. 214.

133. J. Kuptsch, *Durch Wiedergeburt des Volkes zur Wiedergeburt des Reiches: Unsere Stellung zum Volkstum, zur Rasse, zum Vaterland und zum Christentum* [Through rebirth of the people to the rebirth of the Reich: Our attitude to nation, race; homeland and Christianity]. Soldin: 1932. Dedication: "*Unserem Führer / Adolf Hitler / 11. 4. 1932. J. Kuptsch.*" Cited in Wallach, *Adolf Hitlers Privatbibliothek* [Adolf Hitler's private library], p. 43.

134. Richard F. Günther, *Bleibe wach, deutsche Seele!* [Stay alert, German soul!]. Bonn: 1933. Cited in Wallach, ibid., p. 45.

135. Nicholas Goodrick-Clarke, *The Occult Roots of Nazism.* New York: 1992; Anderson, *Hitler and the Occult.*

Chapter 5

Hitler's Works

On entering the storeroom of the Rare Books Collection of the Library of Congress in Washington the first thing that catches one's attention on the shelves is an enormous row of volumes of *Mein Kampf*—for the blind. In fact, not many of Hitler's own works survived. There are the collected speeches bound in brown volumes with a few press cuttings. They are important to Hitler research because they are more complete than any publication so far. They were presumably typed out on the basis of speeches he gave, since here and there the typist missed a word. Looking through them gives one a fuller picture of the horrendous torrent of words with which Hitler talked himself into power before continuing on his path toward destruction. We would have been grateful for a copy of each of the various editions of *Mein Kampf*, but unfortunately only a few survived. However, it might be instructive to examine the remaining copies to see, for example, what linguistic attempts were made to refine the newer editions. No copy of the Führer's first book can be found in the library, although, as we shall see, it is a "fascinating piece" of writing.

Hitler's First Book

We can approach Hitler as we do certain recognized poets, who at first write terrible verse and then consequently disown their first volume— a move that in general most people accept. Expert literature also frequently neglects Hitler's first book. Nevertheless, it was published and remains important. Ernst Nolte attached great importance to it in his analysis of the phenomenology of Fascism.[1] True, Hitler's first book is not entirely his own work. He wrote it in collaboration with Dietrich Eckart. To be precise, this book is a conversation between the two of them, with Eckart saying more. There were some who thought that the whole thing was dreamt up by the poet and journalist Eckart,[2] but those who know the Führer's work have definitively rejected this view.[3]

The title perhaps really was Eckart's idea. It is quite original: *Bolshevism from Moses to Lenin: My Discussions with Adolf Hitler.*[4] Hitler's third book, which was written after *Mein Kampf* and includes his cogitations on external affairs, is published somewhat misleadingly as his second work.[5]

The conversation with Eckart proves to be an important work: it is a self-absorbed but by no means self-contained dialogue. Two Bohemians chat away, whilst the conversation grows increasingly serious. It is a documentary of the rhetorical culture and world of ideals of the contemporary Nazi underworld. Hitler said things here that he later kept quiet about, and thus *Mein Kampf* was in part intended to help the Führer's first work to sink deeper into oblivion. However, even though the Chancellor was not happy about several of his utterances,[6] he felt that overall nothing needed to be changed.[7] He did not even publish his book on foreign politics—the so-called second, but in fact third book. He sensed that if he honestly revealed his real objectives for power then his enemies would use this knowledge against him as a weapon. Indeed, he was right: one of the main reasons *Mein Kampf* was translated into French and English was so that everyone could see who they were dealing with. The grand work is, however, misleading because its author was better at being an expert-politician than a writer: if required he could completely transform himself with amazing agility into a refined French diplomat. When, for example, the public writer Bernard de Jouvenel, who was still active until quite recently, uneasily suggested that the sections referring to France in *Mein Kampf* should be rewritten, the Führer gave the following witty response: "You would like me to correct my book, like a writer does who publishes the reworked version of his text. I, however, am no writer: I am a politician. I shall make the corrections in my foreign politics, which lies in a consensus with France. If I succeed in realizing the German–French approach, that will be proof of a worthy correction. I shall write my correction into the grand book of history."[8] Even the master teacher Eckart would have found this astonishing.

Eckart and Hitler's dialogue signals the entry of the master and his disciple onto the stage. We are all familiar with the situation when the master is almost mesmerized by his disciple. Eckart was happy to act this role out, and to use the jargon of journalism he posed leading questions and was enraptured when "He" answered. Yet he had good reason to be enraptured. This, for him, was self-realization. While Eckart may have appeared hapless, he was in fact a man filled with loathing and hatred: one face full of sentimentalism, the other distorted by anti-Semitism. His drama, *The Frog King* was found amongst Rosenberg's books with a painful dedication to his niece, captured in verse, in which he hopes she will never experience the following feeling:

You seek happiness and wander about
As the waves meander across the sea
Until they are broken on a rock -
A short flicker, a swishing flutter
And above you and your dream
Oblivion dashes over.[9]

He "translated" Peer Gynt into a lamenting melodrama, which he presented to his "dear friend" Hitler.[10]

Eckart appears in Nazi party memory as "Hitler's preacher and apostle," yet it is doubtful that the Führer would have liked this, had he read it.[11] In fact, *Mein Kampf* ends by praising the poet, who in other texts is also labeled with the accolade "unforgettable." Hitler praised no other person with such warm words in his work. However, in 1919 the journalist Konrad Heiden hinted at the kind of leader that Eckart was seeking:

We need a fellow at the helm who can stand the sound of a machine gun. [...] We can't use an officer, because the people don't respect the likes any more. The best would be a worker who knows how to talk. [...] He doesn't need brains, as politics is the most stupid business in the world, and every marketwoman in Munich knows more than the people in Weimar. I'd rather have a vain monkey, who'll give the Reds a piquant answer and won't run away when people begin banging their fists on the table, than a dozen learned professors. He must be a bachelor, that way we'll win over the women as well.[12]

Eckart discovered Hitler, and he took him with him to the obscure Thule Society. The Thule group, among them the man who would become deputy Führer, Rudolf Hess, happened to be discussing the murder of Kurt Eisner, the prime minister of Bayer,[13] not least because he was of Jewish extraction. The Thule motto was: "Remember that you are a German, Keep your blood pure!"[14] As a morphine user Eckart, in particular, might have felt the significance of these words.

The Thule, as we also know from *Faust*, is a mythical ancestral homeland, and as one Nazi myth-poet put it: "In Thule the tribes divided, and some wandered back to the East, others scattered here and there."[15] At the point when Hitler entered the society he was still only taking his bearings. According to Guido Knopp "he was simply a political wanderer." In other words, his behavior was still characterized by "a mixture of confusion, passivity and opportunist adaptation."[16] In late 1918 and early 1919 he agitated for the Socialist Democratic government in Munich. The party leader and the country's president, Kurt Eisner, was—reputedly—shot by an officer who had not been accepted into the counter-revolutionary league because of his suspicious, Jewish, origin and wished to prove himself through this murderous act. A recently discovered newsreel film of the funeral march shows Hitler with the red armband of the Revolutionary Soldier's Council,[17] although earlier, at the front, he had only talked disapprovingly about the Internationalists. Thus it would appear that he toyed a little with the left-wing Bohemians before stepping up to the leadership of the right wing, and it is no accident that members of the SA later dubbed him the "German Lenin." [18] Reportedly he told Rauschning that "I have learnt a lot from Marxism." Obviously he had learnt from its methods, and even then more from its practices than from its theories, since one could hardly imagine him diving into *Das Kapital*. Hitler stressed that: "National Socialism is what Marxism could have become if it had annulled its absurd and artificial bond to democratic order."[19]

Eckart was indeed a prophet. Hitler's conversion was a perfect success. Soon after, in February 1920, they were putting together the twenty-five points of the Nazi Party program. Hitler was also able to take over leadership of the the party with Eckart's support. Many believed that he was Hitler's only friend. Albert Speer, who announced at the Nuremberg trials that if the Führer indeed had a friend then it was Eckart, evaluated the Eckart–Hitler relationship as follows: "In sharing ideas on worldviews Dietrich Eckart was as important for the Führer as Professor Troost was for him in the field of architecture"[20]; (Hitler and Troost planned the aforementioned Brown House).[21] Indeed, the dialogue entitled *Bolshevism from Moses to Lenin* recalls this relationship. The former master becomes a mere tool in his disciple's hands. In the dialogue, with "He" and "I" as the characters, "He" tells everything that has to be told. In the meantime the master drank himself into a state of uselessness, and Hitler consequently relieved him of his leading post at the *Völkisher Beobachter* (The People's Observer) and made Rosenberg its editor.[22]

The most important section in Hitler's first work is his declaration of the experience of revelation:

> "That's it!" He [Hitler] cried out:
> "We are on the right track! Holzweg! The astrologist works differently. [...] He calculates and calculates. [...] But what does the researcher of history do? He explains that which deviates from the set, the existence of the extraordinary statesmen. It does not occur to him that a secret power may be in effect somewhere, which takes everything in a certain direction. That power is, however, here. Since history began it has been here. And you know very well what it is called: it is the Jew."

The reader who had thus far believed that Moses handed over the Ten Commandments to humanity now sees him as the Prophet of Evil, the first Bolshevik. As "He" occasionally cites the *Bible* he expounds the theory that the Jews, upon leaving Egypt, perfidiously revolted against the Egyptian leading stratum and "just as in our case" they won over "the mob" with humanitarian slogans such as the contemporary "Workers of the world, unite!" slogan. Then he explains villainous Jewish deeds, again based on the *Bible*, such as the murderous behavior of Joshua, and so on. At the time it seemed to Hitler a good tactic not to call Jesus Christ an Aryan, as he later did to a smaller circle of people.[23] Instead he stressed that the Jews did not view Jesus as a Jew, and that it was precisely Jewish law that Jesus revolted against. Thus "without any ulterior motives we represent our nation's Christian foundations"—unlike Saint Paul: "[Paulus] goes to the Greeks and the Romans. He takes his own Christianity with him, the one that turns the Roman Empire on its head. All men are equal! Brotherhood! Pacifism! There is no dignity left! And the Jew won!" The Reformation was also part of this process. Hitler, of course, praised Luther, but only for his anti-Semitism. He reckoned that the fruits of the Reformation were all bad: "The puritans, the re-babtizers, the serious Bible researchers are the most juicy. The Jewish worm hides in all of them." What is to be done? Eckart suggested burning down the synagogues and the Jewish schools. Hitler stopped the Master in a state of exasperation: "The burning would mean damn little to us. And that's a fact! Even if there were no synagogues, no Jewish schools, even if the Old Testament had not been compiled, then still the Jewish spirit would be around and in effect. It has been here from the beginnings, and there is no Jew who does not manifest its spirit."[24]

What strikes the reader instantly is the phrase "the burning." Nolte believes that the stress in "the burning" [*Verbrennen*] is not on the noun but on the article, because "if Adolf Hitler was harboring a secret then this is the earliest and perhaps the clearest example of its being exposed."[25] Even Rosenberg had not gone this far yet, even though it was he who discovered the *Accounts of the Zionist Wisemen* for Nazism. Up until that point, it was only Dinter who effectively popularized the myth of blood, that the Jewish spirit is in fact a biological fact. But now it was Hitler's turn to take his first steps in this direction. His next step, which meant the end of this train of thought—at least in terms of its theoretical dimensions—was *Mein Kampf.*

Mein Kampf: My Struggle, *Sein Kampf*: His Struggle: Hitlerian Gnosis

Sadly, tragically, and despite its paltry character, *Mein Kampf* is among the most important works of the twentieth century.[26] This is not simply because it was printed in over ten million copies, but because it is concerned with the Second World War and the massive changes in the world that followed it. True, the author: "[...] appears here as a monomaniacal autodidactic individual, who from the views of his era read together his own conceptual system, the fundamental scheme of which is a primitive form of Darwinism. He was certainly a highly intelligent man, with rapid understanding. That explains why so many followed him. There must have been something appealing in the

closed nature of his thinking. But he lacked any moral or ethical dis-
position."[27]

This judgement from the mid 1980's has been refined several times
recently. Hitler was associated with Marx and Freud, and they were
likened as the three faces of the same era whose common trait was an
overall demand for holistic explanations that traced everything back to
a single source.[28] Undoubtedly, more of the Führer's enemies read his
work than his followers did, perhaps more of them abroad than at
home. Its significance is usually belittled by noting that not even Nazi
leaders browsed through it very much. Speer's statements are also
frequently referred to. The court architect recalled that he, too, gave
up studying the book. Moreover, in 1966 he said that he had never
even known the work.[29] However, in the Hitler-album published in
1936,[30] no one cites *Mein Kampf* more than Speer.[31] Perhaps Speer
quoted him as much as he did because at the time he was not much of
a writer, and did not have an imagination like Goebbels, who characterized his leader, with due respect of course, in a way that evoked and
sustained the suspicion that Hitler had been his creation.[32] However, it
is likely that the memoir-writer Speer, who grew to be a great stylist,
did not in fact read the book. It is as though he was not willing to con-
front every facet of his own past. Had he in fact taken the book into
his hands, he would surely have felt compelled to offer a description
of its character and style.

The German text is at times annoyingly convoluted, and Lion
Feuchtwanger viewed it as 164,000 assaults on German grammar
mainly because of the repetition of words.[33] The English translation is
easily-comprehensible. The French one is elegant, but the Nazis disliked it because they did not consider it faithful enough when they
compared it with the original. What they disliked most was that the
French edition was published without the author's consent.[34] The
French were already trying to campaign against Hitler through the
publication of the work in 1934. The 1939 Romanian translation was
sold secretively as a clandestine work until 1997, and was successful
because it followed the French text. Its Hungarian twin, published
only recently in 1996, was written somewhat guilefully, as the translator simplified the difficult or complicated parts. In 1997 a professional
Romanian translation was published based on the original German
version, with a foreword denouncing both Nazism and the book itself.

It is telling that no critical edition has been prepared as yet. If one should ever be prepared, then surely the 1930 edition that survived in the Hitler library will have to be taken into close consideration during the volume's preparation.

The reason for this is that this particular issue of *Mein Kampf* is unique, because the author's *ex libris* can be found in it, and most of all because somebody carefully underlined sections which they considered important, and marked other parts in the margin. The volume must have been bound in a decorative leather binding *after* it had been read, because the few brief notes scribbled in the margin by this person or people were cut into by the book-binding a little. It is possible that it was Hitler himself who wrote on the margin. Yet all three types of note have a different script. However, we now know that Hitler's handwriting continually changed. Sometimes he changed colors when underlining—using brown and blue. For a closer analysis we should perhaps refer to the examination of a graphologist.

The question arises again as to who would dare to scribble into an *ex libris* book, let alone draw question marks in it? Let us take the first note as an example: the printed text elaborates on the theme that individual races strive for the cleanliness of their race. The thesis is verified empirically: "The fox is always a fox, the goose a goose, the tiger a tiger, and so on, and the difference shows at most in the degree of the individual sample's might, strength, cleverness, skill, endurance, and so on. But no fox will be found which would foster human emotions for a goose, just as there is no cat that would feel a friendly attraction towards a mouse." The reader's note: "*Is the human perhaps a fox?*"

There are two question marks on the margin next to the contemplation according to which "the Jew" has never been "in possession of its own culture," as he has always taken it from others. Then, by another section—which discusses the fact that it is a mere illusion that the instinct for survival is as strong among Jewish people as it is among other peoples, and that it is an illusion that their intellectual capacity is similar to that of other races, although it is no illusion that they lack the idealism necessary to become a cultured people—the "Reader" adds the following note: "*and over here?*" Then there is a statement saying that the Jewish people's will for self-sacrifice does not go beyond pure survival instinct, besides which we can find the note: "*On the contrary!*" The last remark is no less argumentative either: "*See Old Testament!!*" This refers to the statement that the religion of "the Jew" does not know the otherworld, as to him an "Aryan conceptual religion" is unimaginable.

If it was Hitler who made these small remarks then we are witness to some internal dialogue. Would the Führer have re-thought his ideals? In part, yes. As we have seen, he regretted the unrestrained openness of his earlier work. Besides: "Politics for Hitler was merely a tool. He considered [...] *Mein Kampf* no exception to that. He thought that a large part of it was not fitting, and that he should not have written it so soon, and it was this that led me to give up my attempts to read the book." These words were written by Speer, who here obviously faithfully reproduced Hitler's utterances.[35] Indeed, Hitler sometimes said straight out that some parts of his work were "shit" [*scheußlich*].[36] However, this is by no means self-revision. After all, he believed that by thirty years of age one knows everything.[37] At the most he might have had some retrospective doubts and "refined" some details. He could hardly have thought of a newer, amended edition—for political reasons. If he had done that then he would have revealed some form of inner chaos, something against which he had agitated all his life. Nevertheless, it seems that the possible contradictions in his judgments of "the Jew" bothered him.

The "Reader" of *Mein Kampf* put marks mainly by the various pieces of political advice and descriptions of situations that it contains. For example, there is a note beside a section concerning the art of reading. However, we find no marks in places where the reader may have real doubts concerning the authenticity of the content. One such part is the description of the young Hitler's internal battle during his stay in Vienna. The Führer consciously altered details of his own past when he told the story of how he turned into, as he himself confessed, "a fanatical anti-Semite from a weak citizen of the world."

Hitler evaluated becoming "a fanatical anti-Semite" "as the most difficult change" in his life. He claimed that when he came to Vienna he had rejected Lueger's Christian Socialist movement and its anti-Semitism. He saw both of these things as "reactionary." For him Vienna meant the "[...] most difficult change [...] costing the greatest internal struggle, and in this month-long struggle between rationale and emotion, rationale started to win. Two years later emotion caught up with rationale, only to become its most faithful guardian and protector from then on." The scenes in the streets of Vienna "provided an inestimable service." When in the inner city he saw a Jew in a caftan for the first time in his life, the question arose: "Is that a Jew?" This was followed by a second question, "Is that a German?" He bought anti-Semite brochures with his last pennies, none of which helped resolve these questions. But the faces seen in the streets, and life itself did: there were Jews everywhere. The press, art, the theatre, and the cinema were all in their hands. They were also the leaders of the Socialist Democrats. What was impossible to understand was the boundless hatred they expressed "[...] towards their own fellow citizens, how they disparaged their own nation, mocked its greatness, reviled its history and dragged the names of its most illustrious men through the gutter. This hostility towards their own kith and kin, their own native land and home was as irrational as it was incomprehensible. It was unnatural." Nature, as he tells us, follows an aristocratic principle in which "the eternal privilege of force and energy" prevails.

"The Jew" for Hitler is both a symbol and a metaphor of modernity and democracy. What could be true from this first recollection is his internal struggle. There is no doubt that he weighed things up in the manner described above—not in the 1910's, but rather much later. One criticism that was made was that he introduced himself as a cosmopolitan, who did not really know what anti-Semitism was as his father had never spoken about such things at home. On the contrary, it is now suggested that his father did in fact condemn the Jews periodically.[38] However, it is also true that he had a negative relationship with his father. When he began *Mein Kampf* with his almost fairytale-like description of a happy family, he gave way to petit-bourgeois public taste. In fact, the young Hitler protested against both father and authority, not least because his father often humiliated his idolized and adored mother. When Hitler sketched out his own internal struggle he repeatedly enumerated the usual anti-Semitic arguments and phobias. He wisely kept silent about those Jews who helped him, including the Hungarian Joseph Neumann who sold his pictures, or his mother's doctor whom later, after the *Anschluss*, he allowed to escape (his first chauffeur, referred to in *Mein Kampf* as "my brave Maurice"[39] was also reported to have been of Jewish origin). However, the author had to convince and mobilize, and for him the turning point that initiated the experience of revelation was the sight of the Jew in a caftan (this is perhaps reminiscent of the way in which the taste of a madelaine evoked a surge of memory in Proust). The Führer had to demonstrate that the basis of this worldview was long-standing and "solid as granite" (of course, before this "turning point" there was nothing stopping him from entertaining anti-Semite views or scolding the Jews even in Vienna, but ten years were needed until the great turn, the revelation). Thus we can see that the experience of revelation was a retrospective construction.

The lecture in *Mein Kampf* mimics Saint Paul's conversion with typically primitive Nazi atheism. The figure in the "caftan" appearing on the Viennese "road to Damascus" is the central figure of the morbid revelation. Recalling what Wagner emphasized in his article *The Jewry in Music*, it seems as if Hitler gave shape to the following Wagnerian motif: "In everyday life the Jew surprises me with his appearance, which represents a certain unpleasant alienness. No matter which European nationality we belong to we instinctively wish: if only we had nothing to do with people who look like that."[40] Immediately we can see the distorted images of Jews published in anti-Semite brochures flashing up in the background.

The Führer presented only one single figure to us, using his caftan to single out all Jews. He knew a stereotype was required that was not confusing or distracting. In his speeches he also tried to keep a single element in the foreground for the greatest effect. The other "Saint Paulian" element, loosely connected in time and space to Hitler's morbid revelation, is less consciously construed. Just as Saint Paul had lost his vision for three days after the great apparition, Hitler did not see for days after a gas attack; this is a typical symptom of hysteria, a fact that professor Oscar Vogt, who has recently been unjustly ignored, first called our attention to.

It would be far too simple to characterize the Hitlerian revelation as a retrospective construction interwoven with psychopathologic symptoms, especially because the story fits into a kind of Gnostic model or archaic myth.

What is this gnosis then, to which we have repeatedly referred? It is simply knowledge. According to Harald Strohm, who pioneered the mapping out of the relationship between Gnosticism and Nazism, Gnosticism is the second great redemptive religion beside Christianity. Heretic theologians, sword-wielding peasants, romantic writers, poets, philosophers, and Marxist and existentialist thinkers somehow all fit into this spiritual trend alongside strange, obscure and occult magicians and freemasons. But who would dispute the difference between a scholar and a simple murderer? Who would even mention, let alone compare, Albert Camus and Hitler under the same breath? And who would not raise an eyebrow when reading about Hitler being a part of our history of religion,[41] a philosopher, or perhaps even a brilliant ideologist? ("Hitlerism was in fact the doctrine of a brilliant if ruthless ideologue whose ideology was securely rooted in the tradition of political economy."[42]) However, two clear-headed thinkers have given positive answers to the latter two questions—Harald Strohm and Lawrence Birken, whom we mentioned earlier. Both start out from the observation that Hitler's demonization fails to offer an answer to a series of different questions, and apart from that it fails to help rid us of the Nazi virus. What seems to be absurd phantasmagoria has to be taken seriously, because it fits into a tradition of thinking—with some noteworthy elements—that spans back more than a millennium, or at least several centuries. Many of the statements Hitler uttered around the dinner table have to be taken seriously as well, as according to such statements: "I became a politician against my will. Politics for me is only a tool to achieve my aims."[43]

Gnosticism promises redemption through knowledge. One of the best definitions of Nazi gnosis can be read in the obscure explanation of an obscure essay on Odin written for the *Ahnenerbe*. The essay was considered unscientific even by the authorities of the institute run by Himmler (they evidently must have feared that the work of dilettantes would eventually discredit their "science"). In response, the rejected author explained the sense and message of his work in a letter:

> A real religion has to be comprehensible to the people without explanation from priests; priests are not unanimous in their interpretation anyway... For each and every statement found in the *Bible* there is another which—in a typically Jewish manner—communicates the exact opposite. What does the word "belief" mean anyway? It actually refers to something negative. In contrast to this, that which is positive is knowledge. Belief therefore is *not* knowing, or the *non*-acceptance of something as right. All belief is therefore something uncertain, presumed! In opposition to this is the Germanic religion of positive knowledge, which is based on events that sweep everything along with them [*Allmachtgeschehen*], events that we can see and experience in the shaking of the foundations of archaic sacrament. This is the sense of having to believe something, for we all believe or want to believe![44]

The Gnostic does not view the universe as the result of divine creation. In fact he sees it as precisely the work of evil, of Satan, as humans somehow fell out of the world of completeness and became alienated as the result of some external interference. But the chosen ones shall become enlightened, and the world of light shall penetrate the darkness. Hitler might have said something along the lines that he would continue Christ's work,[45] and when he proudly pontificated on how he began to politicize when he was thirty, he did so primarily for the sake of propaganda, because the Savior also rose at that age.[46] However, he must have grown bored with being apostrophized as a messiah or a prophet, because on one evening at his military headquarters, during an after-dinner conversation, he denied to his dining companions that he would wish to appear as either a messiah or a prophet.[47] He considered himself to be a genius. He was proud of his skull, although he grew his strange little moustache to counterbalance his protruding nose. And typically, he also considered Stalin to be a genius (of course only "in his own way," as he said one evening in July 1942 at the table):[48] "A genius [he asserted in 1937] differs from the masses by unconsciously pre-sensing truths which the majority of people will become aware of only later."[49] This confession was also just part of the stage act. He entered the political scene with the clear knowledge that the revelation was simply a Gnostic comedy.

"The genesis of the [Hitlerian] worldview can be seen as a slow progression from the ordinary to the extraordinary," writes an expert on Hitler's early years.[50] And let us add, that here progression means Hitler's arrival at the point where he organized readily available segments of a racist subculture into a worldview. For example, the "sin of blood contamination" was the novelist Dinter's "discovery." But the enlightened Führer of *Mein Kampf* placed this into a Gnostic construction, which says that "blood contamination" is the original sin for which the Aryan, who no longer has pure blood, fell from Paradise, and so on.

The blood-dogma meant that "the Jew" in his physical reality was blood, and that consequently he spread contamination through blood: thus the notion of intellectual contamination was also given a biological basis. This dogma appears in *Mein Kampf* in its radical simplicity and clarity.[51] Accordingly "the Jew" is an infectious poison: he pollutes the soul and the body, seduces German women, and so on. By denying the order of nature "the Jew" himself is "non-nature" itself. Consequently he must be annihilated... In *Mein Kampf* Hitler "only" writes that the gassing of fifteen thousand Jews at the right time would have been enough to win the War.[52] But with this thought we arrive at "rational anti-Semitism," or more precisely, "to the anti-Semitism of the intellect" as he put it. He had expressed this demand earlier in September 1919, while rejecting anti-Semitism based on *emotion*. The "rationale" of his anti-Semitism is revealed in the "removal" of the Jews "according to plans and regulations," or in other words as a state and an authoritative act.[53] The rationale of the "demagogic genius" mobilized emotions in accordance with these plans.

The Führer established his theory of races in Munich. A former fellow soldier reckoned that "Hitler did not contribute any new concept to the complex of ideals called National Socialism. These had all been aired before Hitler was born. He did nothing but translate these ideals into the language of the people."[54] In this "translation" the voice of the literature of anti-Semitic brochures and occult subculture can undoubtedly be heard, just as the influence of Dinter's novel can, too. The Führer, however, gave shape to this chaos by employing a technique of superseding that which he also wished to preserve. He moved on from Dietrich Eckart's so-called esoteric anti-Semitism,[55] which cloaked itself in mysteriousness. As Eckart wrote: "Nothing on Earth shall remain in darkness, if somebody sheds light onto the secret of the Jews."[56] He believed that the Jews were evil by nature. The morphinist poet also argued that "There is no doubt that Mephisto, as Chamberlain says, embodies nature, since like an animal (as he calls himself on one occasion in *Faust*) he is self-interested, quite brutal, insidious, and quite without shame and sorrow; in brief, it is as if he is soulless, and there is just as little debate that he symbolizes Jewish existence which is rooted in nature. Wilhelm Busch calls the Jew 'deeply rotten and soulless,' and this is just how nature appears to the discerning eye."[57]

Yet Hitler discovered that the key to success lay in classifying "the Jew" as being an *un*natural rather than a natural creation. In doing this he connected to some extent with the conservative tradition that referred to natural order as opposed to revolution, but to a greater extent he connected with Nietzsche (Nietzsche qualified Christianity as unnatural and abusive to humans, hailing Dionysus as the ideal instead of Jesus Christ). This meant a qualitative turn in the Nazi worldview because it was not just the dethronement of rationale but the dethronement of morality as well. Both philosopher and politician applied the cunning tactic of declaring precisely what it was they wanted, because they knew that not all of what they said would be believed. When Hitler called himself a "fanatic anti-Semite," he was making a concession to his former emotional anti-Semitism. He was speaking in the language of the people. For "there would be no Hitler today without people's hatred of the Jews," as Irene Harand wrote in her response entitled *Sein Kampf*.[58] (She is unjustly a little known figure of Catholic anti-Fascism, beautiful and strong in her delicacy.[59]) However, it is also true that "In the hands of Adolf Hitler the German revolution was transformed into an anti-Jewish revolution."[60] Meanwhile anti-Semitism was just the starting point for the theory of races which would not wage war against just the Jews.[61]

Typically Hitler could define "the Jew" in a "precise way," but not the Aryan. Self-definition was fundamentally hidden in denial. His assertion was of the preservation of pure blood. Since that is an unachievable ideal, history could only be viewed as deterioration, and purification lay in holding those responsible to account and annihilating them. War and the destruction of the enemy fit the criteria of the Gnostic archaic myth. War in its concrete reality meant redemption for a Bohemian from Vienna and Munich who had traveled to Germany a few years earlier from Austria to escape his military service: because of this he simply did not want the war to end later on...

All of what seems a mythical phase that fits into a more than one thousand year old trend of heretics is, in a paradoxical way, also connected to the rationality of the Enlightenment:

> Hitler spoke in the language of philosophers, a language that had almost passed out of existence in the rarefied strata of the grand intelligentsia. But perhaps that was the only language the masses could really understand. For if the common people of Voltaire's time were in many ways still living in the age of Rabelais, the masses of Einstein's time were in many ways still living in the age of Voltaire. [...] Hitler's success, at least in part, stemmed from the fact that he preserved (even as he vulgarized) the optimism of the philosophers in an increasingly pessimistic world. Hitlerism was not nihilism but a defense against nihilism.[62]

We have to add though, that the nihilists' defense is the other side of so-called philosophical optimism: the death cult. Nazi optimism is a constant devotion to death—in words and with pretence. Hitler, too frequently toyed with the idea of suicide, he thought that if he ever failed he would turn a pistol on himself.

The Führer felt at his best during the midst of death ceremonies. Their pomp and ecstatic mood validated his gnosis.

But can gnosis and nihilism come under the same umbrella? Dostoyevsky demonstrated that they could, when he remarked in a draught of *Crime and Punishment*: "Nihilism is the servitude of thought. The nihilist is the servant of thought."[63] This "thought" leads to redemption. Nazi self-redemption comes not from the mercy of belief as it does for Christians, but through art.[64] Art is a monumental construction. The process of construction is technologized destruction (an ideal typical of the nouveau riche). All this was decorated with a distorted eclecticism. In amalgamating scenes from Wagnerian operas and ceremonies from the Catholic Church, a kind of horrific parody was created. At times, their buildings became the frightening caricatures of memorials from ancient times.

Nihilist optimism, or the flaunting of the aesthetics of death, was supplemented by an ideological construction connected to the Gnostic

myth. It is as if Dostoyevsky felt what was coming when he had Sha-
tov (the hero closest to his heart) talk in the following way in *The
Devils*: "Semi-science is a tyrant that has never sat on our shoulders
before. A tyrant with its own priests and slaves, to whom everybody
bows their head with love and with thus far unimaginable superstition;
from whom even science itself trembles, shamefully nodding in assent
to it in all matters."[65] But what are the aforementioned elements that
are connected to Enlightenment? Above all, there is the physiocratic
view of space and soil. Soil is the source of all prosperity. An even
more fatal factor was that physiocrats divided the populace into cate-
gories of "productive" or "nonproductive" according to their relation
to the soil. Hitler did the same. His cult of nature is the distorted continuation of the Enlightenment's cult of nature. Since he put nature in
the place of God, his belief is deistic,[66] or perhaps more precisely it is
atheistic deism. This is because Hitler was basically a polytheist, a
pragmatic believer in religious pluralism. For him the gods represented the anthropomorphized powers of nature, and they existed to
talk in the name of and announce the laws of nature. Usually Hitler's
social Darwinism is discussed, but Birken points out that there is no
imposed hierarchy among the races in the Darwinian fight for existence. The Darwinian theory was too egalitarian for Hitler, while the
Christian world was too hierarchical. He proclaimed that humanity
had to control its own development itself, and he saw fighting, that is
war, as the natural form of life. Hitler rejected egalitarianism because
it annulled the difference between the beautiful and the ugly, amongst
other things. Beauty for Hitler was race itself. In this sense Walter
Benjamin was right to view Fascism as "turning politics into aesthetics."[67] Yet the skeleton of dogmas and axioms, clearly visible but not
quite noticed, hid behind this aesthetic.

Birken stated that Hitlerian anti-Semitism was a "secular theodicy"[68] with a structure resembling the teachings of Marx and Freud.
Marx replaced the concept of God with the notion of work. Christians
condemned alienation from God while Marx and Engels blamed distance from work. Capital was the vampire of dead work. Terrestrial
Paradise was the reestablishment of the natural order. The young
Freud saw evil in the sexual desire of the child, something he felt to be
unnatural and thus the result of external temptation. Hitler's Jew,
Marx's capitalist, and Freud's seducer all resemble one another. Evil

and its various manifestations are no more than "Three radically different styles of thought to what was in the broadest sense the same intellectual niche: namely the theoretical space between Christian absolutism and post-Christian relativism."[69] The Führer proudly preached: "With the concept of 'nation' France expanded its grand revolution beyond its borders. With the concept of 'race' National Socialism shall take its own revolution to the realization of a new world-order."[70] He was also proud of discovering and raising awareness of "the Jew." On a long January evening in 1941 he dwelled at length upon the fact that "Ten years ago our entire intellectual world had no idea what a Jew was."[71] He also claimed in *Mein Kampf* that "in 1918 there could be no question of systematic anti-Semitism."[72]

Thus he had reason to feel that he had written the best Nazi book ever, one worthy of a leader. The foundations of his style of leadership rest on this book. The simple man speaks up, when necessary, and when his time has come: in prison where he is suffering for his ideals. Such confessional works have literary traditions, and Hitler's work is lifted above the average Nazi intellectual level by its subjectivity and its confessional features. It has a good scenario: he becomes enlightened, he is healed, and this forecasts the healing of the nation.

The theology of blood is absurd when written down and comical when uttered. He did not go into detail in his public speeches. In 1923, having paid his respects at Wagner's grave, he remarked to the composer's widowed daughter-in-law that "I am making a religion out of *Parsifal*."[73] He explained the following to Rauschning: "The king is suffering from the incurable ailment of corrupted blood. The uninitiated but pure man is tempted to abandon himself in Klingsor's magic garden to the lusts and excesses of corrupt civilisation, instead of joining the *élite* of knights who guard the secret of life: pure blood." The Führer claimed that he would refer to Wagner at every point of his life. The conclusion was as follows: "Only a new nobility can introduce the new civilization for us." And the moral of *Parsifal* is that selection and rebirth must be a perpetual struggle. The knight wants to fight, whilst the masses want peace: "The masses, however, are doomed to decay and self-destruction. At the turning point of our revolutionary world the masses are the sum total of a sinking civilization and its dying representatives. We must allow them to die with their kings, like Amfortas."[74] He kept quiet about this *Parsifal* story in

Mein Kampf. Perhaps he was afraid of looking ridiculous, or offering a rod to the critics. Still the essence is there in the tone of his declaration, and the fact that racial contamination is humanity's original sin is also obvious in the work.[75] As he said to Rauschning: "All of us are suffering from the ailment of mixed, corrupted blood."[76]

One psychoanalytic conclusion suggests that Hitler reflected his typically infantile complex onto the world. He considered his mother's sexual life degrading, and saw her illness, cancer, as an infection that could have been cured. After that, the living organism of the nation became the mother that he wanted to cure by cleansing its blood.[77] Contributing to this analysis, yet to some extent also making it relative, was the fact that this dogma about blood, i.e. the demand for the cleanliness of blood and its absolutism, was very much public knowledge. It is probable that it was a product of an ideological interpretation of suffering in First World War trenches, since in the world of war the contamination of blood might have been a source of everyday fears. Similarly, sometime earlier syphilis began to spread with the growth of urbanization, and it became intertwined with the notion of the process of blood contamination. Perhaps the Führer also felt uneasy with Rosenberg who attempted to formulate this demand for cleanliness, point by point, as a religion.[78] In this way Rosenberg sparked unnecessary arguments over belief; moreover, he also questioned the Führer's originality.

The mazes of theology obviously failed to attract Hitler. Consequently he never worked out the finer details of the theology of the blood religion. But the dogma of blood also determined his everyday life. After the great love of his life, Angela Raubal, committed suicide—under circumstances that remain unclear—he became an even stricter vegetarian, because the blood found in meat horrified him. Meanwhile he was also reported to have been scared of having Jewish blood. Several articles were published about his, so to say, semi- or quarter-Jewish origin. This fear complex also crops up in expert literature, since Hans Frank confessed at the Nuremberg trials that Hitler had launched a secret investigation into the matter. According to most general Hitler folklore the Führer's great-grandfather had been Jewish. Expert literature has convincingly demonstrated this claim to be without foundation. Interestingly, the source for his statement never emerged, although there was indeed an investigation. However, no one was looking for his Jewish ancestors. What had happened was that a relative had blackmailed the Führer with the knowledge that there were several lunatics in his family. The Gestapo then collected family photographs and letters that might have proved this to be true,[79] and Frank might have heard something about it. Thus perhaps this grand revelation was the result of the deceptive play of memory, or perhaps he simply made it up, to make the Jews appear as collaborators in the holocaust by presenting the whole thing as the work of a "quarter Jew" (of course, the accusations of psychological disorder must have proved awkward for the Führer, since genocide began with the mentally ill, and even primary school children were given tasks in which they had to calculate things such as how much it would cost to support 300,000 mentally ill per year if one mentally sick person cost 4 Reich Marks per day).[80]

For Hitler the Grail-myth appeared in a negative light when compared to the dogma of blood and the pragmatism of genocide. He did not want to find clean Christian blood, but rather wanted to annihilate contaminated blood.

Since the Gnostic divides people on principle, the Jews were cast in the role of those to be excluded from gnosis. The Führer's political pragmatism was coupled with a strong ideological dogmatism. Einstein's expulsion from Germany was a lost war in itself. The elimination of the Jews in Eastern and Central Europe was intended to eliminate the region's middle class and thus enable the more effective subjugation of subordinate peoples (such as the Czechs, the Croatians, the Hungarians, and the Romanians, amongst others). At the same time the Jews became symbolic figures to some, since it was believed that if this new Great War should be lost, then the war against the Jews would be won instead. Hitler was forced into a war fought simultaneously against the United States of America and the Soviet Union by his Gnostic dogmatism and physiocratic rationalism, since he saw the threat of Jewish endeavor for world power in both countries. Meanwhile he needed space. As he said at his general headquarters in February 1942: "I would be happier to walk to Flanders than travel on wheels to the East. Only rationale commanded us to go eastward."[81] At the same time, instinct and rationality filled Hitler with an ominous sense of self-destruction. He prophesied his own demise in his confessional messages but hid the prediction between the lines. The human logic at work in the subconscious might have suggested that both of his creations, "the Jew" and "the new man," were bound to turn against him.

By placing "the Jew" outside nature Hitler made him into a supernatural power higher than even he himself; however, at the same time he continuously reprimanded him and tried to rub him into the dirt. The logic was limp, but the symbolization was perfect. "The Jew" became the whole world that he wanted to annihilate. "The Jew" was a unit of opposites: he was both capitalist and communist at the same time. In the end the paranoid is always right in some sense. He organizes the world against himself, and then cannot win in that world. Paradoxically it seems that "Unfortunately, Hitler believed the Jews were winning that struggle."[82] By anthropomorphizing the evil that moved the world he failed to notice that the evil was he himself. Inevitably he projected himself upon the symbol to be annulled. As Jung highlighted: "The figure of Ahasver of the Middle Ages took over the role of the restless wanderer, which is not a Jewish but a Christian myth, and thus the motif of the wanderer, something which Christianity rejected, was projected onto the Jews, just like the way in which we regularly discover contents trapped deep in the unconscious in others."[83] John Lukacs also considers this explanation to be correct, and as Marlis Steinert put it, "everything that he hates in himself, the Führer projects onto the Jews; everything that causes him or Germany suffering is the fault of the Jews."[84] In other words, anti-Semitism is "something like a German self-hatred transferred onto the Jews."[85] Hitler viewed the diasporic nature of the Jewish people as unnatural, although to a considerable extent the Germans also had a diaspora scattered around the world. "The Jews are our misfortune," declared the Nazi slogan as the Jews served as the scapegoat for German "misery."[86] The Jews are amoral, turn daylight into nighttime, lie and so on—we hear these accusations from Hitler who made amorality his political moral, a man who would happily stay up late to the distress of the people around him.[87]

György Ránki found Hitler's characterization of Churchill, his most hated enemy, to be the best self-portrayal of the Führer: "He is the most bloody-handed dilettante in all of history [...] As a soldier he is a miserable politician, and as a politician he is a miserable soldier [...] he has only one ability, but in that he is unique: to lie with a pious face."[88] By preaching the omnipotence of nature he eliminated what we refer to as moral, thus drawing the line between truth and lie in a different place to where Jewish-Christian public opinion did. Some time had to pass before western statesmen and diplomats were able to realize that instead of the usual political rationality, absurd and dishonest axioms, or rather obsessions lay behind Hitlerian demagogy.

Another fitting self-portrayal is the one Hitler provided his master Eckart with. He spoke of "the Jew" in response to Eckart's query as to what the aim of "the Jew" might be:

> To annihilate the world. He believes that he has to force the whole world underneath him, in order, as he persuades himself, to be able to create Paradise on Earth. Just give him the chance and he will make himself believe it, and all this will certainly come to pass. One can easily tell by the tools he uses that he is striving to achieve some secret goal. Whilst he imagines that he elevates humanity, he chases it into despair, into insanity and downfall. If no one commands him to halt, he will destroy all. This is his calling, this is what he strives to achieve, although deep down he suspects that he too will be annihilated in the attempt. There is no way out for him, this is what he has to do. This feeling of the inevitable dependency of his existence on that of his victim's seems to me to be the prime reason for his hatred. To want to annihilate somebody with all one's might, and to meanwhile suspect that the act will lead to one's own downfall is, if you like, the tragedy of Lucifer.[89]

What is this real-life Lucifer like? In the world of the occult, as Abdruschin put it, "Lucifer, against all opinions, is proud and beautiful, supernaturally beautiful; solemn majesty surrounds him, he has clear, big, blue eyes which, however, reveal the ice-cold expression of love's absence."[90] This resembles Hitler on stamps and photographs, hugging children in a deadly looking embrace.

Self-destruction, however, could only be the result of destruction. He wanted to destroy all that was different. Let us recall the section from *Mein Kampf* cited earlier that recalled the Jew in a caftan,[91] and the description of the sight of otherness that legitimized his annihilation. At the same time, Hitler wanted to create something completely new, something "other," as he thinks that Nazism is "more even than a religion: it is the will to create mankind anew." A religion in the service of which new God? That of godman, because, "Man is becoming God—that is a simple fact. Active man is god." Not the creative human, as the Romantics believed, but the human *race*. It is interesting that the Führer did not deny that "in a scientific sense there is no such thing as race." But since "The concept of the nation has become meaningless," he and the masses needed something else. He explained the following to Rauschning:

> But you, as a farmer and cattle-breeder, cannot breed your animals successfully without the concept of race. And I as a politician need a concept which enables the order which has hitherto existed on a historical basis to be abolished; which enables the enforcement of an entirely new and anti-historical order and gives it an intellectual basis. [...] I have to liberate the world from its dependence on its historical past. Nations are the outward and visible forms of our history. Thus I have to fuse these nations into a higher order if I want to get rid of the chaos of an historic past that has become an absurdity. And for this purpose the concept of race serves well.[92]

He was not interested in the *Accounts of the Zionist Wisemen* being a forgery, as its "intrinsic truth" was what mattered: "I instantly realized that we had to copy it, evidently in our own way," said the Führer.[93] In any case, as we know, it contains nuggets of "wisdom" where politics and morals have nothing to do with each other.[94] Yet the insane dialectics that stressed the Nazi concept of "otherness" inevitably struck back. Hitler—who declared that National Socialism was "more even than a religion: it is a will to create mankind anew," recoiled in horror from his own creation: "I will tell you [Rauschning] a secret. I have seen the vision of the new man—fearless and formidable. I shrank from him!"[95] No wonder, for if we think of the stone and bronze athletes representing the Nazi ideal, and if we try and imagine how the Nazi coryphaeus on his plinth might have appeared without his uniform and mask, then it is not hard to envisage what would have happened (if we accept the social Darwinist ideology of competitiveness) had these ideal, statue-like "moral eunuchs," as C. C. Mann put it,[96] come to life.

The following statement opens some accounts of certain events concerning internal affairs in the progress report entitled *The Political Power of Racial Concept*. As mentioned earlier, in the secondary school of Benshein "at least 50 percent of benign students show signs of racial inferiority complexes to a greater or lesser degree."[97] We could poke fun at the "superior" children suffering from feelings of inferiority, were it not all part of such a terrible catastrophe. A more serious issue was the notion of the myth of blood as a counterbalance to states of physical imperfection or feelings to that effect. How true Emmanuel Levinas's 1934 diagnosis appears: "Hitler's philosophy is primal. But driven by some elemental power, the primitive forces seething in it force the miserable phraseology apart. [...] Hitlerism is more than an epidemic or a madness, it is the revelation of elemental passions." Nazism is a power instinct on the loose which questions "man's humanity."[98]

The Nazi creation could not be anything but destruction. And self-destruction at that, for Nazi executors had to beware of both one another and their creations. Meanwhile war served as the illusion of a common aim, and it preoccupied everybody, including those who would have otherwise not only realized the true nature of Nazism, but also turned against it. It is natural that under such circumstances the Führer read less and less. In the winter of 1942 his nervous system began to break down. "He was destroyed by his own image," as he could still have made peace with Stalin in Moscow, stressed Alan Bullock in the moral to his grand monograph.[99] It was actually a fortunate coincidence in the history of mankind that Franco did not attack Gibraltar, because otherwise he "might have transformed the subsequent shape of the world," and "If Hitler had won this war, can we doubt that his philosophy, which is now stone dead, would have been reinvigorated, or would have become the orthodox belief on the Continent?" Commented Hugh Trevor-Roper in the early 1980s, when Communism also seemed so unshakable.[100]

After Stalingrad, perhaps even Hitler realized that the end was nigh, though as early as the autumn of 1941 it was clear to him that he could not win the War. When his secretary, Bormann announced to him that his wife had brought a child into the world, the Führer started to cry and ramble on about how he would be happiest reading and visiting museums.[101] At such times he preferred to contemplate, look at pictures and make plans.

Notes

1. Nolte, *Der Faschismus* [Fascism], pp. 404–409.
2. Konrad Heiden, *Der Führer* [The Führer]. Boston: 1944, p. 280; Margarete Plewnia, *Auf dem Weg zu Hitler: Der 'völkische' Publizist Dietrich Eckart* [On the way to Hitler: The 'folk' publicist Dietrich Eckart]. Bremen: 1970, pp. 101–110.
3. Maser, *Adolf Hitler*, p. 188.
4. Dietrich Eckart, *Der Bolschewismus von Moses bis Lenin: Zwiegespräch zwischen Adolf Hitler und mir* [Bolshevism from Moses to Lenin: Dialogue between Adolf Hitler and I]. Munich: 1924. (In the Library of Congress unfortunately I was only able to use the type written copy of the original.)
5. Gerhard L. Weinberg, Hans Rothfels, eds., *Hitlers Zweites Buch: Ein Dokument aus dem Jahr 1928* [Hitler's second book: A document from the year 1928]. Stuttgart: 1961.
6. Otto Wagener, *Hitler: Memoirs of a Confidant*. Ed. Henry Ashby Turner, Jr., New Haven, London: 1978, p. 273.
7. Fest, *Hitler*. 1998, p. 309.
8. Grigol Robakidse, *Adolf Hitler von einem fremden Dichter gesehen* [Adolf Hiter seen by a foreign poet]. Jena: 1939, p. 44.
9. Dietrich Eckart, *Der Froschkönig* [The frog king]. Leipzig, Berlin: 1904. Dedication: *"Du suchst das Glück und irrst umher, / So wie die Welle irrt im Meer, / Bis sie zerschellt am Felsgestein — / Ein kurzes Leuchten, ein flüchtiges Schaum, / Und über dich und deinen Traum / Bricht die Vergessenheit herein. / Daß dir die Erkenntnis dieser Worte / so spät wie möglich, am besten niemals / kommen möge, wünscht dir, lieber Mizzi, / von ganzem Herzen / Dein getrauer 'Onkel' / 17. Juli 1907. / Dietrich Eckart."*
10. Henryk Ibsen, *Peer Gynt. In freier Übertragung für die deutsche Bühne eingerichtet, mit Vorwort und Richtlinien von Dietrich Eckart.* [Adapted for the German stage in a free adaptation with forewords and directions from Dietrich Eckart]. München: 1917. Dedication: *"S. l. Freund / Adolf Hitler / herzlichst / Dietrich Eckart / München. 22. Oktober 1921."*
11. Walter M. Espe, *Das Buch der N. S. D. A. P.* [The book of the N. S. D. A. P.]. Berlin: 1933, p. 47.
12. Heiden, *Der Führer*, p. 20.
13. Henry Grosshans, *Hitler and the Artists*. New York, London: 1983, p. 57.
14. Oswald Claassen, *Die Ahnen des Mondes: Eine indianische Edda* [The ancestors of the worlds: An Indian Edda]. Krefeld: 1933, p. 95.
15. Fest, *Hitler*. 1998, p. 136.
16. Knopp, *Ne féljünk Hitlertől!* [Let's not be afraid of Hitler!]. pp. 134–35; Comp. A. Joachimstaler, *Korrektur einer Biographie: Adolf Hitler 1908–1920* [Edited Biography: Adolf Hitler 1908–1920]. Munich: 1989, p. 215.
17. Reich, *Massenpsychologie* [Mass psychology], p. 148.
18. Fest, *Hitler*. 1998, p. 201.

19. Petra Tauscher, *Nekrophilie und Faschismus: Erich Fromms Beitrag zur sozio-biographischen Deutung Adolf Hitlers und weitere sozialpsychologische Interpretationen* [Nechrophylia and fascism: Erich Fromm's contribution to the socio-biographical meaning of Adolf Hitler and further socio-psychological interpretations]. Frankfurt am Main: 1985, p. 71.

20. Albert Speer, "Die Bauten des Führers" [The constructions of the Führer]. In *Adolf Hitler: Bilder* [Adolf Hitler: Pictures]. p. 74.

21. Grosshans, *Hitler*, p. 59.

22. Picker, *Hitlers Tischgespräche* [Hitler's roundtable], p. 154.

24. Eckart, *Der Bolschewismus* [Bolshevism].

25. Nolte, *Der Faschismus* [Fascism], p. 408.

26. Michael D. Biddis, *Histoire de la pensée européenne. 6. L'ère des masses* [History of European thinking. 6. The era of the masses]. Paris: 1980, p. 224.

27. K. O. v. Aretin, "Vorwort" [Forword]. In Rainer Zitelmann, *Hitler: Selbstverständnis eines Revolutionärs* [Hitler: Self-evidence of a revolution]. Hamburg, New York: 1987. p. viii.

28. Birken, *Hitler*.

29. Maser, *Adolf Hitler: Legende* [Adolf Hitler: Legends], p. 186.

30. Speer, *Erinnerungen* [Recollections], p. 136.

31. Speer, "Die Bauten" [The constructions].

32. Joseph Goebbels, *Unser Hitler* [Our Hitler]. In ibid.

33. Dietrich Strothmann, *Nationalsozialistische Literaturpolitik* [National socialist politics of literature]. Bonn: 1960, p. 383.

34. LC CMD, German Captured Documents, Miscellany, Reel 499.

35. Speer, *Erinnerungen* [Recollections], p. 136.

36. Eitner, *Hitler*, p. 94.

37. Ibid., p. 91.

38. Werner Maser, *Hitlers Mein Kampf: Entsehung, Aufbau, Stil, Änderungen, Quellen, Quellenwert, kommentierte Auszüge* [Hitler's Mein Kampf: Origins, structure, style, versions, sources, source value, commented excerpts]. Munich, Esslingen: 1966, p. 141.

39. Hitler, *Mein Kampf*, p. 566.

40. Marc A. Weiner Snr., *Richard Wagner and the anti-Semitic Imagination*. Lincoln, London: 1995, p. 57.

41. Harald Strohm, *Die Gnosis und der Nationalsozialismus* [Gnosis and the national socialism]. Frankfurt am Main: 1997, p. 275.

42. Birken, *Hitler*, p. 46.

43. Picker, *Hitlers Tischgespräche* [Hitler's roundtable], p. 167.

44. Berlin: Bundesarchiv, *Ahnenerbe*, Ns 21, p. 359.

45. Fest, *Hitler*. 1998, 371.

46. Domarus, *Hitler*, p. 24.

47. Picker, *Hitlers Tischgespräche* [Hitler's roundtable], p. 316.

48. Ibid., p. 468.

49. Domarus, op. cit., p. 8.

50. Eberhard Jäckel, *Hitler's World View*. Cambridge (Mass.), London: 1981, p. 120.

51. Richard A. Koenigsberger, *Hitler's Ideology: A Study in Psychoanalytic Sociology*. New York: 1975.

52. Eberhard Jäckel, *David Irving's Hitler: A Faulty History Dissected*. Port Angeles: 1993, p. 23.

53. Fest, Hitler, p. 181.

54. Ludecke, *I knew Hitler*. p. 695.

55. Klaus Backes, *Hitler und die bildenden Künste: Kulturverständnis und Kunstpolitik im Dritten Reich* [Hitler and fine arts: Understanding of culture and politics of art in the Third Reich]. Köln: 1988, p. 28.

56. Iván Berend T., *Válságos évtizedek: Közép- és Kelet-Európa a két világháború között* [Decades in crisis: Central and Eastern Europe between the two World Wars]. Budapest: 1983, pp. 190–91.

57. Dietrich Eckart, *Das ist der Jude! Laienpredigt über Juden- und Christentum* [That is the Jew! Lay preaching about Jews and Christianity]. Munich: 1921, p. 3.

58. E. Sandvoss, *Hitler und Nietzsche* [Hitler and Nietzsche]. Göttingen: 1969, p. 198.

59. Irene Harand, *"Sein Kampf": Antwort an Hitler* ["His struggle:" Answer to Hitler]. Vienna: 1935, p. 342.

60. Mosse, *The Crisis*, p. 294.

61. Sarah Gordon, *Hitler, Germans, and the 'Jewish Question'*. Princeton: 1984, pp. 92–104.

62. Birken, *Hitler*, p. 42.

63. Fyodor Mikhalyovich Dostoyevsky, *Ördögök* [Devils]. With György Bakcsi's notes. Budapest: 1983, p. 866.

64. Fest, *Hitler*. 1998, p. 545, 720.

65. Dostoyevsky, *Ördögök* [Devils], p. 304.

66. Birken, *Hitler*, p. 68.

67. Ibid., p. 63.

68. Jeffrey Burton Russel, *Mephistoles: The Devil in the Modern World*. Ithaca, London: 1986, p. 142.

69. Birken. *Hitler*, p. 76.

70. Fest, *Hitler*. 1998, p. 972.

71. Picker, *Hitlers Tischgepräche* [Hitler's roundtable talks], p. 152.

72. Hitler, *Mein Kampf*, p. 628.

73. Grosshans, *Hitler*, p. 20.

74. Rauschning, *Hitler Speaks*, pp. 227–28.

75. Koenigsberger, *Hitler's Ideology*, p. 28.

76. Op. cit.

77. Koenigsberger, *Hitler's Ideology*, p. 53.

78. James Biser Whisker, *The Social, Political and Religious Thought of Alfred Rosenberg*. Washington: 1982, pp. 82–89.; Andreas Molau, *Alfred Rosenberg: Der Ideologe des Nationalsozialismus* [Alfred Rosenberg: The ideologist of national socialism]. Koblenz: 1993, pp. 95–99.

79. LC CMD, German Captured Documents, Rehse Collection, Reel 163.

80. Harald Focke, Uwe Reiner, *Alltag unterm Hakenkreuz* [Everyday life under the Hakenkreuz]. Hamburg: 1991, p. 89.

81. Picker, *Hitlers Tischgepräche* [Hitler's roundtable], p. 174.

82. Birken, *Hitler*, p. 82.

83. C. G. Jung, *Aufsätze zur Zeitgeschichte* [Writings on contemporary history]. Zurich: 1946, p. 5.

84. Lukacs, *A történelmi Hitler* [The Hitler of History], p. 199.

85. Christian Graf von Krockow, *Von deutschen Mythen* [About German myths]. Stuttgart: 1995, p. 85.

86. Birken, *Hitler*, p. 38.

87. Mosse, *Jewish Emancipation*, p. 12.

88. Ránki György, *Hitler hatvannyolc tárgyalása 1939–1944. I.* [Hitler's sixty-six briefings 1939–1944. I]. Budapest: 1983, p. 100.

89. Eckart, *Der Bolschevismus* [Bolshevism], p. 51.

90. Abdruschin, *Im Lichte der Wahrheit* [In the light of truth], p. 292.

91. Rauschning, *Hitler*, p. 242.

92. Ibid., p. 229.

93. Ibid., p. 235.

94. John S. Curtis, *An Appraisal of the Protocols of Zion.* New York: 1942, p. 97.

95. Op. cit., p. 243.

96. Mann, Hitler's Three Struggles, p. 72.

97. LC CMD, German Captured Documents, SS und Polizeiakten [SS and Police Files], Reel 58, Die Politische Tragweite des Rassegedankens [The political significance of the concept of race].

98. Emmanuel Levinas, *Quelques réflexions sur la philosophie de l'hitlérisme* [Some thoughts about the philosophy of Hitler]. Paris: 1997, p. 7, 26.

99. Rosenbaum, *Explaining Hitler*, p. 90.

100. Hugh Trevor-Roper, "History and Imagination." In *Essays in Honour of H. R. Trevor-Roper.* Eds. Hugh Lloyd-James, Valerie Pearl, Blair Worden. London: 1981, p. 362.

101. Fest, *Hitler.* 1989, p. 949.

Chapter 6

On the Führer's Taste:
Artistic Albums and Catalogues

Hjalmar Schacht acted as the Reich's economic minister between 1934–1937. At the Nuremberg trials he declared that Hitler "read an endless amount, gathered enormous knowledge, and juggled with this knowledge as a virtuoso in debates and lectures."[1] Today's reader can barely discern any juggling in his *Kulturrede* from the Nuremberg Party Rally. The rhetoric mentions names, but no citations are apparent, although many recall just how much he was able to conjure up from memory. Still, the fact that the rhetorician did not quote directly from others may indicate a wise use of tactics—if the style of the quote stood out against his own style it might motivate the audience to enter into an interpretative debate and render the Hitlerian annunciation relative. However, maybe it was precisely this that was effective. Speer marveled over these speeches "not so much for their rhetoric sheen, but more for their carefully thought-through content and quality"[2] (of course Speer had to convince himself that he was sure of his own actions, and this could be why he exaggerated the Führer's intellectual magic). Today these speeches surely give the impression of monomaniacal rambling, as the sections cited earlier demonstrate. Thomas Mann was right after all when in his famous article entitled *Brother Hitler* from the mid-thirties he carefully avoided the word "artist" in his analysis of the Führer's artistic attitude. To make it even more ironic, "A brother [...] a somewhat awkward and shameful brother; he gets on our nerves, it is an intensely uncomfortable relation."[3] And the question arises: why were Hitler's speeches unpublished for so long (that is in their entirety rather than as extracts as Max Domarus published them), especially his *Kulturrede* which most vividly reveal "the artist"? Is it perhaps because the torrent of words might deceive the semi-erudite and the frustrated? Might those words cause them to fall under his influence and say, along with a contemporary Hungarian analyst, that "It is the almighty, mentioned so beautifully by Hitler, and the eternal in art that calls to what is eternal in us"?[4]

The myth of the Führer reading is partly the product of sympathy for him, and partly the result of the reflex to fend off responsibility. Those who served him raised him onto a pedestal if only to redeem themselves. The führer principle [*Führerprinzip*] survived the Führer. The self-seeking of the Romantic ego ended in the Leader. His own self-esteem required him to be perfect. Even in reading.

Actually, after 1933 the Führer must have had less and less time for reading, although as we have seen, he carefully underlined the things that raised his interest in certain books, and the proportion of books with his markings in them was higher after 1933 than before. Still, the 1938 *The Führer in Weimar* album is typical. The only cultural reference in it is to Hitler's appearance at the celebratory performance of *Aida*.[5] They did not take a photograph of Goethe's house, although the Führer frequently referred to it on the cultural day of the Nuremberg party congress. The album paints a picture of the meetings and marches. The Führer was working. First and foremost he was building.

After the death of Troost, Hitler's principle architect, the Führer found a worthy successor in the person of Albert Speer. Subsequently the two of them planned away together in self-abandonment. The young architect did not understand at the time why his father was horrified when he glanced at plans of Nazi monoliths that invoked Greek forms. "You are both completely mad," he said, and later a terrible trembling overcame him when he was introduced to the Führer who held his son in such high esteem.[6] Yet "this son" was simply happy to be building, as he got anything he asked for—instantly. The mania of monumentality also lifted him above the depressing world of economic crisis.

Hitler, the great master builder, declared several times that no one had done as much for German artists as he had, and that only George Clemenceau was interested in the arts to such a great extent.[7] Meanwhile Hitler kept quiet about his own oeuvre as a painter, even though he mercilessly endorsed his own tastes. First he waited. He allowed various artistic styles and tendencies to collide. Goebbels for example supported modernity, because he wanted to exploit it (yet perhaps he even liked it since he, too, was a fallen bohemian, a frustrated writer). Speer borrowed a few pictures by Nolde from the National Gallery to decorate Goebbels's apartment, but when the Führer saw them and sharply criticized them he naturally had them taken away immediately.[8] This incident reveals the fate of artists in general. Emil Nolde, who was slightly racist himself,[9] and who was reported to Goebbels by Paul Troost and his wife Gerda, was—as one Hitlerian adjutant put it—"otherwise exceptionally progressive."[10] Troost and his wife warned Goebbels that "Nolde and his comrades" were creations of the Jewish revolution and the Weimar state, that they were the Führer's sworn enemies, and that what was happening (i.e. that in 1934 they were allowed to exhibit) was a betrayal of the Führer, "leading to despair and embitterment among artists." Furthermore it meant "the deception of the artistically sensitive circle of people."[11] Goebbels on the other hand, apart from overlooking the report, was powerless to do anything after Hitler had declared his standpoint, and he instead continued to serve faithfully. Thus Nolde was forbidden to paint, and the Gestapo regularly checked his brushes to see whether the smell of fresh oil could be traced on them. That was the point when Nolde turned to aquarelle, because the traces were easier to hide.[12] He was only able to see some of his own oil paintings again at the 1937 exhibition of "degenerate art."

For many years this strange exhibition with its deterrent aim was the last review of modern art in Germany. In the meantime Hitler's paintings were also out of circulation, and their distribution was also forbidden, although that was little comfort for artists who had been banned. Among Hitler's works was a small album entitled *Aquarelle* that had been compiled by his court photographer, and although the works had been slightly retouched, he kept a copy for himself in his library.[13] There were several reasons for banning the distribution of Hitler's pictures. One of these was that some forged copies of his paintings appeared, despite Goebbels stating, perhaps slightly maliciously, that "a real expert" can instantly differentiate between the original and the forgery.[14] Furthermore, people might have realized that the hosanna-like explanations to the pictures in the aforementioned little album contained a certain amount of irony. For example, the words to a watercolor painting representing a suburban yard in Lille read as follows: "Only a true German artist's eyes are capable of thus seeing an unfamiliar place in the glitter of summer sunshine. The picture is grand and yet intimate at the same time." Then there is the explanation that is even more disturbing to the ink drawing of the Gothic church and the houses of Ardoye: "This is an unconscious reference to the extraordinary and outstanding architectonic talent of a then unknown soldier in the Great War, who for us has risen to become the master builder of the Third Reich." This latter annotation represents a more faithful characterization of the Führer.

The Führer was planning and contemplating. Reading grew increasingly difficult for him, and reports were prepared for him with a typewriter that typed with large letters. Also, rather than using glasses he used a magnifying glass.[15] Of course, if some important reading material came to his attention he put his glasses on. This was probably the case when Sven Hedin's book *America in the Battle of the Continents* was given to him. The book did not survive in his library, but he thanked the author for the dedication in which he shunted responsibility for the War over to Roosevelt[16] (it is interesting to note that photographs of the Führer with his glasses on were not allowed to enter the public sphere).[17]

Hitler, with his rapidly deteriorating eyesight, must have been happier to look at his picture albums than to read. He was practically ecstatic when he was able to obtain Makart's painting *The Plague of Florence*, which those around him viewed with distaste.[18] Still, he remained the "master builder" all the way through to the end, even when his magnifying glass was not enough and he stopped reading altogether.

In his last days Goebbels, for example, read Carlyle's *Frederick the Great* to comfort his leader, and not without effect. The Führer, who two years before that had amused his body of officers and his table companions with Carlyle's prediction of enormous European chaos,[19] was now brought to tears when the Minister of Propaganda reached the death of the enemy Czarina Catherine the Great.[20] Then news of Roosevelt's death filled the leader and those around him in the concrete bunker with intense euphoria. In the midst of all the destruction around them he stated that if he could not be certain of the rebuilding of the city he would shoot himself.[21] Equally typical (Erikson also cites this fact) is that Trevor-Roper, who later published an important work on the Führer's last days, came across a book in the Hitler-bunker in Berlin containing architectural plans, mainly of opera houses.[22]

As late as the end of 1945 Hitler was still gazing at a model of Linz in his bunker in Berlin. He wished to transform the town of his childhood and teenage years into a German Budapest.[23] It is curious as to why exactly Budapest should have provided the model he wished to follow, since not long before he had wanted to turn it into a Nazi Stalingrad, and he must have had little pity for the city because of his hatred for the Jews. Budapest was the rival of his beloved Vienna, and Viennese anti-Semite jargon simply referred to it as Judapest—after the renowned mayor Karl Lueger. Even so, in August 1942 he regularly thought about Budapest: "The Hungarians realized the importance of three things in Budapest: firstly they remained faithful to their river; secondly they erected their beautiful buildings in prominent locations; and thirdly they built wonderful bridges!"[24] Then he deliberated on Budapest's wonderful ornamentation:

> The whole of the Hungarian Baroque could hold its own in Austria, too. Rudolf Hapsburg was a German Kaiser. He needed a dynastic reign, otherwise his power would not have endured. Hungary arose from the eastern part of the Empire only 25 years ago. Up to then it had failed in its attempts to do so. The Empire needs a real capital. At the moment Budapest is the most excellent one imaginable. There is nothing that compares with it in the entire German Reich. There is the Parliament, the Castle, the Basilica, the bridges, and it looks vast in the night-illuminations. Vienna gives a similar impression, but it is not situated along the river. Also, the builders of the city are all Germans. We can see the importance of turning a town into a capital. Buda and Pest had been peasant haunts. The number of its inhabitants grew from 140 thousand to 1.3 million in a hundred years. Apart from the City Hall, all its buildings are twice the size of those in Vienna. Berlin must be the capital![25]

His most intelligent secretary, a woman who was enchanted by Hitler's architectural knowledge, remembered her boss as follows: "he was of the opinion that Paris and Budapest exceeded all other capitals from the perspective of urban architecture."[26]

The Führer endeavored to destroy everything that he marveled at. His relation to Budapest is characterized by the same duplicity that characterizes his anti-Semitic race cult. He characterizes the situation of the Hapsburg Empire (and then within that the situation of Budapest) in the following way:

> With the exception of Hungary there was no political tradition evoking memories of a great past in any of the various affiliated countries. If there had been, time had either wiped out all trace of it, or at least, rendered it obscure. In contrast to this, it was only during the age of nationality that national instincts developed in the various countries affiliated under the Hapsburg Empire. It was difficult to suppress these newly awakened national forces, as on the borders of the Dual Monarchy new nation states were springing up whose people were either related or identical to the various peoples who constituted the Hapsburg Empire. These new states had a greater appeal than that of the Austrian Germans.
>
> Even Vienna could not hold out for a lengthy period in the conflict. It found itself a new rival in the shape of Budapest, which was developing into a metropolis, yet the mission of this metropolis was not to help hold together the various divergent parts of the Empire, but rather to strengthen just one part of it. Within a short time Prague followed Budapest's example, and later Lemberg, Laibach, and others followed too. By raising these former provincial towns to the rank of national cities, new centers were provided for the independent cultural life of each country. In this way local national instincts acquired a spiritual foundation and therewith gained a more profound hold on the people. The time was bound to come when the individual interests of those various countries would become stronger than their common Imperial interests. Once that stage had been reached, Austria's doom was sealed.[27]

But the author of *Mein Kampf* hated the Vienna of his youth more than "Judapest," a term he never used in his work, despite viewing the Hungarians as just another subordinate people. He detested multicultural Vienna: "This conglomerate spectacle of heterogeneous races which the capital of the Dual Monarchy represented was repugnant to me as it comprised of a motley crew of Czechs, Poles, Hungarians, Ruthenians, Serbs and Croats, etc., and then everywhere there was that eternal, disruptive element of human society—the Jew, along with more Jews. The gigantic city seemed to be the incarnation of mongrel depravity."[28]

The Führer never wrote anything of the sort about Budapest. The rapid rise of the city appealed to him, and he liked its geographical position and its buildings. He planned a gigantic gallery in Linz, along with a library of a quarter of a million volumes.[29] In his will he left his pictures to what was to become the Führermuseum in Linz. It would have held more than four times the number of artifacts than the Louvre, which he planned to loot.

It is difficult to decide what caused greater damage, Hitler's theft or support of artwork. The grandest event in the Nazi artistic calendar was the annual exhibition at the House of German Art in Munich. The survey of the 1937 exhibition offers a sense of the thematic treatment of its material, and we may add that the proportional arrangement of the material probably varied very little. The thematic division of paintings was roughly as follows: landscapes 40%; women, men, sports people, youth 20%; portraits 15.5%; animals 10%; working peasants 7%; craftsmen, construction 1.7%; functionaries 1.5%; workers 0.5%.[30]

Hitler genuinely marveled at Nazi art, even if perhaps he did not hold its contemporary representatives in high esteem: "Our contemporary artists will never work with the patience and care of the painters of the grand artistic periods," he said, according to his secretary. For him the cradles of culture were Greece and Rome. He preferred Antiquity and the Romantic period. As his secretary further recalled: "He rejected the Renaissance, because it was too intertwined with Christianity."[31] In any event, he remained a great patron of Nazi painters.

If we leaf through the albums from 1938–1944 which were offered to him for purchase or contained artifacts that he had bought, then a weird amalgam of kitsch and anachronism is revealed to us through the Führer's eyes.[32] As for the style of the paintings, it is hard to define. The best term would be "Nazi Realism." However, Nazi artists and ideologists did not use the term "Realism," partly because the Socialists had made it their own, and partly because they had to create works of eternal lasting value which transcended mere style. They felt that the belief that art must serve the people's tastes was untrue, and that in fact the opposite was true: art should *define* the people's tastes.[33] As the youth leader Baldur von Schirach stressed: "Art is in the service not of reality but of truth [...] The artist who believed that he would have to paint for the sake of an era and serve its tastes misunderstood the Führer." The value judgement of a most thorough monograph on the matter says that "the painting of German Fascism does not reflect reality any more, but paralyzes the consciousness"[34] with its hieratic, as it puts three-dimensional perception into the service of the motionless. It stiffens the dynamic of the events that it strove to eternalize, while officially the principle demand might have been the life-like representation of figures and objects. At times a little impressionistic, expressionistic, or perhaps cubist modernity helped: sharp lighting, the dissecting of space into units. It reveals a taste for encyclopedic coverage. "Everything" is there from still life to battle scenes. The thematic treatment of the paintings is roughly as follows: two-thirds landscape and tableau. Besides that about 10% is portrait, including of course nudes. The portraits represent all age groups, from weather-beaten faces to women in the prime of life. There is little Greek, and hardly any German mythology either. The Middle Ages are represented by, contrary to the Wagner cult, only one armored knight per year and by one genre picture, for example the picture of Saint Genevieve with some deer. Perhaps by mistake one year a picture of *Samson and Delilah* was also included in the collection. Only once did a cross appear in the background to a group of village people. First World War battle scenes are also uncharacteristic. This gives us all the more reason to highlight the one army dispatcher image per annum.

As we know, Hitler was an army dispatcher, and although he was unable to climb the ranks (something that later proved to be rather fortunate for him, as he was then able to play the role of the simple soldier from the front to the public) he learnt a lot. He picked up the ins and outs of military strategy (later he was sharply critical of his having had to fulfil his duties as an army dispatcher during daylight hours, as many had perished that way). His techniques of political manipulation were also formed by his war experiences. As Hermann Schmitz wrote: "As an army dispatcher Hitler learnt to put his schizoid autism to the service of the military community, and from a relatively peaceful state he suddenly launched himself into merciless individual actions managed with skillful tactics."[35]

Hitler usually bought a couple of pictures which could well have been photographs. This might be connected to his experience of copying postcards in Vienna and Munich. No other autobiographical element is traceable, unless in reverse form: though he was a vegetarian, there is the odd animal picture, for example of slain or dead birds. In 1938 the new war broke into the Nazi art of painting. The main themes became ruins, tanks and most of all submarines. Next to landscapes there are pictures of buildings, and then factories appear. The praise of peasant work is coupled with the elevation of industrial pro-duction. It is telling that in the 1934 album there are no war pictures; however only part of that album survived.

The photographic album of the Führer's private picture gallery be-gins as a family album, and could be the subject of a separate study.[36] His father, whom he hated, appears first, while his beloved mother appears second. However, this order had to be kept as an anti-feminist act. Third comes the love of his life, Geli Raubal, who committed suicide under mysterious circumstances. In fact there are two photo-graphs of her. There is a Memling: "The Biblical Eve," a Dutch still life, an Italian town scene, and a few works by his favorite painter Franz von Stuck. Also, there is a painting of Bismarck and Frederick the Great, and even one of Hindenburg in civilian clothing; in addition there is one of his most faithful chauffeur and doppelganger Julius Schreck, who is thought to have become the victim of the attempt to assassinate the Führer.[37]

There is a uniquely ludicrous figure in an armored knight's outfit, which looks as if he had just come out of the barbers' with a poorly set aristocratic hairdo. The presence of this armored man is a mystery. Why was there not a more handsome figure portrayed on horseback? Once Hitler, too, was depicted as an armored horseman, thus evoking the false illusion that he supported the very same Teutomania that he condemned. Perhaps it was on account of this that the idea of a horseman irritated him. But of course the Führer could not be irritated (accordingly a Nazi journal published one of Hitler's letters from 1915 with three dots in place of the sentence: "Now I am very irritated").[38] People knew how to please him, but somehow they seem to have misjudged the issue of the knight from the Middle Ages. The armored gear demanded a lot of exercise, and Hitler did not like sports activi-ties at that time. When he was warned about putting on weight, he only remarked that he would loose it during his speeches. Moreover, he may also have disliked the idea of a horseman because it might have reminded him that he had served as a foot soldier; on top of all that it evoked the figure of Don Quixote. Hitler had read the story. In 1909 he sent the a copy of the novel to his elder sister Paula,[39] and on one long night in 1942 he qualified the following books, besides the *Bible*, as universal works: *Robinson Crusoe, Gulliver's Travels, Uncle Tom's Cabin*; at the top of the list was *Don Quixote*. "Cervantes's book is a most excellent parody which records a society doomed to extinction," and Robinson's story "is somehow the history of human development."[40]

Stephen H. Roberts, the aforementioned Australian journalist, reported with great satisfaction that a colored Hitler portrait (which was decorated with the silver ornaments of the Knights of the Grail) which he saw in Munich during the year of the 1936 Olympic Games had been hastily removed because it revealed too much of the Führer's "true mentality."[41] Even so, as indicated earlier, it was public knowledge that the Führer considered Wagner to be his intellectual predecessor. Nevertheless, he endeavored to avoid seeming anachronistic. He embraced the cult of the Middle Ages for tactical reasons (at the most), and even then he only did so on certain occasions to win over old-fashioned officers. He rejected the occult because it provided only incalculable things that lacked any "science." Of course, people in the Führer's service obviously tried to adapt to his taste. This is probably why we would not think the athletic male nude statue with a modern hairdo exhibited in 1943 was Parsifal had it not been written down underneath it.[42] The Führer's collection of over seventy pictures is dominated by nineteenth-century Romantic and Realist landscape paintings. Overall the collection represents the fantasy world of the Biedermeier petit bourgeois, or at least of one who grew rich and accumulated goods (he also received a few valuable pictures as gifts, we know of a Tiziano from Mussolini, and a small Makart from László Bárdossy). This is the fantasy world of a member of the petit bourgeois who fought through the First World War, who with an unflagging instinct for power, and in spite of a deeply wounded soul, discovered the "ideal" that he then began to serve. Looking back from today he seems somewhat similar to the *nouveau riche*. As a flight technician born in 1915 recalls: "He had an effect on me in certain situations. I lived in Holland and Belgium during the Nazi period, thus my perspective is broader. I always match Adolf with the nouveau riche. Nothing is ever enough for them. Not that it is for the old rich either, but they are not always in such a hurry."[43] Hitler detested the nobility, like all parvenus. He was a dispatcher who had climbed the social and political ladder, who gave his world-conquering orders himself. He learnt about the significance and strength of command as a mediator of commands. He recognized the efficacy of a self-confident air in the crisis following the First World War: "No American super-salesman could have been more efficient then he was in selling his political thoughts. His articulateness, fluency and self-assurance have deserved the highest praise." Wrote Emil Lengyel in his warning on the Nazi danger.[44] Lengyel must have wanted to mobilize public opinion in the West by additionally highlighting Hitler's business attributes; perhaps in today's world of "robber capitalism" Hitler's entrepreneurial nature is one reason for Hitler research.

Hitler actually wanted to be an artist. Or at least he said, as the war raged at its heights, that he would have liked to wander about "as an unknown painter" in Italy [45] Still, during the War he said something along the lines that "his happiest day would be when he could take off the uniform and devote himself to art."[46] Had he not been refused admission to the Academy of Arts in Vienna for a second time, many things may well have turned out differently. In his 1937 grand *Kulturrede* we can sense intermittent flashes of the kind of artist he would have become. He rebuked modern copiers because they copy "the nonsense" instead of "the honorable." The autobiographical motif is more striking in outbursts such as the following: "These pen pushers were against the honest and restrained common man, and were the main reason for the disappearance of those truly great artists who help humanity in its progress. It is undeniable that as the nineteenth century grew into the twentieth century the number of really great artists began to decrease in proportion to the extent that artistic literature expanded!"

He was ultimately right when he complained to his friend in 1911 that it was the world that lost out when he was refused admission to the Academy of Arts in Vienna.[47]

Hitler's collection was very valuable and it is clear that this collection of painting and other artworks, including his own works, is better than his library. Yet this was not solely Hitler's achievement. It was the result of various genres. Yet as one browses through Hitler's books, one sees the way in which each little vein grows into a repulsive flood that sweeps all else away and merges it into one thing: his own work.

Literature is obviously only one manifestation of Nazi art. It is like water carrying litter with its various words and their assemblages bobbing on the surface. Nazi painting is the representation of nihilism in pictorial form. Film is the document of motion and dynamics *in vacuo.*[48] Architecture is the manifestation of absurd strivings for monumentality. The fact that "God is dead" and the consequences of that fact can only be expressed through words. And when the "melody of life" begins, to use the euphemistic Nazi slogan, the plot of the self-perpetuating novel begins. The resulting work, the Second World War, is authentic in its own inimitable way. Let us think about its principle creator, Hitler, who has not yet been successfully represented in a literary work. He is an indescribably original phenomenon. The amalgam of his humane and inhumane nature makes him impossible to copy. He has been termed a genius on numerous occasions. Perhaps he was indeed a genius in one respect: in simplification, in the simplification of false ideals. According to the creator of his psychogram or psychological profile his talent for "artistic simplification" was one of his chief characteristics.[49] He was proud of this, too, according to one interesting product of Hitler folklore, Eva Braun's apocryphal diary.[50] In it we can also read, certainly fitting even if it is perhaps untrue, that Himmler asked his Leader whether Jacob Burckhardt's writing, which predicts the coming of the terrible simplifiers, should be banned. Hitler, however, silenced his devotees by saying that it would make good propaganda for the movement.[51] The end result is well-known, but retrospective eyes shall scan the path that led to this outcome for a long time to come. It is a kind of Calvary that must be endured alongside this criminal.

John Lukacs wrote that "Hitler, the fanatical ideologue, went to ruin, among other things, because of his undiminished belief in *Realpolitik*, believing until the end that his opponents were thinking in terms of a balance of power in Europe, too."[52] Was it not perhaps simply his hatred that was packed into his ideology? Did he have an ideology at all?

Hermann Rauschning's studies and accounts make for an illuminating read in their own right, let alone for their content on Hitler. His main thesis is that Hitler's ideology is nihilism. However, it is as if even the author found this hard to accept, as he tries to read elements of some occult or esoteric persuasion into the Führer's utterances— albeit not very successfully (it is interesting to note that questions regarding the degree of Hitler's occultism never arose in the interviews Rosenbaum carried out with so many outstanding historians, writers and theologians on the subject of techniques used to interpret

Hitler.[53] However, he does cite Lucy S. Dawidowicz's characterization, which claims that Hitler's language is esoteric, by which the author only meant that Hitler used coded or call-words to refer to the Jews, words such as "usurers," "grand-capitalists," "international monetary power," "November Criminals," [fighters of the German Revolution in November 1918] Communists, or Social-Democrats).[54] However, experts and serious authors have been hard pressed to uncover or reconstruct more genuine esoteric elements in the Führer's pronouncements, which were rather marked by his instinct for power, and were aimed at an "all or nothing" approach. From which dark stratum of human existence might this have erupted?

When Jung examined and compared Hitler's and Mussolini's faces with passionate fascination, the Führer's expressionless features astonished him. The whole man evoked the impression of a robot for the psychologist, who thought: "He is the loud-speaker which magnifies the inaudible whispers of the Germanic soul until they can be heard by the German's conscious ear. He is the first man to tell every German what he has been thinking and feeling all along in his unconscious about German fate, especially since the defeat in the World War, and the one characteristic which colors every German soul is the typically German inferiority complex, the complex of the younger brother, of the one who is always slightly late to the feast. Hitler's power is not political; it is magic."

As Jung sees it, the Führer was like a prophet from the *Old Testament,* moreover, he was a messiah who wanted to build the foundations for a religion that would stand in opposition to the Christian Church, like Islam. Hitler is a "spiritual being, semi-god, or even more: a myth." "He is not an individual, but a whole nation."[55] Thus criticism of Hitler becomes his apologia—and an accusation leveled at Germany simultaneously. As Joseph Roth wrote in contemplation of the "wandering Jew" in 1934: "National Socialism is right when it says that it is the sole representative the German people. At this hour, it is by all means right."[56] Posterity did find some objectionable aspects in Jung's attitude to Nazism. It was hardly a good idea to write about differences between Jewish and Christian psychoanalysis at a time of raging racial legislation. Indeed, Jung may have sensed that. There is a sharp change in the perspective of his articles entitled *Wotan* from 1936, and *Post-Catastrophe* from 1945.

For example, in 1936 Jung posited that Wotan himself was resurrected in Hitler, who embraced the people in his power like the Germanic god. Yet this happened without external malefice, because Wotan is:

> [...] an ancient Germanic archetype, the unexcelled personification of one of the fundamental particularities typical of the German people. [...] [Thus:] What makes a deep impression in the German phenomenon is exactly that a person, who is overtly possessed, empowers the entire nation in a way that everything is set into motion, everything starts rolling and inevitably on a dangerous slope. [...] [Thus:] We outsiders are too busy judging the Germans of our era as an active party responsible for what happened, even though it would perhaps be fairer to view them as victims in all that happened.[57]

However, in 1945 Jung's diagnosis of Hitler was one of *pseudologia phantastica*. This is a form of hysteria in which the victim believes his or her own lies. In this way Wotan disappeared from the level of the Jungian explanation. "It seems to me that the story of the past twelve years is the case history of a hysteric."[58] The main issue for Jung was the question of collective responsibility and the individual's psychological liberation from it. The psychotherapeutic treatment of this continues even today.

Jung's statements seem to reflect the great intellect's struggle and wavering, how he sought the answer to the questions surrounding the relation between the individual and the community. If we simplify Jung's Hitler theory, as he did in his interview, then it is nothing more than a medium-thesis. According to this thesis, Hitler was a medium, the mouthpiece of others. To cite a later version of the thesis: "In a medium energies travel, the efficacy and direction of which the medium does not necessarily comprehend. The medium dances to music that is not his own."[59] Julius Evola, who was familiar with and practiced Fascism, added to this explanation by refuting the views which claimed that the Führer was a member of some secret society.[60] Also, no matter how obscure Abdruschin's book may be, his following observation is of great import: "People do not easily allow a medium to walk the mid-course."[61]

It is no accident that the great books of the era concern the conflict between the world of human instincts and civilization. Henri Bergson's *The Two Sources of Morality and Religion* seems to precede what Freud later discussed in detail in his book *Mal Feeling in Culture*. What *élan vital* is for Bergson is what instinct is for Freud. Freud wrote neither about Hitler nor about Nazism. Nonetheless, he said most about his era in his explanation of the operation of the human world, where Eros and Thanatos, i.e. the instincts for life and death, arise as all-determining powers. His discussion of the horrors of the Hitlerian world with Stefan Zweig is characteristic: "The outburst of bestiality deeply shocked him as a humanitarian but as a thinker he was in no way astonished. He had always been scolded as a pessimist, he said, because he had denied the supremacy of culture." Now he saw—though it did not make him feel proud—that his "opinion that the barbaric, the elemental destructive instinct in the human soul was ineradicable," and that this opinion "has become confirmed most terribly."[62] It is as if in the course of this discussion Freud had forgotten Romain Rolland's letter to him, which sent him into a long period of contemplation at the time. The French writer commented on Freud's writings which analyzed "religion as an illusion" (and neurosis):[63]

> He [that is to say Romain Rolland, writes Freud] responded that he would tend to completely agree with my views on religion, but he was sorry that I did not deal with the actual source of religiosity. He believed this source to be a strange feeling that he was never able to let go of, and he found that many others—probably millions of people—professed the same thing. This feeling, which he would call a vague impression of "eternity," is one without borders or limits, and is similar to a sort of "ocean-like" feeling. This feeling is a clearly subjective fact, not a belief; no insurance for the individual's survival is connected to it, yet it is the source of religious energy which the various Churches and religious systems seize upon and direct into defined channels that they then no doubt make use of. One can call oneself religious only on the grounds of this ocean-like feeling, even if one rejects all other beliefs and illusions. [64]

Freud was unable to discover this feeling in himself.

Yet is Hitler's desire for eternity not some kind of ocean-like feeling, or to be more precise its ebb? Or is it rather a caricature of it, since for him the individual lived on in the race? He acted under the auspices of the eternal validity of that statement, as in the end—faithful to his social Darwinist concepts—even the race he held divine would nod in approval of his downfall, because in the struggle for existence he was proved to have been weaker than his enemies, and according to him the weak had to perish... Consequently, this enormous ocean-like ebb and flow endeavored to seize everything in its path and drag it towards its oblivion. Thus Hitler could well be a classic example of the death instinct. Several authors followed this line of thought after following Freud's theories and examining Fascism as a symptom of collective frustration.[65] Wilhelm Reich rewrote his work on *The Mass Psychology of Fascism* many times between 1933 and 1942. In the last edition he attributes Hitler with the significance of symbolizing the beginning and ending of an era: "The fact that Hitler was a political genius unmasks the nature of politics in general as no other fact can. With Hitler, politics reached its highest stage of development. We know what the fruits of politics are, and we know how the whole world reacted to them. In short, it is my belief that, with its unparalleled catastrophes, the twentieth century marks the beginning of a new social era, free of politics."[66]

Contrary to this Erich Fromm arrived at the following conclusion: "[...] his [Hitler's] talents were nothing extraordinary. Extraordinary was the socio-economic situation which allowed him to become outstanding. Hundreds of Hitlers live among us who are waiting to step forward instantly should the clock of history signal their hour."[67] However, thus far no one else has been able to unite the energies of the universe so effectively for negative purposes.

Notes

1. Maser, *Adolf Hitler: Legende* [Adolf Hitler: Legends], p. 197.

2. Speer, *Erinnerungen* [Recollections], p. 73.

3. Mann, *Reden* [Speeches], p. 849.

4. Ladislaus Köszegi, *Die Begegnung des deutschen, ungarischen und italienischen Kunstgeistes in Hitler's Ästhetik* [Encounter with Hitler's aesthetics in the German, Hungarian and Italian artistic spirit]. Budapest: 1939, p. 6.

5. *Der Führer in Weimar 1925–1938*. Weimar: 1938, p. 46.

6. Speer, *Erinnerungen* [Recollections], p. 148.

7. Grosshans, *Hitler*, p. 19.

8. Op. cit., pp. 40–41.

9. Robert Pois, *Emil Nolde*. Washington: 1982, pp. 187–88.

10. Hildegard von Kotze ed., *Heeresadjutant bei Hitler 1938–1943: Aufzeichnungen des Majors Engel* [Adjutant to Hitler 1938–1943: Major Engel's notes]. Stuttgart: 1974, p. 50.

11. LC CMD, German Captured Documents, Paul Ludwig and Gerdy Troost Papers Reel 447.

12. Jonathan Petropoulos, *Art as Politics in the Third Reich*. Chapel Hill, London: 1996, p. 95.

13. LC Prints and Photographs Divison, Heinrich Hoffmann, ed., *Adolf Hitler: Aquarelle*. w. y; Hermann Nasse, *Zum Geleit* [Guidance]. In ibid. *Aquarelle*.

14. Joseph Goebbels, "Der Führer und die Künste" [The Führer and arts]. In *Adolf Hitler: Bilder* [Adolf Hitler: Pictures], p. 68.

15. Henry Picker, Heinrich Hoffmann, *Hitlers Tischgespräche im Bild* [Hitler's roundtable talks in picture]. Munich, Berlin: 1980, p. 25.

16. Werner Maser, *Hitlers Briefe und Notizen* [Hitler's letters and notes]. Düsseldorf, Vienna: 1973, p. 201.

17. Hans Bernd Gisevius, *Adolf Hitler: Versuch einer Deutung* [Adolf Hitler: Attempt for meaning]. Munich: 1963.

18. Zoller, *Hitler Privat*, p. 51.

19. Köhler, *Wagners Hitler*, p. 118.

20. Trevor-Roper, *The Last Days*, p. 159, 293; Fest, *Hitler*. 1998, p. 1035.

21. Petropoulos, *Art*, p. 310.

22. Erikson, *Luther*, p. 123.

23. Speer, *Erinnerungen* [Recollections], p. 113.

24. Hitler, *Monologe*, p. 362.

25. Ibid., p. 371.

26. Schroeder, *Er war mein Chef* [He was my boss], p. 219.

27. Hitler, *Mein Kampf*, p. 77.

28. Ibid., p. 135.

29. Ernst Kubin, *Sonderauftrag Linz: Die Kunstsammlung Adolf Hitler* [Special edition in Linz: Adolf Hitler's art collection]. Vienna: 1989, p. 13.

30. Hinz, *Die Malerei* [Painting], p. 44.

31. Schroeder, *Er war mein Chef* [He was my boss], p. 217.

32. LC Prints and Photographs Divison: 11395 F [1938] "Haus der Deutschen Kunst (Neuer Glaspalast)" [House of German Art (New Glass Palace)], Anstalt des öffentlichen Rechts in München. Ankäufe des Führers aus der "Großen Deutschen Kunstausstellung 1938" (Duplikat für das Haus der Deutschen Kunst) [The Führer's purchases at the "Great German Arts' Exhibition, 1938" (Copy to the House of German Art)]; 11396 F [1939] "Haus der Deutschen Kunst (Neuer Glaspalast)" [House of German Art (New Glass Palace)], Anstalt des öffentlichen Rechts in München. Ankäufe des Führers aus der "Großen Deutschen Kunstausstellung 1939" (Duplikat für das Haus der Deutschen Kunst) [The Führer's purchases at the "Great German Arts' Exhibition, 1939" (Copy to the House of German Art)]; 11397 F [1940] "Haus der Deutschen Kunst (Neuer Glaspalast)" [House of German Art (New Glass Palace)], Anstalt des öffentlichen Rechts in München. Ankäufe des Führers aus der "Großen Deutschen Kunstausstellung 1940" (Triplikat für das Haus der Deutschen Kunst) 2. vol. [The Führer's purchases at the "Great German Arts' Exhibition, 1940" (Copy to the House of German Art) vol. 2.]; 11398 F [1941] "Haus der Deutschen Kunst (Neuer Glaspalast)" [House of German Art (New Glass Palace)], Anstalt des öffentlichen Rechts in München. Ankäufe des Führers aus der "Großen Deutschen Kunstausstellung 1939" (Duplikat für das Haus der Deutschen Kunst) [The Führer's

purchases at the "Great German Arts' Exhibition, 1941" (Copy to the House of German Art)]; 11398 F "Große Deutsche Kunstausstellung 1941" Werke, die dem Führer zum Ankauf angeboten wurden ["Great German Arts' Exhibition, 1941," works that the Führer was offered for purchase]; 11399 F Vom Führer für sich persöhnlich aus der "Großen Deutschen Kunstausstellung 1943" angekaufte Werke ["Great German Arts' Exhibition, 1943," works that the Führer personally purchased for himself].

33. Harold James, *A German Identity 1770–1990*. London: 1989, p. 145.

34. Hinz, *Die Malerei* [Painting], p. 74, 95.

35. Schmitz, *Hitler*, p. 266.

36. LC Prints and Photographs Divison, 11373 H Katalog der Privat-Gallerie Adolf Hitlers [Catalogue of Adolf Hitler's private gallery].

37. Ludecke, *I knew Hitler*. p. 468.

38. LC CMD Hitler Collection; Eberhard Jäckel, Axel Kuhn, eds., *Hitler: Sämtliche Aufzeichnungen 1905–1924* [Hitler: Collected notes 1905–0924]. Stuttgart: 1980, p. 68.

39. Kershaw, *Hitler*, p. 75.

40. Grosshans, *Hitler*, p. 19; *Hitler: Monologe*, p. 281.

41. Roberts, *The House*, p. 10.

42. *Große Deutsche Kunstausstellung im Haus der Deutschen Kunst zu München* [Great German Arts' Exhibition, Munich]. Munich: 1943, p. 119.

43. Walter Kempowski ed., *Haben Sie Hitler gesehen?* [Have you seen Hitler?]. Munich: 1973, p. 67.

44. Emil Lengyel, *Hitler*. London: 1932, p. 243.

45. Fest, *Hitler*. 1998, p. 138.

46. Schroeder, *Er war mein Chef* [He was my boss], p. 219.

47. J. Sydney Jones, *Hitler in Vienna 1907–1913*. New York: 1982, p. 228.

48. David Reich, *The Third Reich: Politics and Propaganda*. London, New York: 1993.

49. Eitner, *Hitler*, p. 92.

50. Waite, *The Psychopatic God*, p. 529.

51. Paul Tabori ed., *The Private Life of Adolf Hitler: The Intimate Notes and Diary of Eva Braun*. London: 1949, p. 97.

52. Lukacs, *The Last European War*, p. 344.

53. Ron Rosenbaum, *Explaining Hitler: The Search for the Origins of his Evil*. London: 1998.

54. Lucy S. Dawidowicz, *The War against the Jews 1933–1945*. New York: 1979, pp. 202–203.

55. Knickerbocker, *Is tomorrow Hitler's?*, pp. 46–49.

56. Joseph Roth, "Der Segen des ewigen Juden" [The blessing of the wandering Jew]. In *Ahasvers Spur: Dichtungen und Dokumente vom 'Ewigen Juden'* [Ahasvers Spur: Poetry and documents from 'The Wandering Jew']. Eds. Mona Körte, Robert Stockhammer. Leipzig: 1995, p. 208.

57. Jung, *Aufsätze* [Writings], pp. 13, 22–23.

58. Ibid., p. 93, 101.

59. Pauwels, Bergier, *Le matin* [The dawn], p. 357.

60. Julius Evola, *Hitler e le societè segrete. Il Conciliatore* [Hitler and the secret society]. 1971, p. 15. Cited in Galli, *Hitler.* p. 85.

61. Abdruschin, *Im Lichte der Wahrheit* [In the light of truth], p. 97.

62. Zweig, *Die Welt* [Yesterday's world]. Chap. 16, 17.

63. Sigmund Freud, *Gesammelte Werke* [Collected works]. London: 1955, p. 422.

64. Sigmund Freud, *Esszék* [Essays]. Budapest: 1982, pp. 329–30.

65. Reich, *Massenpsychologie* [Mass psychology]; Erich Fromm, *Escape from Freedom.* New York: 1941.

66. Reich, *Massenpsychologie* [Mass psychology]. pp. 394–95.

67. E. Fromm, *Anatomie der menschlichen Destruktivität* [Anatomy of human destructiveness]. Hamburg: 1981, p. 486.

Farewell to the World of Hitler and His Library

Hitler's library documents a sinful and criminal subculture. Our browsing through the library has shown how the thoughts buried there became part of the "granite foundation"—to use an expression from *Mein Kampf*—of the Hitlerian world view, a view that at times sacrificed acknowledgement of its actual sources, as in the cases of Dinter or Feder, for example. Something that Nazi authors shared beyond their worldview was their fate: they were immensely pathetic, unhappy, and pitiful people. Hitler was deeply honest in his letter (with all its linguistic and spelling mistakes) to the Magistrate of Linz in 1914, in which he made excuses for going to Germany instead of completing his military service: "Youth, and what that beautiful word means, I have never known."[1] These same pitiful people were often ridiculous too, and having acquired terrible knowledge they covered up their ridiculousness, first with demonic poses and later with horrifying crimes. They justified their sins with their worldview, and the central figure of this "worldview" could only be the Führer. His command called for the committal of sin and gave absolution from those sins. Hitler's "granite worldview"—as he called it, which was assembled from his readings—is a burden that still weighs upon humanity today. His expressionless face hides dark dimensions.

It is interesting, however, to reflect on just how little the contemporaries who dealt with Hitler and his movement's relationship to arts or intellectual trends attended to the meaning of what he said: they missed the internal mental structure operating amidst his torrents of words. Ernst Nolte, one of Heidegger's students who praised Hitler for a while, drew attention to such mental structures in his often-cited

work (with its very apt title): *Fascism in its Own Era*. Its view is a
phenomenological one, and the essence of this view is expressed by a
hero from one of the grand novels investigating consciousness written
by the deceased Nazi writer Ernst von Salomon: "It is difficult to give
any specific definition of National Socialism, and there is no other
option than to call it a 'phenomenon,' a distorted monster of life,
which knows no limits and spreads in all directions."[2] So Hitler was a
unique phenomenon with his theology of nature and his neo-pagan
polytheism. This phenomenon was not the logical continuation of past
processes, but something new and different, and it is to be studied as a
product of its own era and measured against its own contemporaries.

Victor Klemperer, a lecturer in French literature, approached Nazism from a linguistic perspective. During the 1930's he happened to
be studying precisely the Enlightenment when he was made to live
through the "Brownshirt" period in a Jewish house in Dresden (his
wife was an Aryan). His "working conditions" were harsh, as it was
forbidden for a Jew to read any work by Hitler or his colleagues. Thus
he listened primarily to radio speeches, or rather he did when he
could, as for obvious reasons he did not always have the opportunity
or the inclination to do so. Thus *Mein Kampf* remained a secret. On
February 10, 1944 he noted: "I really got stuck into *Mein Kampf* (the
first 200 pages from the 800), and it is as fascinating as it is repulsive
and depressing—the publication of this book made this man the
Führer and gave him eleven years of power! The German upper class
is never to be forgiven for that!"[3] The alpha and omega of Klemperer's analysis is language, because language "rules my emotions and
it guides my entire existence," as he put it in 1957 in his work entitled
the *LTI* (*Lingua Tertii Imperii*, meaning "The Language of the Third
Reich"), which summarizes his experiences as written in his diary.[4] He
found the origins of the Nazi world to be rooted in the eighteenth and
nineteenth centuries by examining the use of language, vocabulary,
and the shifts in the meanings of words. Klemperer explained Nazism
as a perverted form of Romanticism, and he believed that the Nazi
Hitler and the Zionist Herzl were both products of this Romanticism.[5]
But by the time his book was published, the author was bound to silence by Communist Party discipline. However, in his diaries, where
these same thoughts can be found, more can be found on the subject.
One of the best examples is an apt—perhaps too apt—definition of

Fascism as "zoology + business."[6] His description of the development of Nazi language is a masterpiece: "The language of the Third Reich was at first lyrical and ecstatic, then it became a military language; finally it grew to be mechanistic and materialistic."[7] However there are only a few Nazi citations in Klemperer's work. He does not reconstruct conceptual structures because he is too horrified by Nazi ideology's purposefully monolithic nature and demagogic torrent of words. Indeed, it was common for researchers dealing with the Führer's language to either view it as confused demagoguery heaving with grammatical errors and linguistic clumsiness, or be dazed by the whole experience, and give themselves over to the Führer. Indeed, in 1939 one of the greatest Hungarian poets, Lőrinc Szabó, anticipated solving the problems of the world with the alliance of the two great totalitarian empires. This time the painter of words went seriously off track! However, his words give a certain "sense" of the magic of the Hitler-myth:

> *Hitler* stresses his words sharply. He does so in accordance with meaning, but often the stress connotes different shades of meaning. The same text has a different effect on the reader and the listener, especially during sarcastic sections. His voice is usually serious, and has an objective tone even during lyrical parts; his anger, however, tends to make his voice a little dull. It is obvious that he knew his speeches by heart, as he frequently looked up and recited long sentences in that manner. With Hitler, reading out loud and oration often flow into one, as with many modern performance artists who recite poetry on stage, half of it by heart, and half of it from the book.
>
> He is wonderful at conveying subtle nuances. As certain parts of a relief lit from the side, so stand out the verbs, adjectives or stresses in the sentence, as he requires. He builds excellent crescendos and decrescendos. He uses his voice as a Saljapin [a great Russian bass]. He can be epic, he can rush, fall, rise, rattle, flood, thunder, meander, hiss, harm, and boil: this is the play of a self-conscious sea, of the rising and falling of waves, ever-changing and captivating even when one does not pay full attention to the contents.
>
> His gestures are much more monotonous, and they mainly underpin the passionate parts of the speech, the outbursts. I often observed that the rhythm of the syllables was measured out regularly over periods of roughly half a minute in length: the rhetorician's body language and vocal expressions probably converge in them.
>
> Yet all this gives little impression of being theatrical. He moves about in such a naturally "relaxed" manner as if he were in an intimate atmosphere, even when amongst hundreds of thousands of people. Of course, occasionally, at the grand military parades, he has to behave somewhat like a statue, but in general he gives

the impression of total familiarity. If there is something else, then I think there is a little tension in him, indeed—and I say it out of respect—he exhibits some appealingly child-like characteristics.

He is a human and a president who feels the Goethe-like call of the anvil or the hammer through every inch of his body. When he speaks, he is an artist wrestling with fate.[8]

If we think in terms of what has been cited from Hitler's *Kulturreden* or *Mein Kampf*, then the following question springs to mind in our astonishment: which Hitler was Lőrinc Szabó writing about? Why did he write these things? Could he, too, have been the victim of his own inspiration?

Inevitably we think of Gottfried Benn's answer to the question (Benn supported the Nazis for a short time):

Was it Hitler who established the movement, or was it the movement that created him? This question is typical, and its two parts are indivisible, because they are the same. Indeed the magic coincidence of the individual and the ordinary is apparent here, which Jakob Burckhardt discusses in his work *Contemplation on World history*, when he cites the great players of world history:[9]

Great individuals are the coincidence of the ordinary and the particular, of permanence and change in one personality. They embody states, religions, cultures and crises. [...] During times of crisis the existing and the new (revolution) find forms of expression in great individuals. The existence of such individuals is a true mystery of world history, their relation to their era is *ieros gamos* (holy matrimony), something that almost only comes about during those terrible times which are the sole measure of greatness, and it is that very greatness that they long for.[10]

According to one analyst's diagnosis of the "medical" world in Auschwitz, the First World War led to the development of war magic, and soon "Hitler became an agent of this transcendence, because of both his oratorical-demagogic genius and the German hunger for transcendence."[11] Is this really what made people blind and deaf? Is this really what re-stylized the world? It may be a cliché, but it is also true to say that if all this did not concern us then it would be comical, but as it does it is tragic. Yet it all seems so simple, especially the "dethroning" of morality. In August 1939 Klemperer wrote about Machiavelli with Hitler in mind at the time: "People always say: dividing moral and political science was his discovery. [We saw that this is wisdom taken from the *Accounts of the Zionist Wisemen*, as an example of—as we have indicated—how he played the role of "the perfect Jew.] But highly amoral politics turns into political stupidity."[12]

On one January night in 1942 Hitler amused his companions by telling them that if he had not been discovered, or to be more precise, "if someone else had been found, I would never have entered politics; I would have become an artist or a philosopher." Earlier he posed the question: "Why do things that exist, exist? Why is there not nothing instead?"[13] This reminds us of Heidegger's well-known question that was inspired by Schelling: "Why is there the extant rather than the nothing?" Hitler's response was destruction. What he left behind in the souls of Germans is nothing more than, as his *Psychogram* shows, nothing.[14]

Thus our impressions after having browsed through the Hitler-library are of comedy becoming tragedy and horror. In the Führer's insignificant appearance and drab everydayness the ghost of some terrible figure of synthesis emerges, one who reads all kinds of things that were produced by odious mediocrity and vulgar hatred. In his own way he drew on the *Bible* and the *Old Testament*: he highlighted those aspects of its implacability that appealed to him, and acquired some elements from the logic of the *New Testament*. He substituted love with hatred, and gave an explanation of the issues of modern alienation using the mythical accessories of gnosis whilst at the same time keeping alive schemes for a mechanistic and scientific world-view; he poured out words with the confidence of a prophet, partly saying out loud and partly keeping secret what it was he really wanted. He stopped at nothing in achieving his goals, as for him there was no turning back.

The question of "how what happened could have happened" refers to a non-finished past. Indeed, this would certainly appear to be the case if we refer to the writing of John Lukacs, who states that "If western civilization should once falter and collapse, the future will hold two dangers. A strong upswell of barbarism could raise Hitler's esteem once more in the eyes of everyday citizens; he could become in their eyes a kind of Diocletian, the last strong architect of Reich order [*Reichsordnung*]."[15] Today he is simply a fallen superman, since, as it is often noted, the simplistic thinking of a Superman is very close to that of the ideal Nazi hero, especially with the red letter "S" glowing in prime position on his costume.[16] However, this type of person does not even read any more, since in the age of the Internet reading is not necessary as it was then to maintain a good image.

Erich Voegelin, who fled from Nazism to America, weighed up one thousand years of European development with bitter disappointment: "Neither cognizance nor Christian determination resolves the mystery of God and existence. Divine creation embraces evil, its rule over existence disturbs the creation; the order of the community is built with hatred and blood, in misery and abandonment from God. Schelling's main question 'Why is there something and why is there not nothing?' which is followed by his next 'Why is it as it is?', is a question of theodicy."[17]

It is no accident that Harald Strohm closed his book analyzing the relation between Nazism and gnosis with Wittgenstein's seemingly mysterious but actually merciless observation: "With a clear mind one cannot harbor anger against Hitler; and one can do so even less against God."[18]

Even so, is Freud's bitter warning and question valid even today? "In their reign over the powers of nature people came so far that with the help of these powers it is easy for them to eradicate each other down to the last man. It is from here that originates a great part of their current restlessness, unhappiness, and anxiety. And now we must wait for the second of the two 'heavenly powers,' for the eternal Eros to gather his strength and conquer his similarly immortal enemy in the fight. But who can foresee the result, the final outcome?"[19]

Are more or fewer people waiting for the victory of Eros in this day and age? Or are Eros and Thanatos the two faces of one singular entity? Maybe that certain "ocean-like" feeling exists after all, and maybe it will sweep us along in the right direction...

Notes

1. Fest, *Hitler.* 1998, p. 108–109.

2. Ernst von Salomon, *Fragebogen* [Questionnaire]. Hamburg: 1991, p. 636.

3. Victor Klemperer, *Ich will Zeugnis ablegen bis zum letzten: Tagebücher 1942–1945 II.* [I want to offer evidence to the last detail: Diaries 1942–1945]. Eds. Walter Nowojski, Hadwig Klemperer. Berlin: 1997, p. 484.

4. Victor Klemperer, *LTI. Notizbuch eines Philologen* [LTI. Notebook of a philologist]. Leipzig: 1996, p. 26.

5. Ibid., pp. 270–74.

6. Klemperer, *Ich will Zeugnis ablegen I.* [I want to offer evidence I], p. 21.

7. Ibid., p. 132.

8. Lőrinc Szabó, *Magyar sors és fehér szarvas* [Hungarian fate and white stag]. Budapest: 1994, p. 85.

9. Fest, *Hitler.* 1998, p. 1079.

10. Jakob Burckhardt, *Weltgeschichtliche Betrachtungen* [Deliberations on world history]. Stuttgart: 1921, pp. 231–32.

11. Robert Jay Lifton, *The Nazi Doctors: Medical Killing and the Psychology of Genocide.* New York: 1986, p. 474.

12. Klemperer, *Ich will Zeugnis ablegen I.* [I want to offer evidence I], p. 480.

13. Eitner, *Hitler*, p. 55, 159.

14. Ibid., p. 253.

15. Lukacs, *A történelmi Hitler* [The Hitler of History], p. 284; *Hitler: Geschichte*, p. 354.

16. Doucet, *Im Banne des Mythos* [Under the spell of the myth], p. 271.

17. Erich Voegelin, *Die politischen Religionen* [The political religions]. Stockholm: 1939, p. 65.

18. Harald Strohm, *Die Gnosis und der Nationalsozialismus* [Gnosis and National Socialism]. Frankfurt am Main: 1997, p. 274.

Selected Bibliography

Alleu, René, *Hitler et les sociétés secrètes: Enquête sur les sources occultes du nazism* [Hitler and the secret society: An inquiry into the occult sources of Nazism]. Paris: 1969.

Alter, Peter, *Nationalism*. London, New York: 1991.

Anderson, Ken, *Hitler and the Occult*. New York: 1995.

Arendt, Hannah, *The Origins of Totalitarianism*. Cleveland, New York: 1962.

Backes, Klaus, *Hitler und die bildenden Künste: Kulturverständnis und Kunstpolitik im Dritten Reich* [Hitler and fine arts: Understanding of culture and politics of art in the Third Reich]. Cologne: 1988.

Berend T., Iván, *Válságos évtizedek: Közép- és Kelet-Európa a két világháború között* [Decades in crisis: Central and Eastern Europe between the two World Wars]. Budapest: 1983.

Biddis, Michael D., *Histoire de la pensée européenne: 6. L'ère des masses* [History of European thinking: 6. The era of the masses]. Paris: 1980.

Binion, Rudolph, *Hitler among the Germans*. New York, Oxford, Amsterdam: 1976.

Birken, Lawrence, *Hitler as Philosopher: Remnants of the Enlightenment in National Socialism*. Westport: 1995.

Bracher, Karl Dietrich, *The German Dictatorship*. New York: 1976.

Breuer, Stefan, *Anatomie der konservativen Revolution* [Anatomy of the conservative revolution]. Darmstadt: 1993.

Bullock, Alan, *Hitler: A Study in Tyranny*. New York: 1964.

Bullock, Alan, *Hitler and Stalin: Parallel Lives*. New York: 1992.

Bülow, Paul, *Adolf Hitler und der Bayreuther Kulturkreis* [Adolf Hitler and the cultural circle of Bayreuth]. Leipzig, Hamburg: w. y.

Burri, Margit, *Germanische Mythologie zwischen Verdrängung und Verfläschung* [German mythology between supression and liberation]. Zurich: 1982.

Cornish, Kimberley, *The Jew of Linz: Wittgenstein, Hitler and their Secret Battle for the Mind*. London: 1998.

Dahrendorf, Ralf, *Society and Democracy in Germany*. New York, London: 1965.

Daim, Wilfried, *Der Mann, der Hitler den Ideen gab: Jörg Lanz von Liebenfels* [The man that gave Hitler his ideas: Jörg Lanz von Liebenfels]. Vienna: 1994.

Dawidowicz, Lucy S., *The War against the Jews 1933–1945*. New York: 1979.

Doucet, Friedrich W., *Im Banne des Mythos: Die Psychologie des Dritten Reiches* [Under the spell of the myth: The psychology of the Third Reich]. Esslingen am Neckar: 1979.

Eatwell, Roger, *Fascism: A History*. London: 1995.

Eberan, Barbo, *Luther? Friedrich 'der Große'? Wagner? Nietzsche...? ...? wer war an Hitler Schuld? Die Debatte um die Schuldfrage 1945–1949* [Luther? Frederick 'the Great'? Wagner? Nietzsche...? ...? who was to blame for Hitler? The debate of the question of blame 1945–1949]. Munich: 1983.

Eitner, Hans-Jürgen, *Hitler: Das Psychogramm* [Hitler: The psychogramm]. Frankfurt am Main, Berlin, 1994.

Erikson, Erik H., *Luther avant Luther* [Luther before Luther]. Paris: 1968.

Fest, Joachim C., *The Face of the Third Reich*. New York: 1970.

Fest, Joachim C., *Hitler*. New York: 1973.

Fest, Joachim C., "Um einen Wagner von aussen bittend: Richard Wagner" [Of a Wagner from the outside]. In *Der Ring von Niebelungen. Ansichten des Mythos* [The circle of Niebelungen. Views of the myth]. Eds. Udo Bermbach, Dieter Borchmeyer. Stuttgart, Weimar: 1995.

Fest, Joachim C., *Hitler: Eine Biographie* [Hitler: a biography]. Berlin: 1998.

Fromm, E., *Anatomie der menschlichen Destruktivität* [Anatomy of human destructiveness]. Hamburg: 1981.

Galli, Giorgio, *Hitler e il nazismo magico* [Hitler and his nazi magic]. Milano: 1989.

Gisevius, Hans Bernd, *Adolf Hitler: Versuch einer Deutung* [Adolf Hitler: Attempt for meaning]. Munich: 1963.

Goodrick-Clarke, Nicholas, *The Occult Roots of Nazism*. New York: 1992.

Gordon, Sarah, *Hitler, Germans, and the 'Jewish Question'*. Princeton: 1984.

Grosshans, Henry, *Hitler and the Artists*. New York, London: 1983.

Günther, Hans F. K., *Rasse und Stil* [Race and style]. Munich: 1926.

Kempowski, Walter, ed., *Haben Sie Hitler gesehen?* [Have you seen Hitler?]. Munich: 1973.

Haffner, Sebastian, *The Meaning of Hitler*. London: 1978.

Hamann, Brigitte, *Hitlers Wien: Lehrjahre eines Diktators* [Hitler's Vienna: A dictator's apprenticeship]. Munich: 1996.

Harand, Irene, *"Sein Kampf:" Antwort an Hitler* ["His struggle:" Answer to Hitler]. Vienna: 1935.

Harris, Robert, *Selling Hitler: The Story of the Hitler Diaries*. London: 1986.

Hartung, Günter, "Artur Dinter: A Successful Fascist Author in Pre-Fascist Germany." In *The Attractions of Fascism*. Ed. John Milfull. New York, Oxford, Munich: 1990.

"Historikerstreit." *Die Dokumentation der Kontroverse um die Einzigartigkeit der nationalistischen Judenvernichtung* [The documentation of the controversy of the uniqueness of the national socialist genocide against the Jews]. Munich: 1987.

Hoffmann, Hilmar, *"Und die Fahne führt uns in die Ewigkeit"*: *Propaganda im NS-Film* ["And the banner leads us into eternity": Propaganda in NS-film]. Frankfurt am Main: 1991.

Horváth, Iván, "Gondolatok a könyvtárról" [Thoughts from the library]. *2000*. Part I., 1997 December; Part II., 1998 January.

Jaccard, Roland, "Wittgenstein, philosophe de classe d'Hitler et espion soviétique" [Wittgenstein, class philosopher of Hitler and soviet spy]. *Le Monde*, 1988 April 21.

Jäckel, Eberhard, *David Irving's Hitler: A Faulty History Dissected*. Port Angeles: 1993.

Jäckel, Eberhard, *Hitler's World View*. Cambridge, Mass., London: 1981.

Jaffé, Aniela, *Aus Leben und Werkstatt von C. G. Jung* [From the life and workshop of C. G. Jung]. Zurich: 1968.

James, Harold, *A German Identity 1770–1990*. London: 1989.

Joachimstaler, A., comp., *Korrektur einer Biographie: Adolf Hitler 1908–1920* [Edited Biography: Adolf Hitler 1908–1920]. Munich: 1989.

Jones, J. Sydney, *Hitler in Vienna 1907–1913*. New York: 1982.

Josephson, Paul R., *Totalitarian Science and Technology*. New Jersey: 1996.

Kelley, Douglas M., *22 Männer um Hitler*. [22 men around Hitler] Olten-Bern: 1947.

Kershew, Ian, *Hitler 1889–1936*. Stuttgart: 1998.

Klemperer, Klemens von, *Germany's New Conservatism*. Princeton: 1968.

Knopp, Guido, *Ne féljünk Hitlertől!* [Let's not be afraid of Hitler!]. Budapest: 1997.

Koenigsberger, Richard A., *Hitler's Ideology: A Study in Psychoanalytic Sociology*. New York: 1975.

Köhler, Joachim, *Wagners Hitler: Der Prophet und sein Vollstrecker* [Wagner's Hitler: The prophet and his executor]. Munich: 1997.

Kotze, Hildegard von, ed., *Heeresadjutant bei Hitler 1938–1943: Aufzeichnungen des Majors Engel* [Adjutant to Hitler 1938–1943: Major Engel's notes]. Stuttgart: 1974.

Krockow, Christian Graf von, *Von deutschen Mythen* [About German myths]. Stuttgart: 1995.

Kubin, Ernst, *Sonderauftrag Linz: Die Kunstsammlung Adolf Hitler* [Special edition in Linz: Adolf Hitler's art collection]. Vienna: 1989.

Lang, Jochen von, *The Secretary: Martin Bormann, The Man Who Manipulated Hitler*. Athens, Ohio: 1981.

Langer, Walter C., *The Mind of Adolf Hitler*. New York: 1972.

Leske, Monika, *Philosophen im 'Dritten Reich'* [Philosophers in the 'Third Reich']. Berlin: 1990.

Levinas, Emmanuel, *Quelques réflexions sur la philosophie de l'hitlérisme* [A few thoughts about the philosophy of Hitler]. Paris: 1997.

Lewy, Guenter, *The Catholic Church and Nazi Germany*. New York, Toronto: 1968.

Lifton, Robert Jay, *The Nazi Doctors: Medical killing and the Psychology of Genocide*. New York: 1986.

Lukacs, John, *Az európai világháború 1939–1941* [The European World War 1939–1941]. Budapest: 1995.

Lukacs, John, *The Hitler of History*. New York: 1997; in Hungarian: *A történelmi Hitler*. Budapest: 1998.

Lukacs, John, *Hitler: Geschichte und Geschichteschreibung* [Hitler: History and history writing]. Munich: 1997.

Maidenbaum, Aryeh, Stephen A. Martin, eds., *Lingering Shadows: Jungians, Freudians, and Anti-Semitism*. Boston, London: 1991.

Mann, Cuthbert Carson, *Hitler's Three Struggles: The Neo-Pagan Revenge*. Chicago: 1995.

Mann, Golo, *Deutsche Geschichte des neunzehnten und zwanzigsten Jahrhunderts* [German history of the nineteenth and twentieth centuries]. Frankfurt am Main: 1959.

Mann, Thomas, *Reden und Aufsätze 4*. [Speeches and essays 4]. Frankfurt am Main, 1974.

Marchand, Wolf R., *Joseph Roth und völkish-nationalistische Wertbegriffe* [Joseph Roth and folk-national concepts of value]. Bonn, 1974.

Maser, Werner, *Hitlers Mein Kampf: Entsehung, Aufbau, Stil, Änderungen, Quellen, Quellenwert, kommentierte Auszüge* [Hitler's Mein Kampf: Origins, structure, style, versions, sources, source value, commented excerpts]. Munich, Esslingen: 1966.

Maser, Werner, *Hitlers Briefe und Notizen* [Hitler's letters and notes]. Düsseldorf, Vienna: 1973.

Maser, Werner, *Adolf Hitler: Legende, Mythos, Wirklichkeit* [Adolf Hitler: Legends, myth, reality]. Munich: 1989.

Molau, Andreas, *Alfred Rosenberg: Der Ideologe des Nationalsozialismus*. [Alfred Rosenberg: The ideologist of National Socialism]. Koblenz: 1993.

Molau, Harald, Uwe Focke-Reiner, *Alltag unterm Hakenkreuz* [Everyday under the *swastika*]. Hamburg: 1991.

Mosse, George L., *The Crisis of German Ideology*. New York: 1964.

Mosse, George L., *The Nationalization of the Masses*. New York: 1975.

Mosse, George L., "Jewish Emancipation." In *The Jewish Response to German Culture*. Jehuda Reinharz, Walter Schatzberg, eds. Hannover, London: 1985.

Müller-Gangloff, Erich, *Horizonte der Nachmoderne* [Horizon of the postmodern]. Stuttgart: 1964.

Nolte, Ernst, *Der Faschismus in seiner Epoche* [Fascism in its era]. Munich: 1963.

Nolte, Ernst, *Der Europäische Bürgerkrieg 1917–1945: Nationalsozialismus und Bolshewismus* [The European civil war 1917–1945: National Socialism and Bolshevism]. Frankfurt am Main, Berlin: 1989.

Ormos, Mária, *Nácizmus—fasizmus* [Nazism—fascism]. Budapest: 1987.

Ormos, Mária, "Betegek és betegségek a történelemben" [The ill and illnesses in history]. *Korunk*, 1997. No. 7.

Ormos, Mária, *Hitler*. Budapest: 1997.

Ormos, Mária, *A Hitler életrajz buktatói*. Budapest: 1993.

Pauley, Bruce F., *From Prejudice to Persecution: A History of Austrian Anti-Semitsm*. Chapell Hill, London: 1991.

Pauwels, Louis, Jacques Bergier, *Le matin des magiciens* [The dawn of the magicians]. Paris: 1960.

Payne, Robert, *The Life and Death of Adolf Hitler*. New York, Washington: 1973.

Pechel, Rudolf, *Deutsche Widerstand* [German opposition]. Zurich: 1947.

Petropoulos, Jonathan, *Art as Politics in the Third Reich*. Chapel Hill, London: 1996.

Phelps, Reginald H., "Die Hitler-Bibliotek" [The Hitler library]. *Deutsche Rundschau*, 1954 September.

Phelps, Reginald H., "Before Hitler Came: Thule Society and Germanen Orden." *The Journal of Modern History*, 1993. No. 3.

Picker, Henry, *Hitlers Tischgespräche im Führerhauptquartier 1941–1942* [Hitler's roundtable talks at the Führer's headquarters]. Stuttgart: 1963.

Picker, Henry, Heinrich Hoffmann, *Hitlers Tischgespräche im Bild* [Hitler's roundtable talks]. Munich, Berlin: 1980.

Pois, Robert, *Emil Nolde*. Washington: 1982.

Pritz, Pál, *Pax Germanica: Német elképzelések Európa jövőjéről a második világháborúban* [Pax Germanica: German ideas on the future of Europe during the Second World War]. Budapest: 1999.

Ravenscroft, Trevor, *A végzet lándzsája* [The harpoon of destiny]. Budapest: 1993.

Reich, David, *The Third Reich: Politics and Propaganda*. London, New York: 1993.

Reich, Wilhelm, *Massenpsychologie des Faschismus* [Mass psychology of fascism]. Kopenhagen: 1934.

Rosenbaum, Ron, *Explaining Hitler: The Search for the Origins of his Evil*. London: 1998.

Russel, Jeffrey Burton, *Mephistoles: The Devil in the Modern World*. Ithaca, London: 1986.

Sandvoss, E., *Hitler und Nietzsche* [Hitler and Nietzsche]. Göttingen, 1969.

Schmitz, Hermann, *Adolf Hitler in der Geschichte* [Adolf Hitler in history]. Bonn: 1999.

Schramm, Percy Ernst, *Hitler: The Man and the Military Leader*. Chicago. 1971.

Shircr, William L., *Berlin Diary: The Journal of a Foreign Correspondent 1934–1941*. New York: 1984.

Stehle, Hansjakob, "Bischof Hudal und SS-Führer Meyer" [Bishop Hudal and the SS-Leader Meyer]. *Vierteljahreshefte für Zeitgeschichte*, 1989. No. 2.

Steinert, Marlis, *Hitler*. Paris: 1991.

Stern, Fritz, *Kulturpessimismus als politische Gefahr* [Cultural pessimism as a political hazard]. Bern, Stuttgart, Vienna: 1963.

Sternburg, Wilhelm von, *Fall und aufstieg der Deutschen Nation* [Fall and rise of the German nation]. Frankfurt am Main: 1993.

Stierlin, Helm, Adolf *Hitler: Familienperspektiven* [Hitler: A family perspective]. Frankfurt am Main: 1997.

Strasser, Otto, *Mein Kampf: Eine politische Autobiographie* [My struggle: A political autobiography]. Frankfurt am Main, 1969.

Strohm, Harald, *Die Gnosis und der Nationalsozialismus* [Gnosis and National Socialism]. Frankfurt am Main: 1997.

Strothmann, Dietrich, *Nationalsozialistische Literaturpolitik* [National Socialist politics of literature]. Bonn: 1960.

Syring, Enrico, *Hitler: Seine politische Utopie* [Hitler: His political utopia]. Berlin: 1994.

Tauscher, Petra, *Nekrophilie und Fascismus: Erich Fromms Beitrag zur soziobiographischen Deutung Adolf Hitlers und weitere sozialpsychologische Interpretationen* [Necrophylia and fascism: Erich Fromm's contribution to the sociobiographic meaning of Adolf Hitler and further socio-psychological interpretions]. Frankfurt am Main: 1985.

Taylor, A. J. P., *The Origins of the Second World War*. New York: 1987.

Thies, Jochen, "Nazi Architecture—a Blueprint for World Domination: the Last Aims of Adolf Hitler." In *Nazi Propaganda: The Power and the Limitations*. Ed. David Welch. London, Canberra: 1983.

Toland, John, *Adolf Hitler*. New York: 1976.

Trevor-Roper, Hugh, "History and Imagination." In *History and Imagination: Essays in Honour of H. R. Trevor-Roper*. Eds. Hugh Lloyd-James, Valerie Pearl, Blair Worden. London: 1981.

Ulshöfer, Helmut, *Liebesbriefe an Adolf Hitler: Briefe in den Tod* [Love letters to Adolf Hitler: Letters into death]. Frankfurt am Main: 1994.

Vondung, Klaus, *Magie und Manipulation* [Magic and manipulation]. Göttingen: 1971.

Waite, Robert G. L., *The Psychopatic God*. New York, 1977.

Wallach, Jehuda L., "Adolf Hitlers Privatbibliothek" [Adolf Hitler's private library]. *Zeitgeschichte*, 1992. No. 1–2.

Weiner, Marc A., *Richard Wagner and the anti-Semitic Imagination*. Lincoln, London: 1995.

Weiss, Hohn, *Ideology of Death: Why the Holocaust Happened in Germany*. Chicago: 1996.

Whisker, James Biser, *The Social, Political and Religious Thought of Alfred Rosenberg*. Washington: 1982.

Wilson, Colin, *Rudolf Steiner: The Man and his Vision*. Wellingborough: 1985.

Winckler, Lutz, *Studie zur gesellschaftlichen Funktion faschistischer Sprache* [A study of the social function of fascistic speech]. Frankfurt am Main: 1970.

Wulff, Wilhelm, *Zodiac and Swastika*. New York: 1973.

Zitelmann, Rainer, *Hitler: Selbstverständniss eines Revolutionärs* [Hitler: Self-evidence of a revolution]. Hamburg, New York: 1987.

Zoller, Albert, *Hitler Privat: Erlebnisbericht seiner Geheimsekretärin* [Private Hitler: an account of his private secretaries experiences]. Düsseldorf: 1949.

Name Index